Regions and Innovation Policies in Europe

NEW HORIZONS IN REGIONAL SCIENCE

Series Editor: Philip McCann, *Professor of Urban and Regional Economics, University of Sheffield, UK*

Regional science analyses important issues surrounding the growth and development of urban and regional systems and is emerging as a major social science discipline. This series provides an invaluable forum for the publication of high quality scholarly work on urban and regional studies, industrial location economics, transport systems, economic geography and networks.

New Horizons in Regional Science aims to publish the best work by economists, geographers, urban and regional planners and other researchers from throughout the world. It is intended to serve a wide readership including academics, students and policymakers.

Titles in the series include:

Innovation in Developing and Transition Countries
Edited by Alexandra Tsvetkova, Jana Schmutzler, Marcela Suarez and Alessandra Faggian

Globalization, International Spillovers and Sectoral Changes
Implications for Regions and Industries
Edited by Charlie Karlsson, Andreas P. Cornett and Tina Wallin

Transportation, Knowledge and Space in Urban and Regional Economics
Edited by Kakuya Matsushima and William P. Anderson

Cities and Sustainable Technology Transitions
Leadership, Innovation and Adoption
Edited by Marina van Geenhuizen, J. Adam Holbook and Mozhdeh Taheri

Resilience, Crisis and Innovation Dynamics
Edited by Tüzin Baycan and Hugo Pinto

Geography, Open Innovation and Entrepreneurship
Edited by Urban Gråsjö, Charlie Karlsson and Iréne Bernhard

Economic Crisis and the Resilience of Regions
A European Study
Edited by Gillian Bristow and Adrian Healy

Knowledge, Policymaking and Learning for European Cities and Regions
From Research to Practice
Edited by Nicola Francesco Dotti

Global City Makers
Economic Actors and Practices in the World City Network
Edited by Michael Hoyler, Christof Parnreiter and Allan Watson

Resilience and Urban Disasters
Surviving Cities
Edited by Kamila Borsekova and Peter Nijkamp

High Speed Rail and China's New Economic Geography
Impact Assessment from the Regional Science Perspective
Zhenhua Chen and Kingsley E. Haynes

Smart, Sustainable and Inclusive Growth
Political Entrepreneurship for a Prosperous Europe
Edited by Charlie Karlsson, Daniel Silander and Brigitte Pircher

Regions and Innovation Policies in Europe
Learning from the Margins
Edited by Manuel González-López and Bjørn T. Asheim

Regions and Innovation Policies in Europe

Learning from the Margins

Edited by

Manuel González-López

Associate Professor of Applied Economics, ICEDE Research Group, University of Santiago de Compostela, Galicia, Spain

Bjørn T. Asheim

Professor of Economic Geography and Innovation Theory, University of Stavanger Business School and the Stavanger Centre for Innovation Research, University of Stavanger, Norway

NEW HORIZONS IN REGIONAL SCIENCE

With the support of the Erasmus+ Programme of the European Union

Cheltenham, UK • Northampton, MA, USA

The European Commission's support for the production of this publication does not constitute an endorsement of the contents, which reflect the views only of the authors, and the Commission cannot be held responsible for any use which may be made of the information contained therein

Published by
Edward Elgar Publishing Limited
The Lypiatts
15 Lansdown Road
Cheltenham
Glos GL50 2JA
UK

Edward Elgar Publishing, Inc.
William Pratt House
9 Dewey Court
Northampton
Massachusetts 01060
USA

A catalogue record for this book
is available from the British Library

Library of Congress Control Number: 2019956674

This book is available electronically in the **Elgar**online
Social and Political Science subject collection
DOI 10.4337/9781789904161

ISBN 978 1 78990 415 4 (cased)
ISBN 978 1 78990 416 1 (eBook)

Typeset by Servis Filmsetting Ltd, Stockport, Cheshire
Printed and bound by CPI Group (UK) Ltd, Croydon, CR0 4YY

Contents

List of contributors   vii

Introduction: regional innovation systems and regional
innovation policies   1
Manuel González-López and Bjørn T. Asheim

1   The role of the Regional Innovation System approach in
    contemporary regional policy: is it still relevant in a globalised
    world?   12
    Bjørn T. Asheim, Arne Isaksen and Michaela Trippl

2   Advancing place-based regional innovation policies   30
    Robert Hassink

3   Policy learning in regions: the potential of co-generative
    research methodologies to help responsible innovation   46
    Ainhoa Arrona, James Karlsen and Miren Larrea

4   Regional autonomy and innovation policy   66
    Elisabeth Baier and Andrea Zenker

5   EU regional development policy, from regional convergence
    to development through innovation   92
    Cristina Ares

6   An overview of the European Union innovation policy from
    the regional perspective   113
    María del Carmen Sánchez-Carreira

7   Regional Innovation Systems and regional disparities in the
    Euro area: insights for regional innovation policy   139
    Óscar Rodil-Marzábal and Xavier Vence-Deza

8   The effects of projects funded by the EU Framework
    Programmes on regional innovation and scientific performance   162
    Pedro Varela-Vázquez and Manuel González-López

9   Evolution and change of the Galician innovation system and
    policies   188
    Manuel González-López

10 The evolution of regional innovation policy in a peripheral
    area: the case of Apulia region   207
    Ivano Dileo and Francesco Losurdo

11 Regional innovation system and policy in Malopolska, Poland:
    an institutionalised learning   225
    Marta Gancarczyk, Marta Najda-Janoszka and
    Jacek Gancarczyk

12 The Agder region: an innovation policy case study   252
    Roger Normann, Sissel Strickert and Jon P. Knudsen

Index   271

Contributors

Cristina Ares is Senior Lecturer of Political Science and Public Administration at the University of Santiago de Compostela (Galicia, Spain).

Ainhoa Arrona is a researcher at the Orkestra-Basque Institute of Competitiveness (Basque Country, Spain).

Bjørn T. Asheim is Professor of Economic Geography and Innovation Theory at the University of Stavanger (Norway).

Elisabeth Baier is Professor for Business Administration at the Hochschule für Wirtschaft, Technik und Kultur (hwtk) University of Applied Sciences (Berlin, Germany).

María del Carmen Sánchez-Carreira is Assistant Professor in the Department of Applied Economics at the University of Santiago de Compostela (Galicia, Spain).

Ivano Dileo is Associate Professor in the Department of Political Sciences at the Università degli Studi di Bari Aldo Moro (Italy).

Jacek Gancarczyk is Adjunct Professor at the Institute of Entrepreneurship, Jagiellonian University (Krakow, Poland).

Marta Gancarczyk is Associate Professor at the Institute of Economics, Finance and Management, Jagiellonian University (Krakow, Poland).

Manuel González-López is Associate Professor in the Department of Applied Economics at the University of Santiago de Compostela (Galicia, Spain).

Robert Hassink is Professor of Economic Geography at Kiel University (Germany).

Arne Isaksen is Professor in the Department of Working Life and Innovation at the School of Business and Law at the University of Agder (Norway).

James Karlsen is Professor at the University of Agder (Norway) and Senior Associate Researcher at the Orkestra-Basque Institute of Competitiveness (Basque Country, Spain).

Jon P. Knudsen is Associate Professor at the University of Agder (Norway).

Miren Larrea is Senior Researcher at the Orkestra-Basque Institute of Competitiveness (Basque Country, Spain).

Francesco Losurdo is Professor in the Department of Political Sciences at the Università degli Studi di Bari Aldo Moro (Italy).

Marta Najda-Janoszka is Associate Professor at the Jagiellonian University (Krakow, Poland).

Roger Normann is Senior Researcher at the NORCE Norwegian Research Centre, Social Science Department (Norway).

Óscar Rodil-Marzábal is Associate Professor in the Department of Applied Economics at the University of Santiago de Compostela (Galicia, Spain).

Sissel Strickert is Strategy Advisor and researcher at the NORCE Norwegian Research Centre, Social Science Department (Norway).

Michaela Trippl is Professor of Economic Geography at the University of Vienna (Austria).

Pedro Varela-Vázquez is Lecturer in the Department of Applied Economics at the University of Santiago de Compostela (Galicia, Spain).

Xavier Vence-Deza is Professor in the Department of Applied Economics at the University of Santiago de Compostela (Galicia, Spain).

Andrea Zenker is a researcher and project manager at the Fraunhofer Institute for Systems and Innovation Research ISI (Karlsruhe, Germany).

Introduction: regional innovation systems and regional innovation policies

Manuel González-López and Bjørn T. Asheim

During the last two decades interest in regional innovation policies has progressively increased within the field of regional innovation studies. Such growing interest, which has been mostly European, is observed in the pattern of mentions of the term "regional innovation policy" in scientific papers (González-López et al. 2019).

Regional innovation policies studies are narrowly linked to the regional innovation system (RIS) approach (Cooke 1992; Cooke et al. 1997; Asheim and Isaksen 1997; Howells 1999; Asheim and Gertler 2005). The RIS approach, which emerged in the 1990s, linked to both the Innovation Systems (IS) literature and contemporary contributions on Economic Geography and Cluster Theory. The IS approach underlines that nations, regions and sectors show distinctive patterns of innovation, due to diverse technological and institutional trajectories (Lundvall 1992; Edquist 1997). Linked to the post-Schumpeterian views of the Evolutionary School (Nelson and Winter 1982; Dosi and Nelson 1994), innovation and economic changes are understood as a dynamic and path-dependent process, which contributes to explaining why each sector or territory follows different innovation trajectories, shaping different systems of innovation. Moreover, the IS literature draws also on the so-called "interactive learning theories" (Lundvall and Johnson 1994), where innovation is understood as a phenomenon that is the result of multiple interactions and continuous learning processes in which multiple agents participate. At the regional or national level, firms, higher education institutions or technological centres (among others) are the relevant agents that interact and give rise to learning processes and innovations.

The other basis for the RIS approach concerns several Economic Geography schools that, particularly since the 1980s, have emphasised the importance of innovation for regions' and territories' competitiveness. Among others, we can include here the New Industrial Districts school (Becattini 1990), the Flexible Production Systems approach (Scott 1988; Storper and Harrison 1991) and the Learning Region approach (Asheim

1

1996; Morgan 1997). All these perspectives highlight the distinctive character of the factors influencing regional development (institutions, technologies, external connections, etc.). A similar perspective is also present in Cluster Theory, developed particularly by Porter, which has also served to influence both the RIS approach and regional innovation policies (Porter 2000; Cooke 2001). From these perspectives, each territory not only shows a particular economic trajectory, but also demands specific and place-based policies.

Unlike neoclassical economics, the Evolutionary and IS approaches are not only focused on market failures in order to underpin S&T (Science & Technology) policies, based on a linear view of innovation. Rather, they also focus on the need to address systemic failures based on the understanding that learning processes needed for innovation are the result of multiple interactions in systems where different agents and institutions are involved (Metcalfe and Georghiou 1997). Such interactions, for instance between universities and industries, are not always fluid and sometimes they do not even exist. When this happens, a policy intervention is needed.

Therefore, the systemic approach leads to other kinds of innovation policies, which are different and more complex. There is a broad range of different instruments that attempt to strengthen interactions and support the creation and expansion of innovative enterprises. Among them, it should be highlighted, are support infrastructures for innovation, such as technological parks and technological centres, in addition to the provision of services by innovation centres or agencies for innovation. Another relevant issue is the fostering of cooperation among the different elements and players involved in innovation, as well as the articulation and coordination of the IS. In this sense, the structures that encourage cooperation, mainly between enterprises and universities, are useful tools (collaborative projects, researchers' mobility, etc.). Interactions with the financing system are relevant as well.

SMART SPECIALISATION STRATEGIES AND PATH TRANSFORMATION

The dominant paradigm for regional innovation policies in recent times has been, at least in Europe, the so-called Smart Specialisation (SS) approach. As indicated by Bjørn Asheim (2019), the SS approach is coherent with the RIS approach and somehow a logical extension of it. In fact, it can be considered a natural link between regional development policies and innovation policies. SS refers to "the capacity of an economic system (a region for example) to generate new specialities through the discovery of new domains of opportunity and the local concentration and agglomeration of resources and competences in these domains" (Foray 2014, p. 1). Meanwhile Smart Specialisation Strategies (S3) refers to those actions and measures (policies) that promote this kind of process. As noted by McCann (2015, p. 175), "the smart specialization logic argues that in order to foster innovation and growth regions should aim to prioritise those activities fostering and enhancing entrepreneurial search initiatives in activities which are aimed at technologically diversifying those activities which are both highly embedded within a region and also highly connected to other regions".

SS became a key pillar for the Cohesion Policy of the European Commission (EC) for the period 2014–2020. According to McCann (2015), S3 rationale fitted very well with the European Union (EU) Cohesion Policy due to two reasons. Firstly, it provided a policy prioritisation framework in line with the Europe 2020 strategy. Secondly, it followed a "place-based" logic, like the Cohesion Policy did. The place-based approach assumes that policy priorities should vary between different types of regions. It also suggests that regional policies should build on local capabilities and promote innovative strategies, based on local and non-local actors and knowledge (Rodrik 2005; Barca et al., 2012). This is what S3 do when applying a bottom-up approach such as the entrepreneurial discovery process.

The S3 approach also stresses the importance of a coherent design of regional strategies, based on the active participation of key stakeholders. This is quite a novelty with regard to regional innovation policies because, as pointed out by Uyarra (2010), Evolutionary scholars are usually biased towards normative analysis (what policymakers ought to do), disregarding the positive analysis (i.e. what policymakers actually do). S3 also refers to regional structural change and path development and transformation (Foray 2014). As noted by authors like Boschma and Lambooy (1999) and Neffke et al. (2011), the location of emerging industries is not a random process; existing industrial paths explain the new paths. This "related variety" or "related diversification" pertains to the existence of knowledge spillovers from existing sectors to new ones (Frenken et al. 2007; Boschma and Iammarino 2009). From the regional innovation policy perspective, the previous concepts and studies comprise a very useful instrument in order to prioritise industries or technologies with high potential.

THE CONTENTS OF THIS BOOK

The present book has as its standpoint the research activities developed by academics from different European institutions, which benefited from the support of the Jean Monnet project "EURIPER" (EU Regional and Innovation Policies and Peripheral Regions). This project, which took place between 2017 and 2019, was funded by the EC, coordinated by the University of Santiago de Compostela in Galicia (Spain), and enjoyed the participation of researchers from Norway, Italy, Poland, Germany and Denmark.

This book is composed of twelve chapters, which discuss regional innovation policies combining theoretical and empirical analyses. The chapters are organised in three main parts. The first part focuses on the foundations of regional innovation policies and it comprises four chapters. These chapters deal with interesting issues concerning regional innovation policies, such as regional path transformation, place-based strategies, learning policy and regional autonomy. The second part of the book (made up of four chapters) addresses the role of EU institutions in the promotion of regional development and innovation, as well as the combination of cohesion and competitiveness goals. The third part of the book presents four case studies of the regional innovation systems and policies of non-core European regions: Galicia (Spain), Apulia (Italy), Malopolska (Poland) and Agder (Norway).

The contents and contributions of each chapter are briefly described below.

Bjørn T. Asheim, Arne Isaksen and Michaela Trippl discuss the role of the RIS approach in contemporary regional policy. They pose two insightful questions: is the regional level still relevant for policymaking in a globalised world and is the RIS approach continuing to be a powerful tool for designing and implementing regional innovation policies directed towards promoting transformative changes? The chapter also addresses the transformations of regional innovation policy during three sequential frames (research and development [R&D], innovation system and transformative change). The authors illustrate the discussion about RIS dynamics with compelling examples of regional innovation policies in Europe.

Next, Robert Hassink contributes to the understanding of place-based regional policies by strengthening the conceptualisation of place. This debate is more relevant within a context of economic and political instability, with growing populism, particularly in old industrial and rural areas (e.g. the USA). This instability may be related to uneven regional development in three domains: economic, social and recognition of inequalities. The author asks what regional places are in existence and whether they are still relevant in these unstable circumstances. This chapter discusses a place-neutral policy approach, which emphasises agglomeration economies for regional economic development, and a place-based policy approach, which consists of tailor-made policies. It also aims at a better understanding and improving of place-based policies.

In Chapter 3, Ainhoa Arrona, James Karlsen and Miren Larrea reflect on policy learning, focusing on the role of researchers. Policy learning is one mechanism for explaining policy changes and evolution. The chapter deals with issues such as what policy learning is, who is learning, what they are learning and the result of the learning process. Policy learning is more relevant within the context of responsible innovation, which addresses societal goals in a way that is socially desirable. This requires a change in the rationale of innovation policies, which affects policymakers as well as researchers.

This chapter addresses responsible innovation within regional innovation policies, based on in-depth interviews with policymakers in the Basque Country. The authors depart from the idea that policymakers do not always have the absorptive capacity required to implement policy recommendations delivered by researchers. However, they argue that, behind the low level of effectiveness, lies the need of a better understanding of the policy process by researchers, as much as the need of capabilities by policymakers. The chapter approaches this issue, providing a framework to better understand the policy process and how research can be relevant to improve the interaction. This framework is the action research for territorial development, which is developed in the regional innovation policy field. It proposes knowledge co-generation between policymakers and researchers as a specific form of policy learning, contributing to improve interactions and promote learning.

In the following chapter, Elisabeth Baier and Andrea Zenker discuss the interrelation between regional autonomy and innovation policies across Europe. Regional innovation policymaking is determined by different rationales, institutional structures and framework conditions. The varying degrees of autonomy for regional innovation policy depend on several aspects, such as decision-making power, budgetary responsibility, and region-specific technological and institutional trajectories. These aspects are shaped by different governance levels. The authors use a dynamic perspective within the innovation system framework approach, contributing to the conceptual and the policy-oriented dimensions. The chapter provides a conceptualisation and operationalisation of regional autonomy, proposing an empirical approach to describe and measure regional autonomy through a set of indicators that includes the role of EU funding and national constitutional settings. It also raises the question whether regions with higher degrees of autonomy have better conditions for designing and implementing territory-specific innovation policies. Moreover, the chapter analyses transformation processes concerning regional autonomy, which are mainly triggered by policies on the supra-national level, such as regional cohesion and economic development policy in the EU.

In Chapter 5, Cristina Ares provides an overview of the EU's Regional Development Policy or Cohesion Policy, and its transformations over time. The EU shows socioeconomic heterogeneity at the regional level, which has increased with the accession of new Member States from the 1980s. The reason for launching the Cohesion Policy was the willingness to compensate the less-favoured regions for the adaptation to the single market. However, the EU's Cohesion Policy has changed over time, and mainly since the beginning of the twenty-first century. The main changes are related to the accession of Southern and Eastern Member States, the limited size of the EU budget, and the Great Recession. Moreover, policy innovations have been introduced, with the aim of better investing EU funding. In this sense, S3 have become key instruments. This chapter underlines that the main change in policy rationale has been the progressive substitution of compensation logic based on helping less-favoured regions to converge, for the rationale of enhancing the competitiveness of the EU as a whole by means of regional development through innovation. This change involves investing more common structural budget in those territories where more results can be achieved. Other current trends in the EU's Cohesion Policy are related to underline the contextual factors of each region. Thus, the ERDP (European Regional Development Policy) has moved towards more comprehensive and well-timed strategies for regional development, and more integrated approaches, and to regionally differentiated investments and policy responses. This reorientation is problematic from the point of view of political equality and consequently EU discontent. The chapter supports more place-sensitive policies and empowerment of regional and local representatives in policy and investment prioritising.

Next, María del Carmen Sánchez-Carreira approaches the foundation and evolution of the EU's innovation policy over time, focusing on its key moments, rationales, objectives, tools and trends. Moreover, she tackles the regional perspective within the innovation policy. Traditionally the policy has been focused on research, according to the linear model of innovation. However, innovation has been gradually introduced and a systemic approach emerges. The EU's innovation policy is characterised by a multilevel model and the regions have increasingly become relevant actors in innovation policies. Among other actions, the Framework Programmes (FPs) and the European Structural Funds underline this development. The EU's innovation policy, and mainly the FPs, have hardly considered the territorial dimension, economic development or innovation level of the regions. Several attempts to include some element of cohesion in the policy have been made over time, through different tools. This chapter also deals with the links between EU regional and innovation policies, from their background to the current S3. It concludes that there is considerable potential for leveraging synergies between cohesion policy and innovation policy, as well as among other EC policies, despite the presence of challenges and risks for regional cohesion.

In Chapter 7, Óscar Rodil-Marzábal and Xavier Vence-Deza contribute to reopen the debate about regional convergence and the drivers of regional growth. The EU has been characterised by stages of increasing regional disparities in past decades, as well as since the Great Recession. Despite the diverse nature of factors explaining these differences, innovation is pinpointed as a key determinant. Thus, this chapter focuses on the role of innovative capacity in the growth performance of different regions in the Economic and Monetary Union (EMU) from the introduction of the Euro to the present. It also seeks to identify the relevance of different components of the RIS in the evolution of regional disparities. The authors analyse the growth patterns of the EMU regions considering differences regarding innovation and its effects on economic growth. This is a way to assess whether deeper integration has shown real capacity to promote territorial cohesion and moderate regional inequalities. The empirical study shows a positive association between innovation performance and economic growth. The findings also confirm that innovation performance should be considered in a complex and systemic framework where business plays a key role. Evidence of increasing regional disparities in parallel with deeper EU integration is a challenge both for economic growth theories and for policymakers. In this sense, the objective of boosting European economic growth is highly dependent on improving capabilities and reinforcing complementarities among all RIS components. Likewise, the objective of a more cohesive EU requires reinforcement of the RIS of all European regions. The chapter suggests that policies prioritise business capabilities in R&D and non-R&D innovation activities, as well as promotion of linkages between public and private agents.

In the following chapter, Pedro Varela-Vázquez and Manuel González-López analyse the effects of the 6th and 7th Framework Programmes in regional innovation and scientific performance. The geographical distribution of project coordination and participation shows a high concentration in few hubs across Europe. This fact is coherent with the allocation criteria of the FPs, which are mainly based on scientific excellence and industrial leadership. This geographical concentration of projects has implications on regional cohesion, because it leads to increased regional differences in innovation and scientific performance, as well as in long-term economic growth. Empirical evidence highlights the positive role played by coordination and participation in projects to foster innovation and scientific outcomes. Coordination of projects is more effective in encouraging innovation in less-developed regions than in developed regions, while the opposite happens with scientific publications. Coordination of projects is also more effective in middle-income regions regarding both innovation and scientific performance. Participation in projects shows the highest impact in less-developed regions.

Next, Manuel González-López presents the case study of the innovation system and policies of Galicia, a European region in Northwest Spain. Galicia, which owns relevant legal and political competences on industrial and innovation policies, has progressively built an institutional set-up to support innovation and so to articulate its innovation system. Nevertheless, many structural weaknesses persist, which explains the relatively poor innovation performance of the region in comparison with the EU average. The late 2000s economic crisis, which hit particularly hard in southern European economies, also explains the difficulties involved here in improving innovation performance. All in all, the Galician economic structure has not experienced relevant changes and a conservative pattern has dominated over the last two decades.

In Chapter 10, Ivano Dileo and Francesco Losurdo analyse the evolution of regional innovation policies in the peripheral region of Apulia (Italy). This chapter focuses on legal and institutional frameworks, actions and instruments implemented over the last four EU planning periods. It attempts to understand how to overcome the old policy innovation approach towards the Research and Innovation Strategies for Smart Specialisation (RIS3) model, avoiding some identified risks. The authors present the strengths and weaknesses of the Apulia Research and Innovation (R&I) system and policy, with a special focus on human resources, the fragmentation of research activities and the crisis in traditional manufacturing. Nevertheless, areas such as mechatronics, aerospace, ICT (Information and Communications Technology) and start-ups have created new opportunities to expand R&I activities and increase the rate of skilled human capital. The involvement of local actors and the role of universities, as well as the effort to foster university–industry interaction, underline these developments. The chapter supports the need for new place-based and territorial-oriented approaches.

In the penultimate chapter, Marta Gancarczyk, Marta Najda-Janoszka and Jacek Gancarczyk analyse the evolution of the regional innovation system and policies in Malopolska (Poland) as a learning process. They use a positive perspective to present policy characteristics vis-à-vis the evolution of the Malopolska innovation system after Poland's accession to the EU in 2004. This chapter presents the real processes of formulating, adjusting and implementing innovation policies, including objectives, activities, assessment measures and budgets. It focuses on the dynamics of the innovation system, changes in the innovation policy regarding the regional specialisation, support for entrepreneurial discovery and innovation to open a new development path, and types of learning that stimulated the evolution of the regional innovation policies. Institutional mechanisms of learning were identified as the major drivers of the evolution of Malopolska's innovation policies. The authors' findings point to the increasingly positive potential of Malopolska's innovation system (input characteristics) and its less positive but improving performance (output characteristics). Its industrial specialisation evolved from an unfocused approach to combination of the dominant knowledge base and industries of new opportunities, following the SS concept. Policy measures and budgets increasingly targeted entrepreneurship support. This chapter proposes strengthening the interaction and synergies between the dominant and emerging areas of specialisation, and enhancing the collaborative links among businesses, as well as among businesses and academia.

Finally, Roger Normann, Sissel Strickert and Jon P. Knudsen discuss the emergence of a new set of innovation policies in the region of Agder (Norway), within the context of RIS3 as a dominating paradigm in Europe and a significant regional reform model in Norway. This case is unusual, because Norway does not belong to the EU. The chapter takes account of the status for these processes and asks which steps lie ahead for innovation policy development and learning based on developments in that region. It seeks to identify some of the key features of regional innovation policy, as well as the key challenges. Moreover, it raises the question of how the Agder region's response to RIS3 can be explained. This region had only a symbolic response to RIS3, a fact that may surprise, given that it had proven itself to be a place-based leadership capable of executing and realising complex innovation policy goals. The authors consider the existence of different types of rationales for choosing whether to implement a new policy at the regional level. Access to structural funds is one of the drivers of RIS3 as a policy in the EU. Since Norwegian regions do not have access to EU structural funding, this incentive is missing. RIS3 development was neither required nor encouraged by the national government, while Norwegian regions became increasingly occupied with internal processes, managing the planning and execution of the reform. In addition, cuts in national budgets mean scarcer resources for R&D. RIS3 in Agder had potential to be a useful amendment to existing ways of working, planning, developing and executing a new set of effective regional innovation policies.

ACKNOWLEDGEMENT

This book has received support from the project EURIPER (EU Regional and Innovation Policies and Peripheral Regions), funded by the European Commission under the Jean Monnet Projects Action of the Erasmus+ Programme (Project Reference: 587410-EPP-1-2017-1-ES-EPPJMO -PROJECT).

REFERENCES

Asheim, B.T. (1996). Industrial districts as "learning regions": a condition for prosperity. *European Planning Studies*, *4*(4), 379–400.

Asheim, B.T. (2019). Smart specialisation, innovation policy and regional innovation systems: what about new path development in less innovative regions? *Innovation: The European Journal of Social Science Research*, *32*(1), 8–25, DOI: 10.1080/13511610.2018.1491001

Asheim, B.T., and M.S. Gertler (2005). The geography of innovation: regional innovation systems. In *The Oxford handbook of innovation*, edited by J. Fagerberg, D. Mowery and R. Nelson, 291–317. Oxford: Oxford University Press.

Asheim, B.T., and A. Isaksen (1997). Location, agglomeration and innovation: towards regional innovation systems in Norway? *European Planning Studies*, *5*(3), 299–330.

Barca, F., P. McCann and A. Rodríguez-Pose (2012). The case for regional development intervention: place-based versus place-neutral approaches. *Journal of Regional Science*, *52*(1), 134–52.

Becattini, G. (1990). The Marshallian industrial district as a socio-economic notion. In *Industrial districts and inter-firm co-operation in Italy*, edited by F. Pyke, G. Becattini and W. Sengenberger, 37–51. Geneva: International Labour Organization.

Boschma, R., and S. Iammarino (2009). Related variety, trade linkages, and regional growth in Italy. *Economic Geography*, *85*(3), 289–311.

Boschma, R.A., and J.G. Lambooy (1999). Evolutionary economics and economic geography. *Journal of Evolutionary Economics*, *9*(4), 411–29.

Cooke, P. (1992). Regional innovation systems: competitive regulation in the new Europe. *Geoforum*, *23*(3), 365–82.

Cooke, P. (2001). Regional innovation systems, clusters, and the knowledge economy. *Industrial and Corporate Change*, *10*(4), 945–74.

Cooke, P., M.G. Uranga and G. Etxebarria (1997). Regional innovation systems: institutional and organisational dimensions. *Research Policy*, *26*(4–5), 475–91.

Dosi, G., and R.R. Nelson (1994). An introduction to evolutionary theories in economics. *Journal of Evolutionary Economics*, *4*(3), 153–72.

Edquist, C. (ed.) (1997). *Systems of innovation: technologies, institutions and organizations*. London: Pinter.

Foray, D. (2014). *Smart specialisation: opportunities and challenges for regional innovation policy*. New York, NY: Routledge.

Frenken, K., F. Van Oort and T. Verburg (2007). Related variety, unrelated variety and regional economic growth. *Regional Studies*, *41*(5), 685–97.

González-López, M., B.T. Asheim and M.D.C. Sánchez-Carreira (2019). New insights on regional innovation policies. *Innovation: The European Journal of Social Science Research*, 32(1), 1–7, DOI: 10.1080/13511610.2018.1537121

Howells, J. (1999). Regional systems of innovation. In *Innovation policy in a global economy*, edited by D. Archibugi, J. Howells and J. Michie, 67–93. Cambridge: Cambridge University Press.

Lundvall, B.-Å. (1992). *National systems of innovation: towards a theory of innovation and interactive learning*. London: Pinter.

Lundvall, B.-Å, and B. Johnson (1994). The learning economy. *Journal of Industry Studies*, 1(2), 23–42.

McCann, P. (2015). *The regional and urban policy of the European Union: cohesion, results-orientation and smart specialisation*. Cheltenham, UK and Northampton, MA, USA: Edward Elgar Publishing.

Metcalfe, J.S., and L. Georghiou (1997). *Equilibrium and evolutionary foundations of technology policy*. CRIC Discussion Paper No. 3. Centre for Research on Innovation and Competition, University of Manchester.

Morgan, K. (1997). The learning region: institutions, innovation and regional renewal. *Regional Studies*, 31(5), 491–503.

Neffke, F., M. Henning and R. Boschma (2011). How do regions diversify over time? Industry relatedness and the development of new growth paths in regions. *Economic Geography*, 87(3), 237–65.

Nelson, R.R., and S.G. Winter (1982). *An evolutionary theory of economic change*. Cambridge: Belknap.

Porter, M.E. (2000). Location, competition, and economic development: local clusters in a global economy. *Economic Development Quarterly*, 14(1), 15–34.

Rodrik, D. (2005). Growth strategies. In *Handbook of economic growth*, edited by P. Aghion and S. Durlauf, 967–1014. Amsterdam: Elsevier.

Scott, A.J. (1988). Flexible production systems and regional development: the rise of new industrial spaces in North America and Western Europe. *International Journal of Urban and Regional Research*, 12(2), 171–86.

Storper, M., and B. Harrison (1991). Flexibility, hierarchy and regional development: the changing structure of industrial production systems and their forms of governance in the 1990s. *Research Policy*, 20(5), 407–22.

Uyarra, E. (2010). What is evolutionary about "regional systems of innovation"? Implications for regional policy. *Journal of Evolutionary Economics*, 20(1), 115–37, DOI: 10.1007/s00191-009-0135-y

1. The role of the Regional Innovation System approach in contemporary regional policy: is it still relevant in a globalised world?

Bjørn T. Asheim, Arne Isaksen and Michaela Trippl

1. INTRODUCTION

Schot and Steinmueller (2018) argue that science, technology and innovation policies can be framed in three different ways following the Second World War. The first framing, which they call 'R&D' (research and development), lasted until the 1970s; the second framing, referred to as 'National Systems of Innovation', peaked around 2010, but is still very influential; and the third framing, 'transformative change', has been increasing in importance since 2010, with its focus on how to solve grand societal challenges (Schot and Steinmueller, 2018). The Regional Innovation System (RIS) approach is an outcome of the second framing, and came into dominance in the 1990s (Asheim et al., 2019).

In this chapter we ask whether the RIS approach is still relevant in a globalised world that is increasingly confronted with grand global and societal challenges such as climate change, lack of economic growth, and high levels of social and regional inequality, as well as an ageing population, problems that either were not recognised in the 1980s and 1990s, when the innovation system approach was developed, or were not present during those decades. We also ask, how can the RIS approach still be relevant, and which changes in the approach would have to be implemented, for it to continue to be a powerful tool for designing and implementing regional (innovation) policies directed towards promoting transformative changes?

We seek to answer these questions via several steps. Firstly, we give a short account of how regional (innovation) policy has been transformed during the period of the three framings. In a next step we present in further detail the development of 'RIS-based policy' during the second framing.

We then propose some important changes the RIS approach must undergo to continue to be a relevant tool in the age of transformative change. We use examples from regional (innovation) policy in Europe to illustrate our discussion, and we end with reflections on RIS dynamics and our conclusions.

## 2.	REGIONAL POLICY IN THE THREE FRAMINGS

### 2.1	The First Framing – 'R&D'

In the aftermath of the Second World War, there was a strong focus on rebuilding Europe after the massive destruction that took place during the war years. Abundant economic resources were mobilised, e.g. through the Marshall Plan, to restart the engines of society so as to promote economic growth and increase standards of living as quickly as possible. One instrument of this strategy was allocating resources to R&D as an important way of boosting economic growth. This strategy is an example of the linear model of innovation, in which investments in R&D comprise the key variable in achieving increased competitiveness of firms and nations through new and improved products and processes. This view was launched by the American scientist Vannevar Bush (1945) in a report entitled *Science: The Endless Frontier*. The report expressed a strong belief in the potential economic impact of investments in science (Lundvall and Borrás, 2005). It was the first time science policy became a policy area. Science was looked upon as a productive force that could be economically and socially useful.

This linear view of innovation was a supply-based strategy, in which R&D input into the production system was the most important factor. Thus, the focus was on building the exploration capacity of firms and regions/nations, and no serious considerations were devoted to the diffusion and adoption dimensions of new technologies, nor to the strengthening of the exploitation capacity of firms. It was taken for granted that available new technologies would be automatically diffused and adopted by firms.[1]

In regional policy, this first framing of R&D was only partly manifested in the so-called 'Growth Centre' strategy. This strategy built on work by the French regional economist Perroux (1970) on 'Growth Poles', developing perspectives on concrete geographic and abstract economic space. The background for Perroux's development of his theory was the provision of a theoretical framework for the establishment of the European Coal and Steel Community in 1951, which was a forerunner and model for the formation of the European Economic Community (EEC) in 1957.

Perroux argued that companies exploiting agglomerated external econo-mies, i.e. localisation economies, in concrete geographic space, could intensify the benefits of external economies. Growth Poles in concrete geographic spaces were constituted by firms belonging to the same or closely supporting sectors (e.g. as a result of sector specialisation). Perroux asserted that firms within a Growth Pole were more innovative than firms outside a Growth Pole due to the impact of the 'key' or 'motor' industry of the Growth Pole, which is defined as an over-average innovative firm and which made the whole Growth Pole more innovative by impacting the other firms in the Growth Pole through knowledge spillovers and input–output linkages. This perspective on industrial and innovation policy was later revitalised by Porter's cluster concept in the 1990s.[2]

In the 1960s this was developed into a generalised regional innovation policy approach of Growth Centres, which became an important policy instrument in Europe for a couple of decades, aiming at generating regional multiplier effects that would promote economic growth in the regions (Holland, 1976). In addition to developing Perroux's Growth Pole theory, the Growth Centre approach was informed by Myrdal's (1957) and Hirschman's (1958) perspectives on unbalanced growth. The idea was that Growth Centres should promote spread or trickle-down effects from the centre to the surrounding peripheral regions, but often the result was that the backwash or polarisation effects were stronger, increasing regional inequalities between centre and periphery.

2.2 The Second Framing – 'National Systems of Innovation'

Following the oil shocks of the 1970s and the serious recession at the beginning of the 1980s, it became obvious that the linear model of innova-tion of the 'R&D' framing was not sufficient to generate the necessary level of economic growth. The economic crisis also intensified the competition between countries, which highlighted the differences in countries' innova-tive and productive performance. In this context it is important to note that the concept of innovation systems was introduced focusing on economic competitiveness. The aim of the Organisation for Economic Co-operation and Development (OECD) expert group in the 1980s, which developed the concept, was to provide a dynamic approach to international competitive-ness as an alternative to the static, cost-based view of international trade theory on how to promote competitiveness. Basing their insights on the principle of comparative advantage, protagonists of this traditional view argued that international competitiveness was achieved by having the most cost-efficient production of products and services. The OECD expert group presented a different view, arguing that international competitiveness could be achieved through promoting learning and innovation in societies, i.e. that competition was based on a country's innovativeness (Freeman, 2004). This idea was used ten years later by Porter, who argued for the role of clusters driving innovation, resulting in firms and countries obtaining competitive advantage (Porter, 1990).

Also in other dimensions, the innovation systems approach represents important theoretical and policy advances. Placing innovation at the centre of economic growth, it introduces innovation for the first time as interactive learning processes that take part between multiple actors and organisations (entrepreneurs, firms, universities, public agencies, government and civil society). This stands in contrast to the hitherto-dominating supply-side, linear model of innovation, in which innovation was seen as the outcome of a unidirectional process from basic via applied R&D to new products and processes. Innovation systems, thus, constitute the first explicit innovation policy approach compared with the previously dominating science and technology policies (Lundvall and Borrás, 2005). This is also the first policy approach emphasising that long-term relationships between key stakeholders (university, industry and government/public sector) can play a strategic role in the promotion of innovation and competitiveness, implying that not only the exploration capacity of the national system (i.e. the research infrastructure) was emphasised, but so too was the exploitation capacity of firms. Key to this focus on the exploitation side was the absorptive capacity of firms, which pointed to the educational level of people and firms. To generate employment growth and economic development, new technologies must be considered useful and relevant for industry, which to a high degree depends on the firms' absorptive capacity.

The National Systems of Innovation approach was directly influencing the development of the RIS approach at the beginning of the 1990s (Cooke, 1992; Asheim and Isaksen, 1997). The approach was also informed by the endogenous development that took place in the industrial districts of the Third Italy (the Central and North-Eastern regions of Italy), which was described as a transition from Fordism to Post-Fordism representing a second industrial divide in the history of capitalist industrialisation (Piore and Sabel, 1984). Post-Fordism rests on flexible specialisation as the basic organising principle of industrial production, i.e. semi-customised batch production carried out by a geographically agglomerated network of small and medium-sized enterprises (SMEs). The linear model was instrumental to the Fordist industrial model of large companies, often with their own R&D department, manufacturing standardised mass products.

In the context of the European Union (EU)'s regional policy agenda, the RIS perspective firstly became manifested in policy initiatives promoting technology transfer between university and industry in programmes and initiatives such as the European Commission's Regional Technology Plan (RTP) and further in DG XVII's Regional Innovation & Technology Transfer Strategy scheme and in DG XIII's Regional Information Society Initiative. The outcome of these initiatives, however, was a tendency to favour a one-size-fits-all approach (Tödtling and Trippl, 2005), where all regions opted for the same high-technology clusters, reinforcing the advantage of core regions. The exception in this picture was the Regional Innovation Strategy pilot actions launched by DG XVI, which were part of new policy developments in Europe in the 1990s to promote economic development through innovation in less developed regions within the EU (Bellini and Landabaso, 2007). In this action the concept of Learning Regions was applied as a strategy to develop more complete regional innovation systems, which owes much to the national innovation systems approach, in which capabilities of learning play a central role (Asheim, 2012).

However, the need for a more place-based, differentiated regional innovation policy that appreciated the huge differences within the heterogeneous landscape of regions in Europe, became increasingly more obvious, and in 2004, DG Research established an Expert Group for the purpose of developing a strategy called 'Constructing Regional Advantage' (Asheim et al., 2006; Asheim et al., 2011). The main message of the Constructing Regional Advantage (CRA) approach was to promote competitive advantage through an innovation-based differentiation strategy creating unique products and services, building on the view that this can be achieved in all types of industries and regions, yet based on the industry-specific modes of innovation and knowledge bases.

Thus, the CRA approach represented a broad-based innovation policy. This makes the approach instrumental in designing and implementing an innovation-based policy for promoting diversified specialisation. Moreover, as the aim of the CRA approach was to inform the development of regional innovation strategies, it constituted an explicit spatial, place-based approach.

The CRA approach implies that competitive advantage has to be constructed on the basis of the uniqueness of firms' and regions' capabilities (Asheim et al., 2006). As an important initial strategy for new path development, regions and countries should base their competitive strategy on industries in which they have traditionally been doing well. In designing and implementing the CRA strategy, RIS played a key role.

The CRA approach was followed by Smart Specialisation Strategy (S3), which was launched by the EU as a strategic approach to an innovation-based policy for regional economic development. It is the basis for European Structural and Investment Fund interventions in research and innovation (R&I) as part of the future Regional and Cohesion Policy's ambition for the European 2020 job and growth agenda to achieve a smart, inclusive and sustainable economy. The presence of an S3 strategy is a requirement as part of the next conditionality framework for a member state wishing to use its European Regional Development Fund (ERDF) for innovation activities. This is why all member regions in the EU have had to design and implement this strategy to receive structural funds in the coming years towards 2020.

S3 is probably the single largest attempt ever of an orchestrated, supranational innovation strategy to boost economic growth through economic diversification and new path development, e.g. diversifying the economy into technologically more advanced activities that move up the ladder of higher knowledge complexity and value creation compared with the present level in the region (Asheim et al., 2017). The aim is to plan for economic diversification in the short- and medium term, in addition to establishing a long-term perspective for promoting more fundamental structural changes in the economy through transformative activities. S3 represents an explicit, place-based approach, emphasising prioritisation through non-neutral, vertical policies as well as, for the first time in the EU's history, providing a policy framework for promoting and implementing a broad-based innovation policy. Thus, it could be argued that S3 in many ways builds on insights from the CRA approach (Asheim et al., 2011; Boschma, 2014).

S3 is not about 'specialisation' as known from previous regional development strategies, i.e. a Porter-like cluster strategy, but about diversified specialisation. What this means is that regions (and countries) should identify strategic sectors – or 'domains' – of existing and/or potential competitive advantage, in which they can specialise and create capabilities in a different way from other countries and regions. They should diversify their economies primarily based on existing strengths and capabilities by moving into related and unrelated sectors. S3 should build on 'each region's strengths, competitive advantage and potential for excellence' and 'support technological as well as practice-based innovation' (European Commission, 2014, p. 2).

'Smart' in the S3 approach refers to the identification of these domains of competitive advantage through what is called the 'entrepreneurial discovery' process. However, the emphasis here is not on the role of traditional entrepreneurs, resulting in a policy focus only on firm formation and start-ups as an individual entrepreneurial project. As underlined in the writings on S3, 'entrepreneurial' should be understood broadly to encompass all actors with an entrepreneurial mindset, including innovative

(Schumpeterian) entrepreneurs at the firm and company level, institutional entrepreneurs at universities and in the public sector, and place leadership at the regional level with the capacity to discover domains for securing existing and future competitiveness (Grillitsch and Sotarauta, 2018). Such a broad interpretation of 'entrepreneurial discovery' as a public–private initiative avoids the pitfall of ignoring the systemic nature of innovation as interactive learning involving a number of stakeholders. The systems approach to innovation policies also highlights the role of the public sector in driving innovation, as well as the balance between exploration and exploitation (Asheim and Gertler, 2005; Asheim et al., 2016).

The RIS approach can basically be viewed as an innovation-based theory of competitive advantage, i.e. representing a 'high road strategy' for regional economic development that consists of a process of economic diversification (structural change) in addition to mere economic growth (expansion). Furthermore, it also represents a focusing device for designing this strategy, as it points to the necessary (but not sufficient) components to put in place for implementing such a policy. It has, thus, also been shown to be instrumental for the design and implementation of S3 strategies.

Consequently, the RIS approach can be used for analysing why regions experience positive or, alternatively, less favourable economic development as well as for assessing how well policies for regional economic development have been designed and implemented (Trippl et al., 2019). During the years since the concept's introduction, the approach has mostly been viewed as an instrument for policy analysis, while the original use of the approach to promote innovation, economic growth and competitiveness has been rather ignored or forgotten, especially in academic research, even if it has been used to explain the uneven geography of innovation and economic development (Asheim and Gertler, 2005; Asheim et al., 2016).

However, in policy contexts, e.g. represented by Swedish government agency VINNOVA's regionally focused innovation policy, the growth and competitiveness perspectives have clearly been present. VINNOVA aims to create strong research and innovation milieus with a regional focus but with national and international linkages, which should strengthen Sweden's international competitiveness.

Regional innovation systems have played and will continue to play a strategic role in promoting the innovativeness and competitiveness of regions, which is the overall mission of innovation policy in the second framing. The RIS approach has lately been strengthened by attention being directed towards the need perceived by policy makers at both EU and regional levels to construct regional advantages (Asheim et al., 2006), recently within the framework of its S3 policy as described above. Thus, the RIS approach is still an efficient instrument for the design and implementation of the S3 strategy. It combines horizontal policies (e.g. promoting university–industry collaboration and building capacities in KETs [key enabling technologies]) and vertical place-based, direct and specific policies (e.g. VINNOVA's 'strong' R&I milieus). Moreover, policies inspired by the RIS approach represent a combination of top-down (horizontal) and bottom-up (vertical) approaches, in which the bottom-up part also constitutes an entrepreneurial discovery process involving regional stakeholders.

However, what about the potentials of the RIS approach to meet the requirements of the third framing of innovation policy, i.e. transformative change? Under this approach, the rationale for policy intervention is less to fend off market failure and to correct system failures than to shape and create markets (e.g. through the use of innovative public procurement) to address grand societal challenges and to solve capability constraints and reduce deficits within regional innovation systems with regard to interaction, connectivity and direction (Tödtling and Trippl, 2018; Asheim et al., 2019).

2.3   The Third Framing – 'Transformative Change'

A starting point for this discussion is the EU's ambition to become a smart, sustainable and inclusive economy by 2020, which is the overall aim of the Horizon 2020 funding programme. As Smart Specialisation Strategy (S3) is part of Horizon 2020, this is also the overall aim of S3. The 'inclusive' dimension relates strongly to key parts of the cohesion policy. Here, the aspects of promoting an economically and socially sustainable society take priority by integrating all citizens and regions in benefits resulting from economic growth and prosperity. In a Europe still suffering from too high unemployment, especially of young people particularly in Southern and Eastern Europe, this is a huge challenge. Consequently, an economic and innovation policy within the EU has to be 'smart' also in the sense that it can provide good, stable and well-paid jobs to all its citizens in all its regions.

S3 policies have a greater potential of achieving this than previous linear innovation policies due to the application of a broad-based approach to innovation and to the practice of taking the existing strengths and competitive advantage of regions as a starting point for the design of S3 priorities. This makes it possible to prioritise sectors with different modes of innovation and knowledge bases, and not only to try to boost high-tech sectors, which would only benefit already well-developed regions and only provide high-skill jobs. This would not serve well the majority of regions in the EU, especially in Southern and Eastern Europe, and it would lead to reduced cohesion socially and regionally; thus, it would be neither 'sustainable' nor 'inclusive'. A broad-based approach to S3 could develop a wide number of sectors that provide a majority of jobs in many Southern and Eastern European regions, and, thus, it is vital to the regional economy (e.g. tourism as a classical example) and would represent an 'inclusive' development.

An S3 priority focusing on the tourism sector should then strengthen the sector's competitive advantage by identifying unique regional assets that would differentiate it from the tourism sector of other competing regions, and enable it to climb the value-added ladder. Applying a 'sustainability' dimension in such a strategy would be logical.

Moreover, the success of achieving this depends to no small extent on the way the entrepreneurial discovery process is practised, or, more precisely, how collective this process is. If a narrow interpretation is used, with only entrepreneurs from the business sector being involved, the outcome would probably in the best cases be only 'smart', meaning profitable for the entrepreneur him-/herself but not qualifying as either 'sustainable' or 'inclusive'. A broader involvement of other stakeholders would probably make it easier to achieve, and to use the entrepreneurial discovery process to contribute to solving grand societal challenges as part of a region's S3 strategies.

Many of these societal challenges are related to the health and welfare sector, e.g. ageing and generally increasing public costs of providing sufficient public health services. In welfare states, the public sector is responsible for providing most of these services, and, thus, it represents a large and critical customer. This gives the public sector a strong motivation to drive innovation and entrepreneurial discovery processes as part of a public procurement of innovation (PPI) policy. This sector should also to an increasing degree involve users in developing innovations to improve the lives of patients with chronic diseases. Such user-driven innovations, involving 'ordinary' citizens (i.e. civil society actors), are a very good example of social innovations, including non-profit-seeking actors in the entrepreneurial discovery process. Academia can also play a key role in initiating and accommodating such user-driven innovations, as the 'Patient Innovation Lab' at the business school of the Catholic University in Lisbon illustrates (Oliveira et al., 2015).

To achieve a sustainable and inclusive social and economic development requires a long-term perspective, which is more easily realised with a strong commitment from the public sector. In an EU context this is pursued through a focus on solving grand social challenges such as energy supply, public health, ageing and climate change. In several regions, one or more of these challenges is part of the S3 (Trippl et al., 2019). The policy instrument to achieve this is 'system innovation policy', which the OECD defines as 'a horizontal policy approach that mobilises technology, market mechanisms, regulations and social innovations to solve complex societal problems in a set of interacting or interdependent components that form a whole socio-technical system' (2015, p. 7).

This represents a reorientation of the strategic focus from a place-based to a 'societal change-driven' policy transcending sectoral, geographical and organisational domains, which reflects a recent trend in European innovation policy. The aim of system innovation policy is to secure international competitiveness within thematically coherent but technologically and cognitively diverse areas to promote economic growth and provide solutions for grand societal challenges.

A broad-based innovation policy is better aligned to support a system innovation policy; as such a policy points to the need for reaching a balance between demand-oriented and supply-led strategies, in which place-specific context matters and innovation policy can be attuned to and embedded in the particularities of the regional and national economies it claims to target. However, a shortcoming of a system innovation policy approach is precisely the lack of such place-specific focus. Linking S3 with system innovation policy could, thus, be a solution to achieving a smart, sustainable and inclusive economy in the EU by 2020 (Asheim and Moodysson, 2017).

So, what modifications, adaptations and changes must be undertaken to make the RIS approach able to accommodate the needs for broader stakeholder involvement, stronger presence of agency and an expanding role of the public sector to strengthen the demand side of innovation policies, in addition to a continued upgrading of the importance of non-regional resources, knowledge linkages, and production and innovation networks?

In concrete terms, a broader stakeholder involvement can be achieved by expanding the RIS framework from a triple-helix to a quadruple-helix constellation by including civil society and non-governmental actors and agencies. This is already the ambition of S3 in the promotion of social innovations. An increased role of agency has also been pursued in S3 by the central position of the entrepreneurial discovery process in the implementation of the strategies, especially when using a broad and inclusive understanding of what is an entrepreneur. In the RIS approach this could be accommodated by explicitly allowing for different types of entrepreneurship in the 'boxes' of industry, university, public sector and civil society. And, lastly, the extended role of the public sector not only to correct market and system failures but also to shape and create markets to develop a critical demand for new products and services that can contribute to solving the grand societal challenges is a key factor in the new push for mission-oriented innovation policies (Mazzucato, 2017), which is high on the innovation agenda of the EU and many countries both in developed and emerging economies.

In general, these changes must lead to the RIS approach becoming more dynamic, opening up for continuous experimentation and learning as well as the formation of new bridging networks that link up previously unconnected actor groups and agencies to form coalitions better positioned to solve grand societal challenges (Tödtling and Trippl, 2018; Asheim et al., 2019). This points towards the urgency of coming up with new institutional practices and governance structures that transcend the existing segmented divisions between government, markets and civil society.

3.   RIS DYNAMICS AND REGIONAL STRUCTURAL CHANGE

In this section, we seek to explain how the RIS approach could lead to a better understanding of how regions (need to) reconfigure their organisational and institutional support structures for facilitating regional structural change and dealing with grand societal challenges. This is a key issue as the literature maintains that well-coordinated and stable regional innovation systems often support the further strengthening of dominating regional industries and established practices (Boschma et al., 2017; Weber and Truffer, 2017). Basically, then, RISs sustain regional industrial path extension and to some extent path upgrading rather than new path development, although the ability to initiate new paths differs between types of RISs due to varying degrees of regional organisational and institutional thickness and different capacities to absorb and anchor extra-regional assets (Isaksen and Trippl, 2016; Zukauskaite et al., 2017; Trippl et al., 2018). The 'lock-in approach' (Grabher, 1993) contributes to explaining the fact that RISs tend to support continuity rather than transformation. Lock-in stems from close networks between regional firms and between the political–administrative system and the regional industry. Strong regional industries also become institutionalised over time, in the sense of being embedded in the wider regional economy and society.

Based on these arguments, regional structural change may require that RISs change so that they are better equipped to support the emergence of new regional industries and innovations that contribute to solving grand societal challenges. The transformation of RISs can be of three main types (Tödtling and Trippl, 2013). Firstly, RIS transformation may involve the establishment of new organisations (such as an incubator or a prototype lab) or changes within existing organisations (such as new study programmes offered by existing educational bodies) (Miörner and Trippl,

2017). Secondly, RIS is transformed through new or changed relations between organisations, such as increased interactive learning between firms and between firms and universities (as a result of, for example, cluster policy programmes) or collaborative practices involving a larger variety of players belonging to complex quadruple-helix actor constellations. Thirdly, RIS transformation can include changes in laws and regulations and in informal institutions, such as the emergence of new routines and patterns of behaviour (Tödtling and Trippl, 2013).

Such RIS changes do not, however, occur automatically but call for agency in the meaning of an 'action or intervention by an actor to produce a particular effect' (Sotarauta and Suvinen, 2018, p. 90, drawing on Emirbayer and Mische, 1998). This leads to the understanding that transformative changes must be supported by agency that develops and adapts RISs to better support regional socio-economic structural transformation, in addition to innovative actions on the firm level. The 'role of human agency in new path creation' (Simmie, 2013, p. 171) has also gained increasing attention recently. In this view, new pathways 'require social action by knowledgeable pioneering individuals, universities, companies and/or governments' (Simmie, 2012, p. 769), and mindful deviation from existing structures by entrepreneurs is seen to constitute the heart of path creation (Garud and Karnøe, 2001, p. 6). This approach emphasises the importance of strategic agency of knowledgeable entrepreneurs who mindfully deviate from established ways of doing things. These are entrepreneurs who are able to break with existing social rules, technological paradigms and trajectories.

Isaksen et al. (2019) distinguish between two main types of agency, amongst other things to be able to focus on actions aiming to transform RISs. Firm-level agency considers how actors start new innovative ventures or initiate new activities in existing firms or organisations. Entrepreneurs are traditionally understood as individuals who start new firms more or less on their own. 'Schumpeter's entrepreneur is always a single human being acting strategically' (Weik, 2011, p. 471); Alsos et al. (2014, p. 97) maintain that 'entrepreneurship research traditionally views both the individual and the firm as decontextualized entities'. The innovation system approach has since the 1990s contributed to a change in the understanding of entrepreneurship and innovation activity as driven by individual actors to also include social and economic structures surrounding entrepreneurship and innovation (Lundvall, 1992; Porter, 1998; Spigel and Harrison, 2018). Entrepreneurship is then considered as 'the result of the interaction between individual actors and the surrounding environment' (Bosma et al., 2011, p. 484).

In addition, several studies point to the fact that firm-level agency is most often not a sufficient condition to initiate regional structural change.

In their study of the development of the wind turbine industry in Denmark and the US, Garud and Karnøe (2003), for example, use the concepts of distributed agency. This points towards how successful introduction of a new technology relies not only on those who introduce the technology in the market, but also on those who develop complementary assets and rivalling technology, on customers, on policy actors and so on. Thus, agency is distributed across multiple actors.

Distributed agency points to the second type of agency, i.e. system-level agency, which is linked to the RIS approach. System-level agency includes actions or interventions able to reconfigure RISs, and the 'industrial milieu' more generally, to better support growing industries and socioeconomic restructuring. The defining characteristic of system-level agency is that actors exert influences outside their institutional or organisational boundaries.

The distinction between firm-level and system-level agency and actors resembles the 'trinity of change agency' as put forward by Grillitsch and Sotarauta (2018). The first type of change agents includes innovative entrepreneurs. These are key actors for change as they are able to break 'with existing paths and work towards the establishments of new ones' (Grillitsch and Sotarauta, 2018, p. 11). The second group of change agents in this typology is institutional entrepreneurs. These are individuals, organisations or groups of actors who 'mobilize resources, competence, and power to create new institutions or to transform existing institutions' (Sotarauta and Pulkkinen, 2011, p. 98). Institutions, in the meaning of 'taken-for-granted, culturally embedded understandings' (Garud et al., 2007, p. 958), change slowly and thus tend to support the continuation of existing activities and procedures, and therefore usually support existing paths. Institutional change is then important for 'moulding rules of the game and playing fields for innovative entrepreneurs to surface and succeed' (Grillitsch and Sotarauta, 2018, p. 13). Institutional entrepreneurs may include policy makers, politicians, university leaders and firm leaders, who act intentionally and strategically. A common characteristic is a 'capacity to reflect and act in ways other than those prescribed by taken-for-granted rules' (Garud et al., 2007, p. 961). The third type of change agents are actors performing place leadership (Grillitsch and Sotarauta, 2018). Firms that represent seeds for new regional growth paths need access to sufficient resources and knowledge to be able to grow. 'This calls for a collective mobilisation of resources to support the emergence and growth of new paths' (Grillitsch and Sotarauta, 2018, p. 13), i.e. place leadership.

Similar arguments to those linked to system-level agency and institutional entrepreneurship are also put forward by Musiolik, Markard and Hekkert (2012). These authors regard system building as an important activity in the development of technological innovation systems that are able to support emerging business fields. 'System building is the deliberate creation and modification of broader institutional and organisational structures . . . carried out by innovating actors' (Musiolik et al., 2012, p. 1035). System building is regarded as a collective approach by a number of actors who join forces in networks. A key to changes in technological innovation systems is the interplay and deployment of resources at the organisational, network and system levels.

We have so far argued that regional structural change often requires deliberate initiatives to transform RISs by system-level actors at the same time as firm-level actors establish new firms or conduct innovations in existing firms that contribute to initiating a new path. The distinction between firm-level agency and system-level agency can provide the basis for two different, simple 'roads' to transformation (Isaksen et al., 2019).

A firm-oriented road starts when firm-level actors come up with new ideas, inventions or innovations that can contribute to upgrade existing or create new regional paths. However, two other conditions must be present for a new path to appear. Firstly, the innovation developed by the forerunners has to be employed and possibly adapted and improved by several other firm actors so that a critical mass of firms or organisations using a new technology, producing a new product or service, and so on, emerges (Foray, 2015). Secondly, the RIS needs to be transformed to better fit an emerging new or altered regional path. In this case, firm-level agency as it were 'pushes' forward changes in the RIS. The development starts at the firm level, but, as argued above, system-level agency plays an important role in reconfiguring wider RIS structures.

The other route, i.e. the RIS-oriented road, has its origin in system-level actors developing and adapting RISs to better fit real or assumed needs of possible new industries, technologies, business models and so on. Examples of system-level agency are the establishment of new organisations that contribute to the commercialisation of research ideas or to testing and experimenting with new green technologies, and the adaption of policy tools to support emerging industries or new social practices or to enable regulations to protect firms in new market niches. The idea is then that firm-level actors in new and existing firms respond to new possibilities introduced through RIS reconfiguration, which can lead to the fact that more firms and organisations use new knowledge and skills, and a new regional path can emerge though the diffusion and adaptation of new technologies and social practices.

A possible drawback with the second road is lack of relevant responses from firm-level actors and other organisations. This can lead to a classic 'cathedral in the desert' situation, which occurs when the regional actors lack absorptive capacity to utilise knowledge and technology found in the RIS. This points to the fact that system-level and firm-level agency need to be coordinated, i.e. that competence and other assets should be built on both the system and the organisational levels.

4.   CONCLUSIONS

In this chapter, we have demonstrated that the RIS approach has played – and continues to play – a powerful role in informing the design and implementation of regional innovation policies. RIS scholars have begun to complement their traditional focus on 'innovation for economic growth' by directing more attention to novel solutions that contribute to solving grand societal challenges such as climate change, resource depletion, the ageing of society, and increasing territorial and social inequalities. As shown in this chapter, the RIS approach continues to produce important insights on how to boost regional economic and societal development, not least due to recent advances of the concept that pay more attention to the direction and desirability of innovation and change, take account of new innovation actors not covered by the traditional triple-helix approach, and outline how to think about (and promote) RIS dynamics, i.e. the reconfiguration of regional organisational and institutional support structures in order to meet current and future economic and societal problems.

NOTES

1.   In this context it is quite a paradox that the linear view still has quite a lot of influence in important agencies responsible for (regional) innovation policy. One example is the EU Commission's Directorate-General for Research (DG Research).
2.   Porter has obviously read Perroux, as his cluster theory closely resembles Perroux's 'Growth Pole' approach. In the original presentation of his approach, in *The Competitive Advantage of Nations* (1990), clusters referred mainly to non-agglomerated, national industrial clusters (cf. Perroux's ideas about abstract economic space) (Porter, 1990, p. 149), even if some of the case studies (e.g. industrial districts in the 'Third Italy') referred to agglomerated regional clusters. In his 1998 article in *Harvard Business Review*, he defines clusters as regional clusters only (Porter, 1998) (cf. Perroux's writing on concrete geographic space).

REFERENCES

Alsos, G.A., Carter, S., and Ljunggren, E. (2014). Kinship and business: How entrepreneurial households facilitate business growth. *Entrepreneurship & Regional Development*, 26(1–2), 97–122.

Asheim, B.T. (2012). The changing role of learning regions in the globalising knowledge economy: A theoretical re-examination. *Regional Studies*, 46(8), 993–1004.

Asheim, B.T., and Gertler, M.S. (2005). The geography of innovation: Regional innovation systems, in J. Fagerberg, D.C. Mowery and R. Nelson (eds), *The Oxford Handbook of Innovation*, Oxford, UK: Oxford University Press, pp. 291–317.

Asheim, B.T., and Isaksen, A. (1997). Location, agglomeration and innovation: Towards regional innovation systems in Norway? *European Planning Studies*, 5(3), 299–330.

Asheim, B.T., and Moodysson, J. (2017). Innovation policy for economic resilience: The case of Sweden. CIRCLE Papers in Innovation Studies 2017/5, Lund University, Sweden.

Asheim, B.T. et al. (2006). *Constructing Regional Advantage: Principles – Perspectives – Policies*. Final report from DG Research Expert Group on 'Constructing Regional Advantage'. DG Research, European Commission, Brussels.

Asheim, B.T., Boschma, R., and Cooke, P. (2011). Constructing regional advantage: Platform policies based on related variety and differentiated knowledge bases. *Regional Studies*, 45(7), 893–904.

Asheim, B.T., Grillitsch, M., and Trippl, M. (2016). Regional innovation systems: Past – present – future, in R. Shearmur, C. Carrincazeaux and D. Doloreux (eds), *Handbook of the Geographies of Innovation*, Cheltenham, UK and Northampton, MA, USA: Edward Elgar Publishing, pp. 45–62.

Asheim, B.T., Grillitsch, M., and Trippl, M. (2017). Smart Specialisation as an innovation-driven strategy for economic diversification, in S. Radosevic, A. Curaj, R. Gheorgiou, L. Andreescu and I. Wade (eds), *Advances in the Theory and Practice of Smart Specialisation*, Amsterdam: Elsevier Science Publishers, pp. 74–97.

Asheim, B., Isaksen, A., and Trippl, M. (2019). *Regional Innovation Systems: An Advanced Introduction*. Cheltenham, UK and Northampton, MA, USA: Edward Elgar Publishing.

Bellini, N., and Landabaso, M. (2007). Learning about innovation in Europe's regional policy, in R. Rutten and F. Boekema (eds), *The Learning Region: Foundations, State of the Art, Future*, Cheltenham, UK and Northampton, MA, USA: Edward Elgar Publishing, pp. 231–51.

Boschma, R. (2014). Constructing regional advantage and Smart Specialisation: Comparison of two European policy concepts. *Italian Journal of Regional Science*, 13(1), 51–65.

Boschma, R., Coenen, L., Frenken, K., and Truffer, B. (2017). Towards a theory of regional diversification: Combining insights from Evolutionary Economic Geography and Transition Studies. *Regional Studies*, 51(1), 31–45.

Bosma, N., Schutjens, V., and Stam, E. (2011). Regional entrepreneurship, in P. Cooke, B. Asheim, R. Boschma, R. Martin, D. Schwartz and F. Tödtling (eds), *Handbook of Regional Innovation and Growth*, Cheltenham, UK and Northampton, MA, USA: Edward Elgar Publishing, pp. 482–94.

Bush, V. (1945). *Science: The Endless Frontier*. Washington, DC: United States Government Printing Office.

Cooke, P. (1992). Regional innovation systems: Competitive regulation in the new Europe, *Geoforum*, 23(3), 365–82.

Emirbayer, M., and Mische, A. (1998). What is agency? *The American Journal of Sociology*, 103(4), 962–1032.

European Commission (2014). National/regional innovation strategies for smart specialisation (RIAS3). Brussels: European Commission.

Foray, D. (2015). *Smart Specialisation: Opportunities and Challenges for Regional Innovation Policy*. London and New York, NY: Routledge.

Freeman, C. (2004). Technological infrastructure and international competitiveness, *Industrial and Corporate Change*, 13(3), 541–69.

Garud, R., and Karnøe, P. (2001). Path creation as a process of mindful deviation, in R. Garud and P. Karnøe (eds), *Path Dependence and Creation*, Hillsdale, NJ: Lawrence Erlbaum Associates, pp. 1–38.

Garud, R., and Karnøe, P. (2003). Bricolage versus breakthrough: Distributed and embedded agency in technology entrepreneurship. *Research Policy*, 32(2), 277–300.

Garud, R., Hardy, C., and Maguire, S. (2007). Institutional entrepreneurship as embedded agency: An introduction to the special issue. *Organization Studies*, 28(7), 957–69.

Grabher, G. (1993). The weakness of strong ties: The lock-in of regional development in the Ruhr area, in G. Grabher (ed.), *The Embedded Firm: On the Socioeconomics of Industrial Networks*. London and New York, NY: Routledge, pp. 255–77.

Grillitsch, M., and Sotarauta, M. (2018). *Regional Growth Paths: From Structure to Agency and Back*. CIRCLE, University of Lund, Lund: Papers in Innovation Studies. Paper no. 2018/01.

Hirschman, A.O. (1958). *The Strategy of Economic Development*. New Haven, CT: Yale University Press.

Holland, S. (1976). *Capital versus the Regions*. Basingstoke: Macmillan.

Isaksen, A., and Trippl, M. (2016). Path development in different regional innovation systems: A conceptual analysis, in M.D. Parrilli, R.D. Fitjar and A. Rodríguez-Pose (eds), *Innovation Drivers and Regional Innovation Strategies*, London: Routledge, pp. 66–84.

Isaksen, A., Jakobsen, S.E., Njøs, R., and Normann, R. (2019). Regional industrial restructuring resulting from individual and system agency. *Innovation: The European Journal of Social Science Research*, 32(1), 48–65.

Lundvall, B.Å. (ed.) (1992). *National Systems of Innovation: Towards a Theory of Innovation and Interactive Learning*. London: Anthem Press.

Lundvall, B.Å., and Borrás, S. (2005). Science, technology, and innovation policy, in J. Fagerberg, D.C. Mowery and R. Nelson (eds), *The Oxford Handbook of Innovation*, Oxford, UK: Oxford University Press, pp. 599–631.

Mazzucato, M. (2017). *Mission-Oriented Innovation Policy: Challenges and Opportunities*, Institute of Innovation and Public Purpose (IIPP) Working Paper, 2017-1.

Miörner, J., and Trippl, M. (2017). Paving the way for new regional industrial paths: Actors and modes of change in Scania's games industry. *European Planning Studies*, 25(3), 481–97.

Musiolik, J., Markard, J., and Hekkert, M. (2012). Networks and network resources in technological innovation systems: Towards a conceptual framework for system building. *Technological Forecasting & Social Change*, 79, 1032–48.

Myrdal, G. (1957). *Economic Theory and Underdeveloped Regions*. London: Gerald Duckworth.

OECD (2015). *System Innovation: Synthesis Report*. Paris: OECD.

Oliveira, P., Zejnilovic, L., Canhão, H., and von Hippel, E. (2015). Innovation by patients with rare diseases and chronic needs. *Orphanet Journal of Rare Diseases*, 10(41), 2–9.

Perroux, F. (1970). Note on the concept of Growth Poles, in D. McKee, R. Dean and W. Leahy (eds), *Regional Economics: Theory and Practice*, New York, NY: The Free Press, pp. 93–103.

Piore, M.J., and Sabel, C (1984). *The Second Industrial Divide: Possibilities for Prosperity*. New York, NY: Basic Books.

Porter, M.E. (1990). *The Competitive Advantage of Nations*. London: Macmillan.

Porter, M.E. (1998). Clusters and the new economics of competition. *Harvard Business Review*, 77–90.

Schot, J., and Steinmueller, E. (2018). Three frames for innovation policy: R&D, systems of innovation and transformative change. *Research Policy*, 47(9), 1554–67.

Simmie, J. (2012). Path dependence and new technological path creation in the Danish wind power industry. *European Planning Studies*, 20(5), 753–72.

Simmie, J. (2013). Path dependence and new technological path creation in the economic landscape, in P. Cooke (ed.), *Re-framing Regional Development: Evolution, Innovation and Transition*, London and New York, NY: Routledge, pp. 164–85.

Sotarauta, M., and Pulkkinen, R. (2011). Institutional entrepreneurship for knowledge regions: In search of a fresh set of questions for regional innovation studies. *Environment and Planning C: Government and Policy*, 29, 96–112.

Sotarauta, M., and Suvinen, N. (2018). Institutional agency and path creation: Institutional path from industrial to knowledge city, in A. Isaksen, R. Martin and M. Trippl (eds), *New Avenues for Regional Innovation Systems: Theoretical Advances, Empirical Cases and Policy Lessons*, Berlin: Springer, pp. 85–104.

Spigel, B., and Harrison, R. (2018). Towards a process theory of entrepreneurial ecosystems. *Strategic Entrepreneurship Journal*, 12(1), 151–68.

Tödtling, F., and Trippl, M. (2005). One size fits all? Towards a differentiated regional innovation policy approach. *Research Policy*, 34(8), 1203–19.

Tödtling, F., and Trippl, M. (2013). Transformation of regional innovation systems: From old legacies to new development paths, in P. Cooke (ed.), *Reframing Regional Development: Evolution, Innovation and Transition*. London and New York, NY: Routledge, pp. 297–317.

Tödtling, F., and Trippl, M. (2018). Regional innovation policies for new path development: Beyond neoliberal and traditional systemic views. *European Planning Studies*, 26(9), 1779–95.

Trippl, M., Grillitsch, M., and Isaksen, A. (2018). Exogenous sources of regional industrial change: Attraction and absorption of non-local knowledge for new path development. *Progress in Human Geography*, 42(5), 687–705.

Trippl, M., Zukauskaite, E., and Healy, A. (2019). Shaping Smart Specialisation: The role of place-specific factors in advanced, intermediary and less-developed European regions. *Regional Studies* (in press), doi: 10.1080/00343404.2019.1582763

Weber, K.M., and Truffer, B. (2017). Moving innovation systems research to the next level: Towards an integrative agenda. *Oxford Review of Economic Policy*, 33(1), 101–21.

Weik, E. (2011). Institutional entrepreneurship and agency. *Journal of the Theory of Social Behaviour*, 44(4), 466–81.

Zukauskaite, E., Trippl, M., and Plechero, M. (2017). Institutional thickness revisited. *Economic Geography*, 93(4), 325–45.

2. Advancing place-based regional innovation policies

Robert Hassink

1. INTRODUCTION

We live in times of great economic and political instability in large parts of the world. Some scholars even observe a crisis in global capitalism and neoliberal globalization (O'Sullivan, 2019). Politically, we can observe a rising populism, with increasingly loud anti-establishment, nationalistic voices, particularly in old industrial areas, such as the Rust Belt in the USA and Northern England (Rodríguez-Pose, 2018). Therefore, uneven regional development is clearly seen to be directly related to current times of economic and political instability. According to Barca (2019), three inter-related inequalities are at work here: economic, social and recognition inequalities. The last also refers to issues related to identity (Fukuyama, 2018). Part of the problem, however, also lies in perceptions: "what arouses popular opposition is not inequality per se, but perceived unfairness" (Rodrik, 2018, p. 18). Moreover, Rodríguez-Pose (2018, pp. 204–5) recently stated in this context, "local inhabitants . . . want opportunities rather than assistance and aid; they want a future rather than permanent support. It is in these circumstances when they feel at their most vulnerable", and continued, "territorial inequality, persistent lack of opportunities and incapacity and/or unwillingness to move are at the root of a resentment that is lighting the fire of territorially based populism. Withdrawing intervention in these areas will inevitably add fuel to the fire". At the same time, regional policies, which are supposed to successfully tackle regional economic inequalities, have increasingly moved towards regional innovation policies, particularly in Europe (OECD, 2009, 2010, 2011).

Given the changing circumstances, what regional innovation policies do we have in place and are they still powerful?

First, a place-neutral (or spatially blind, people-based) policy solution is advocated for by geographical economics (see for instance, the World Bank Report "Reshaping Economic Geography" (World Bank, 2009). This approach strongly emphasizes the importance of agglomeration economies in general for regional economic development. However, the policy recommendations derived from geographical economics have been criticized for treating space and scales in a reductionist way, due to strict assumptions, and for their limited explanatory power in the real world (Martin, 2015; Barca, 2019). Moreover, the above-mentioned methodological approach does not account for contextual, geographical differences, leading to a one-size-fits-all approach to regional policy. There is also a belief among the advocates of this policy solution that "institutional reforms should spread 'best-practices' designed independently of particular places" (Barca, 2019, p. 84). Finally, since place-neutral policy solutions are strongly linked to the neoliberal capitalism that is in crisis (Economist, 2016), they are not considered to be in a good position to provide alternative models of development.

This leads to the second approach, which, in contrast to the first approach, consists of tailor-made, place-based policy solutions, which have been advocated for by theories and paradigms in economic geography, often based on heterodox economics (Barca et al., 2012; Pike et al., 2017). These kinds of policies come with different terms in the literature, such as place-based policy, place-based regional policy and place-sensitive policy (Rodríguez-Pose, 2018; Iammarino et al., 2019; Farole et al., 2018). The key strengths of place-based approaches to regional innovation policy (Barca et al., 2012; OECD, 2009) are that they take real places with their unique institutional context seriously and that they aim at providing tailor-made policy solutions. The most recent regional innovation policy concept in Europe, smart specialization (Foray, 2015), situates the place-based approach as one of four key priority-setting rationales next to related variety, revealed competitive advantage and entrepreneurial discovery (Grillitsch and Asheim, 2018).

Although place-based policies have been recently favoured in general to fight the problems in lagging regions leading to populism, more of the same would not be a solution. In fact, improved place-based policies are necessary to fight populism (Rodríguez-Pose, 2018, p. 189). However, how can these policies be improved? And what exactly is meant by place-based policies? This chapter aims to contribute to better place-based policies by creating a firmer understanding and conceptualization of place. In the next section, I describe the general trends in regional innovation policy and its theoretical foundations, before turning to the recent discussion about place-based policies, in section 3. In section 4, I argue in favour of a stronger conceptualization of place for regional innovation policy, and in section 5 I draw some conclusions.

2. REGIONAL INNOVATION POLICIES: GENERAL TRENDS[1]

Regional innovation policies have developed rapidly in Europe since the mid-1980s. This surge is mainly due to the increasing importance of the regional level with regard to diffusion-oriented innovation support policies (Cooke and Morgan, 1998; Landabaso, 1997; Hassink, 1992; Asheim et al., 2003). Partly supported by national and supranational support programmes and encouraged by strong institutional set-ups found in successful regional economies, such as Baden-Württemberg in Germany and Emilia-Romagna in Italy, many regions in Europe have been setting up several regional innovation support measures. They include science parks, technopoles, technological financial aid schemes, innovation support agencies, community colleges and initiatives to support clustering of industries since the second half of the 1980s. The central aim of these policies is to support regional endogenous potential by encouraging the diffusion of new technologies from both universities and public research establishments to small and medium-sized enterprises (SMEs), between SMEs and large enterprises (vertical cooperation), and between SMEs themselves (horizontal cooperation). Over the years, however, these policies have been the target of strong criticism for a variety of reasons. Tödtling and Trippl (2005) criticized one-size-fits-all approaches, on the basis that different regions suffer from different shortcomings, and that innovation policy should be designed with that in mind. Moreover, regional innovation policies suffer from the innovation paradox, as defined by Oughton et al. (2002). This refers to the observed fact that lagging regions are often the ones with less capacity to make effective use of the policy instruments created to increase innovation potential. Therefore, innovation policies are likely to reinforce current regional inequalities, by allowing those firms in core regions to develop even further their potential. As a way to deal with these problems, I suggest a multi-scalar approach that considers not only the regional dimension (Gong and Hassink, 2018), but also the organizational (below the region) and the national (above the region) scales. The effectiveness of innovation policy, particularly in poorer regions, results from the interaction between these three scales of activity.

Regional innovation policies consist of four groups of measures. First, a large range of financial aid schemes, such as support for research and development (R&D), is devised at national and in some countries also at regional level to boost the innovativeness of SMEs. Second, assistance is sought from technology transfer and consultancy agencies, a group that includes all agencies found in a region operating at three different stages of support: the provision of general information, and the provision of technological advice and support for joint R&D projects, between firms (of which technology-following SMEs are the main group) and universities and public research establishments (Hassink, 1996). Agencies that belong to this group try to help to solve innovation problems mainly of technology-following SMEs either by giving them advice themselves or by referring them to other agencies in a further stage of support. Third, in the 1990s, there were technology parks, a land- and property-led technology policy concept, which aimed at encouraging the spatial clustering of high-tech firms and R&D organizations. The parks were very popular among local, regional and national policy makers as a tool to boost regional economic growth. They often adopted different denominations, such as science parks, high-tech centres, incubator centres, technology parks, technoparks or science cities, but their final aim was similar, namely to boost regional technology transfer, innovativeness and hence competitiveness. Fourth, in addition to the three more traditional policy measures, the most recent measures focus on the "smart specialization" of regions (Foray, 2015; Hassink and Gong, 2019). The objective of this new wave of innovation policies is twofold. First, it aims to build on the complementarities that exist in a region and encourage processes of path creation through related variety and cross-sectoral collaboration. Second, it aims to go beyond a narrow emphasis on stimulating the production of codified knowledge (R&D, patenting), to consider not only other types of knowledge (synthetic, symbolic) but also other elements such as good governance and human capital, which are seen as essential to ensure good policy making. For an extensive description of innovation policies in different contexts, see McCann and Ortega-Argilés (2013).

2.1 Regional Innovation Policies: Why Did They Surge?

The increasing importance of regions for innovation policy can be considered as the outcome of a convergence of regional and technology policy since the early 1980s. These two policy fields converged into regional innovation policies because their aim became partly the same, namely supporting the innovative capabilities and thus competitiveness of SMEs. Moreover, there have been decentralization and regionalization trends in innovation policy not only in Europe, but also in the USA and East Asia (Cooke and Morgan, 1998). These trends fit with what Asheim et al. (2003) observed as a shift from a firm-oriented, static allocation of resources for innovation to a trans-sectoral, dynamic and system-oriented, learning-to-innovate policy based on pro-active, multi-actor partnership. Although we can speak of a general phenomenon, there are of course significant differences between individual regions and countries concerning the extent to which these trends take place (see also Prange, 2008). Generally, contributing factors to regional innovation policies are a federal political system, decentralization, strong regional institutions and governance, a marked industrial specialization in the region, socio-cultural homogeneity and thus relationships of trust, large economic restructuring problems, and a robust commitment of regional political leaders (Hassink, 1996).

One of the main arguments supporting the use of the regional level for innovation support has been called the "garden argument" (Paquet, 1998): if the economy is regarded as a garden with all kinds of trees and plants, for the gardener (government) there is no simple rule likely to apply to all plants. Growth is therefore best orchestrated from its sources at the level of cities and regions. At this level, rather than at the national level, policy makers can better tailor policy in relation to demand (Nauwelaers and Wintjes, 2003). Regionalization, therefore, allows for differentiation in policies, which is necessary because of differing regional economic conditions and thus different support needs of industries and firms. Regionalization also raises the enthusiasm and motivation of regional policy makers, as they are now able to devise "their own" policies. Scholars in favour of a place-based approach towards regional development policy (Barca et al., 2012; OECD, 2011) have recently taken up the arguments in favour of regionalization, which unfolds endogenous potential in regions, again.

2.2 Standardization

Despite the above-mentioned garden argument and the plea for tailored regional innovation policy, the use of benchmarking, the creation of partnerships and the search for best practices have led to the standardization of regional innovation policies in Europe (Tödtling and Trippl, 2005). The European Commission strongly supports partnerships and benchmarking between cities and regions in Europe in the framework of several programmes. Moreover, an increasing number of consultancies, such as McKinsey, earn their living through benchmarking exercises and advices to regional governments all over the world with lessons learned in successful regions. There is also a rich literature describing policy initiatives in full detail and trying to come to some kind of comparison in the concluding sections (OECD, 2007, 2010, 2011). Learning from best-practice initiatives is the main credo of many of these studies. Particularly in Europe, one of the main arguments in favour of interregional learning processes has been the institutional diversity in that continent: one should benefit from the strengths of the diversity of innovation policies in regions and nations (Hassink and Lagendijk, 2001). However, according to Coenen and Morgan (2019, p. 3), "the more generic, place-blind policy mobility to emulate and transfer best-practice from successful regions such as Silicon Valley, often resulting in the heroic but naive effort to build high-tech cathedrals in the desert".

The regional innovation paradox (Oughton et al., 2002) is another important, yet relatively ignored argument against standardization and in favour of differentiated, fine-tuned policies. Oughton et al. (2002) identified an important paradox in this field: due to the lack of absorptive capacity, less-favoured regions cannot benefit to the same extent from innovation policies as structurally strong regions, which leads to greater territorial disparities and hence to eroding cohesion. Richer regions make a better use of policy instruments to stimulate further innovative capacity.

National governments, however, often play a significant role in devising policy, not only for innovation but also in many other areas of government intervention. It is true that, in some countries, regions have more autonomy to devise policy (Baier et al., 2013); however, recent research has been unable to find conclusive evidence that strong regional decentralization leads to higher levels of growth in the member countries of the Organisation for Economic Co-operation and Development (OECD) (Ezcurra and Rodríguez-Pose, 2013). In practice, this means that national institutional variation is likely the most important element explaining different growth rates. In another study, Percoco (2013) suggested that the main factor explaining different levels of efficiency in regional development is national institutional settings. Both studies point to the continuing relevance of national policies in explaining different rates of economic growth and should lead us to incorporate this level of analysis when explaining dysfunctions at the regional or local levels.

2.3 Towards a New Understanding of Innovation

Regional innovation policies are embedded in the understanding of innovation of the economy and of society, at large. For a long time, they were embedded in a relatively narrow understanding of market-based, technology-driven innovation, without much questioning of the need and function of innovation (Coenen and Morgan, 2019). The current generation of innovation (e.g., artificial intelligence, radical innovations in green and/or manufacturing technologies, digitalization, etc.) is much more complex than innovation of the previous generations as it is arguably characterized by high uncertainty and high risk. Moreover, high hopes are put on innovation, or innovation-based activities, for solving many of the grand societal challenges, such as climate change, demographic changes, the widening of digital gaps, environmental deterioration and the loss of biodiversity (Schot and Steinmueller, 2018). In this context, states have increasingly been expected to play a more important role in facilitating the new generation of innovation, as the complexity of innovation requires various resources and actors that are beyond the reach of individual firms. Among others, mission-oriented innovation policies have become increasingly popular among policy makers at several spatial levels, both in coordinated and liberal market economies (Mazzucato, 2018; Coenen et al., 2015; Morgan, 2018). In contrast to previous generations of mission-oriented innovation policies, which aimed for instance at nuclear and defence-related projects and were strongly centrally steered and controlled by governmental organizations in a top-down way, the new generation is supposed to be more bottom-up, decentralized and focused on experimentation and learning among a broader group of actors, including niche actors. However, what role regions are supposed to play in this new generation of innovation policies is relatively unclear. Arguably, some of these broader groups of actors, such as experimenting niche actors, can be found particularly at the local and regional level, where they can play a role in regional innovation policies (Tödtling and Trippl, 2018; Uyarra et al., 2019), smart specialization (Foray, 2015) and new path development.

Moreover, Coenen and Morgan (2019) recently argued in favour of opening up innovation to the so-called foundational economy (see also Engelen et al., 2017; Marques et al., 2018). "The foundational economy model focuses on the unfashionable mundane sectors that are designed to keep us 'safe, sound and civilized', such as health, education, dignified care for the elderly, social housing, agrifood, and energy" (Coenen and Morgan, 2019, p.6). Arguing for a move beyond separated social innovations, these authors see potential in fostering market-based technological innovations in the foundational economy, but they are relatively vague on how to achieve this. As the foundational economy, in which the state is often heavily involved, plays a relatively important role in lagging regions, they see potential in reducing inequalities by promoting innovations in the foundational economy of lagging regions (Coenen and Morgan, 2019). Furthermore, this is seen as the part of the economy that is place based and hence fits well with the new policy framework of place-based policies (Heslop et al., 2019).

3.   PLACE-BASED POLICIES

As mentioned above, the place-based policy framework developed by Barca (2009, 2019) and Barca et al. (2012) is an increasingly popular policy framework, in which geographical context, consisting of social, cultural and institutional elements, matters and policy intervention, should include the participation of a broad group of actors, avoiding social exclusion and unevenness. According to Barca (2019, p. 88), place-based policy aims at "giving people in places stuck in an under-development trap the *power* and the *knowledge* to expand their 'sustainable substantial freedom' by improving their access to, and the quality of, essential services, and by promoting the opportunity to innovate, thus reducing economic, social and recognition inequalities" (italics in original).

Barca (2009) suggested a "place-based" approach to regional development that is both strongly supportive of incorporating local knowledge into the design of the policy itself, and that seeks to integrate the different scales of government to ensure good coordination and effectiveness. The latter is necessary, as many key policies for regional development, such as those covering education (including higher education), science and technology, industrial development, labour markets, and others, are primarily devised at the national level, with regions having only a certain amount of input. As a consequence, if we observe deficiencies at the regional level for example in terms of skills, it would be a mistake to take into consideration only the endogenous features of that region.

Moreover, multilevel governance is seen as a key issue in the place-based policy approach, as local actors alone, particularly the local elites (often "rentiers"), are not able or willing to make many important changes, "since they derive power and income from a condition of local backwardness" (Barca, 2019, p. 87). Particularly in structurally weak regions, such as old industrial areas and rural areas, these local elites have been benefiting from so-called "compassionate compensations" to combat inequalities. However, "while sustaining employment and income in the short term, *compassionate compensations*, have produced perverse effects, by turning local elites into intermediaries of public funds and *rentiers*, weakening people's motivation for mobilisation and change" (italics in original) (Barca, 2019, p. 88).

What, then, is the role of national governments? According to Barca (2009, p. 41), their role is to formulate general aims, to monitor and to evaluate, whereas local and regional governments have "the freedom to advance the ends as they see fit" (Barca, 2009, p. 41). By doing the latter, they are supposed to foster untapped resources and potential in regional economies, similar to much older arguments in favour of fostering endogenous potential in regions (Stöhr, 1980). However, the danger is that rentiers and other rent-seeking actors in regions abuse this, by making choices to their own benefit. In order to avoid this, Barca (2019) draws on democratic experimentalism (Sabel and Zeitlin, 2012; see also Morgan, 2018), that is "to make the local decision-making process verifiable, open, experimental and inclusive" (Coenen and Morgan, 2019,

p. 8). Experimental governance is defined as "a recursive process of provisional goal-setting based on learning from the comparison of alternative approaches to advancing them in different contexts" (Sabel and Zeitlin, 2012, p. 169). The experimental approach allows for room for experimentation, but at the same time it involves constant, mutual monitoring and the flexibility and willingness to adapt and change interventions and policies. It combines "bottom-up localism and agent empowerment with the top-down pressure for standards, testing and the dissemination of the results of localized learning beyond the confines of the locality" (Coenen and Morgan, 2019, p. 9). The role of these national and supranational authorities, "as well as committing [themselves] to make sectoral interventions place-aware, must also trigger the endogenous change that the internal economic and political forces of a place [i.e., the local elites] have failed to produce" (Barca, 2019, p. 89). So Barca (2019) stresses that national sectoral policies, such as education, health and agriculture, need to become space aware and place aware, which means tailored towards the specific needs of places. The latter is particularly necessary in relatively centralized political–administrative systems, which will require reforms of these policies, as well as considerable investments in human resources in the national administrations, as they are in most cases not place aware, yet. Barca (2019, p. 91) states further, "one of the objectives of a place-based approach thus becomes the reform of the national and regional sectoral policies in a space-aware direction". This requires huge efforts and often goes against the interests of local elites, but Barca (2019) is convinced that there are currently strong reasons to do so, such as the high and growing degree of regional inequality within countries (Iammarino et al. 2019) and the rising pressure from populist parties.

Barca (2019) also explicitly mentions innovation several times in his latest publication. He also emphasizes the role of public debate in that context. According to him, "much of the knowledge needed for a place to innovative is embedded in the place itself" (Barca, 2019, p. 88). And "for innovation to occur, people must be empowered and engaged in decision-making through a process of heated, informed and reasonable public debate, and this debate must be open to external knowledge" (Barca, 2019, p. 88). In these public online or offline debates, experts and local elites are supposed to be challenged.

In addition to the term place-based policies (Barca, 2019), other, similar terms have been developed. Iammarino et al. (2019, p. 274), for instance, are critical of both spatially blind agglomeration-oriented regional policies and place-based regional policies. They write that the latter often function "more as social rather than economic development policies" (Iammarino et al., 2019, p. 288). They launch, as an alternative, so-called place-sensitive distributed development policies, which are "based on integrated micro (individual)–meso (territorial) logics of tackling diverse development trajectories" (p. 274) and which go beyond the dichotomy between people-based (mobility, education, etc.) and place-based (job development, innovation support, etc.) regional policy. However, place sensitivity is only seen in a categorization of regions concerning their income, from very high income to low income regions. The conceptualization of place remains underdeveloped, both in the suggested place-sensitive distributed development policies and in the place-based regional policies developed by Barca (2019).

According to Coenen and Morgan (2019, p.9), the "place-based approach has not yet delivered the anticipated dividends", due mainly to public sector barriers, such as lack of transparency, rent-seeking behaviour and the like. Moreover, a too limited understanding of place in these new policies might also be a reason for this.

4. ADVANCING PLACE-BASED REGIONAL INNOVATION POLICIES BY TAKING PLACE MORE SERIOUSLY

As has become clear, place-based regional innovation policies put a strong emphasis on several aspects related to place, such as the economic, social and cultural contexts. This indicates deep contextualization (Martin and Sunley, 2015). To take the geographical context seriously is not an entirely new insight for regional innovation policy; it has already been proposed, in fact, in one way or another in concepts such as endogenous potential (Stöhr, 1980) and regional innovation systems (Cooke and Morgan, 1998). Particularly in the literature on regional innovation systems and the related literature arguing against one-size-fits-all regional innovation policy, a region-specific focus has prevailed. For instance, Tödtling and Trippl (2005) discussed innovation barriers in specific types of regions (metropolitan areas, old industrial regions and rural, peripheral regions) in their well-cited paper. Other work referred to the region-specific aspects of the regional innovation systems, such as the specific industrial structure, and the specific knowledge generation in public research establishments and higher education institutes, as well as region-specific intermediaries and promotion agencies. In that literature, the focus is also on the matches and mismatches between the region-specific knowledge production and demand among SMEs and what to do about mismatches with the help of regional innovation policy measures and aid schemes.

Instead of focusing on region-specific aspects of the regional innovation and industrial landscape, the current discussion about place-based policy seems to concentrate more on the place-specific needs, worries and wishes of citizens. However, there is still much fuzziness around the term "place" in this recent literature. What is meant by place in this context? What does Barca (2019) mean when he writes about place- and space awareness of national sectoral policies?

Certainly, from a geographical perspective, place should mean more than a container filled with data, as the term is often used by economists. Taking place more seriously, in the sense of a socially constructed, much more qualitative concept (Williams, 2014; Antonsich, 2011), resonates well with the place-based policy concept in three ways.

First, place is partly conceptualized as a sense of place, related to the feelings, emotions, recognition, identity and imaginations a place evokes (Agnew, 2011; Cresswell, 2014). These play a key role in place-based regional policy, particularly in the era of populism, as has been stated several times above.

Second, place conceptualization affects the relationship between place and the drivers of actors for regional development. A large group of different economic actors decides on the location and development of economic activities. Several, and sometimes conflicting, drivers lie behind these decisions and are a source of economic dynamism and change. Identifying the key actors, but particularly also their drivers, is a key task of research on place-based regional policy. Innovation can be regarded as the most significant driver of economic actors and activities, as has been stressed in the economic geography literature for decades (Shearmur et al., 2016). Innovation, as a driver of economic activities, is obviously linked to place by classical agglomeration advantages as well as by the stickiness of collective tacit knowledge creation in clusters and industrial districts. However, there is a much broader and increasingly heterogeneous range of drivers than just innovation and related entrepreneurship and competitiveness. Currently an increasing number of different, sometimes conflicting drivers both affect economic activities in place and are affected by place-specific context, and therefore belong to the core of place-based policies. They include, for instance, creativity (Gong and Hassink, 2017), financial profit (stock exchange), sustainability, de-growth (Krueger et al., 2018), social entrepreneurship (Smith and Stevens, 2010), social justice (labour unions) and crime (Ganau and Rodríguez-Pose, 2018). Drivers have a high degree of context- and place specificity. One potential reason for different degrees of context- and place specificity of drivers is related to the way economic actors are embedded and influenced by different institutions.

Third, and relatedly, place as a qualitative concept is strongly related to informal institutions (norms, values, conventions and traditions), as well as formal institutions (laws, regulations and organizations). Both institutions are important socially constructed elements of the environment of actors and their economic activities (Gertler, 2018); they have a very high degree of place specificity; and they have both positive and negative effects, such as cognitive and political lock-ins (Hassink, 2010), on economic activities in places.

5. CONCLUSIONS

In the battle for policy frameworks for regional innovation policies, currently in many countries the place-based framework seems to be favoured over a spatially blind framework. Particularly due to rising populism in structurally weak regions, such as old industrial regions and rural areas, the place-based approach, which takes the needs and worries of citizens seriously, appears to be promising. A place-based policy approach, however, clearly goes beyond the governance borders of places and regions. A vertical, multilevel governance model is necessary, in addition to a horizontal (regional) model of coordination and collaboration. The effectiveness of a place-based innovation policy, particularly in structurally weak regions, results from the interaction and interdependence between these scales of activity (Lagendijk, 2011).

However, as has been made clear, because of several reasons the place-based approach still does not deliver the expected results. In this chapter, I have argued that a more advanced conceptualization of place is one promising way to advance place-based regional innovation policies. So far, the theoretical basis for the place-based approach is relatively weak, as it does not focus on place other than stating that it should be tailored to the specific context. Moreover, theory on regional economic inequalities is often discussed only from an economic perspective; little theoretical insight related to place, space and scale is used in these debates. In my view, such insight can strongly contribute to the debate and strengthen place-based approaches and policies. Place is no container; it is socially constructed, which influences the behaviour of citizens, as well as of political and economic actors. If we take place-based approaches seriously, we need to take these conceptual and theoretical considerations into account and operationalize them into regional policies. Such an advancement could lead to more insights into the place-specific drivers and untapped, endogenous potential for development, place-specific informal institutions, such as norms and values affecting the economy in the sense of risk taking or risk aversion, and social innovations and their contribution to the foundational economy.

NOTE

1. This section draws heavily from Hassink and Marques (2016).

REFERENCES

Agnew, J. (2011) Space and place. In: Agnew, J. and Livingstone, D.N. (eds) *The SAGE Handbook of Geographical Knowledge*. London: SAGE, 316–31.

Antonsich, M. (2011). Grounding theories of place and globalisation. *Tijdschrift voor economische en sociale geografie*, 102(3), 331–45.

Asheim, B.T., Isaksen, A., Nauwelaers, C., and Tödtling, F. (eds) (2003). *Regional Innovation Policy for Small–Medium Enterprises*. Cheltenham, UK and Northampton, MA, USA: Edward Elgar Publishing.

Baier, E., Kroll, H., and Zenker, A. (2013). Regional autonomy with regard to innovation policy: A differentiated illustration of the European status quo. Working Papers Firms and Region, No. R3/2013, Fraunhofer ISI, Karlsruhe. Available at https://www.econstor.eu/bitstream/10419/69499/1/73607046X.pdf (accessed on 18 November 2019).

Barca, F. (2009). *Agenda for a Reformed Cohesion Policy*. Independent report prepared at the request of Danuta Hübner, Commissioner of Regional Policy, European Communities.

Barca, F. (2019). Place-based policy and politics. *Renewal: A Journal of Labour Politics*, 27(1), 84–95.

Barca, F., McCann, P., and Rodríguez-Pose, A. (2012). The case for regional development intervention: Place-based versus place-neutral approaches. *Journal of Regional Science*, 52, 134–52.

Coenen, L., and Morgan, K. (2019). Evolving geographies of innovation: Existing paradigms, critiques and possible alternatives. *Norsk Geografisk Tidsskrift* (forthcoming).

Coenen, L., Hansen, T., and Rekers, J.V. (2015). Innovation policy for grand challenges: An economic geography perspective, *Geography Compass*, 9(9), 483–96.

Cooke, P., and Morgan, K. (1998). *The Associational Economy: Firms, Regions, and Innovation*. Oxford: Oxford University Press.

Cresswell, T. (2014). Place. In: Lee, R., Castree, N., Kitchin, R., Lawson, V., Paasi, A., Philo, C., Radcliffe, S., Roberts, S.M. and Withers, C. (eds) *The SAGE Handbook of Human Geography*. London: SAGE, 3–21.

Economist (2016). Place-based economic policies as a response to populism. *The Economist*, 15 December.

Engelen, E., Froud, J., Johal, S., Salento, A., and Williams, K. (2017). The grounded city: From competitivity to the foundational economy. *Cambridge Journal of Regions, Economy and Society*, 10(3), 407–23.

Ezcurra, R., and Rodríguez-Pose, A. (2013). Political decentralization, economic growth and regional disparities in the OECD. *Regional Studies*, 47(3), 388–401.

Farole, T., Goga, S., and Ionescu-Heroiu, M. (2018). *Rethinking Lagging Regions: Using Cohesion Policy to Deliver on the Potential of Europe's Regions*. Washington, DC: World Bank Group.

Foray, D. (2015). *Smart Specialisation: Opportunities and Challenges for Regional Innovation Policy*. Abingdon: Routledge.

Fukuyama, F. (2018). *Identity: Contemporary Identity Politics and the Struggle for Recognition*. London: Profile Books.

Ganau, R., and Rodríguez-Pose, A. (2018). Industrial clusters, organized crime, and productivity growth in Italian SMEs. *Journal of Regional Science*, 58(2), 363–85.

Gertler, M.S. (2018). Institutions, geography and economic life. In: Clark, G., Gertler, M., Feldman, M.P. and Wójcik, D. (eds) *The New Oxford Handbook of Economic Geography*. Oxford: Oxford University Press, 230–42.

Gong, H., and Hassink, R. (2017). Exploring the clustering of creative industries. *European Planning Studies*, 25(4), 583–600.

Gong, H., and Hassink, R. (2018). Co-evolution in contemporary economic geography: Towards a theoretical framework. *Regional Studies*, 53(9), 1344–55.

Grillitsch, M., and Asheim, B. (2018). Place-based innovation policy for industrial diversification in regions. *European Planning Studies*, 26(8), 1638–62.

Hassink, R. (1992). *Regional Innovation Policy: Case-studies from the Ruhr Area, Baden-Württemberg and the North East of England*. Utrecht: Nederlandse Geografische Studies.

Hassink, R. (1996). Technology transfer agencies and regional economic development. *European Planning Studies*, 4(2), 167–84.

Hassink, R. (2010). Locked in decline? On the role of regional lock-ins in old industrial areas. In: Boschma, R. and Martin, R. (eds) *The Handbook of Evolutionary Economic Geography*. Cheltenham, UK and Northampton, MA, USA: Edward Elgar Publishing, 450–68.

Hassink, R., and Gong, H. (2019). Six critical questions about smart specialization. *European Planning Studies*, 27(10), 2049–2065.

Hassink, R., and Lagendijk, A. (2001). The dilemmas of interregional institutional learning. *Environment and Planning C: Government and Policy*, 19, 65–84.

Hassink, R., and Marques, P. (2016). The regional innovation paradox revisited. In: Hilpert, U. (ed.) *Routledge Handbook of Politics and Technology*. London: Routledge, 120–31.

Heslop, J., Morgan, K., and Tomaney, J. (2019) Debating the foundational economy. *Renewal: A Journal of Labour Politics*, 27(2), 5–12.

Iammarino, S., Rodríguez-Pose, A., and Storper, M. (2019). Regional inequality in Europe: Evidence, theory and policy implications. *Journal of Economic Geography*, 19, 273–98.

Krueger, R., Schulz, C., and Gibbs, D.C. (2018). Institutionalizing alternative economic spaces? An interpretivist perspective on diverse economies. *Progress in Human Geography*, 42(4), 569–89.

Lagendijk, A. (2011). Regional innovation policy between theory and practice. In: Cooke, P. (ed.) *Handbook of Regional Innovation and Growth*. Cheltenham, UK and Northampton, MA, USA: Edward Elgar Publishing, 597–608.

Landabaso, M. (1997). The promotion of innovation in regional policy: Proposals for a regional innovation strategy. *Entrepreneurship & Regional Development*, 9, 1–24.

Marques, P., Morgan, K. and Richardson, R. (2018). Social innovation in question: The theoretical and practical implications of a contested concept. *Environment and Planning C: Politics and Space*, 36(3), 496–512.

Martin, R. (2015). Rebalancing the spatial economy: The challenge for regional theory. *Territory, Politics, Governance*, 3(3), 235–72.

Martin, R., and Sunley, P. (2015). Towards a developmental turn in evolutionary economic geography? *Regional Studies*, 49(5), 712–32.

Mazzucato, M. (2018). Mission-oriented innovation policies: Challenges and opportunities. *Industrial and Corporate Change*, 27(5), 803–15.

McCann, P., and Ortega-Argilés, R. (2013). Modern regional innovation policy. *Cambridge Journal of Regions, Economy and Society*, 6(2), 187–216.

Morgan, K. (2018). *Experimental Governance and Territorial Development.* Paris: OECD (background paper for seminar 5: Experimental governance, 14 December 2018).

Nauwelaers, C., and Wintjes, R. (2003). Towards a new paradigm for innovation policy? In: Asheim, B., Isaksen, A., Nauwelaers, C. and Tödtling, F. (eds) *Regional Innovation Policy for Small-Medium Enterprises.* Cheltenham, UK and Northampton, MA, USA: Edward Elgar Publishing, 193–220.

O'Sullivan, M. (2019). *The Levelling: What's Next After Globalization.* New York, NY: PublicAffairs.

OECD (2007). *Competitive Regional Clusters.* Paris: OECD.

OECD (2009). *Regions Matter: Economic Recovery, Innovation and Sustainable Growth.* Paris: OECD.

OECD (2010). *Regional Development Policies in OECD Countries.* Paris: OECD.

OECD (2011). *Regions and Innovation Policy*, OECD Reviews of Regional Innovation. Paris: OECD.

Oughton, C., Landabaso, M., and Morgan, K. (2002). The regional innovation paradox: Innovation policy and industrial policy. *Journal of Technology Transfer*, 27, 97–110.

Paquet, G. (1998). Techno-nationalism and meso innovation systems. In: Anderson, R., Cohn, T. and Day, C. (eds) *Innovation Systems in a Global Context: The North American Experience.* Montreal, QC: McGill-Queen's University Press, 58–75.

Percoco, M. (2013). Strategies of regional development in European regions: Are they efficient? *Cambridge Journal of Regions, Economy and Society*, 6, 303–18.

Pike, A., Rodríguez-Pose, A., and Tomaney, J. (2017). Shifting horizons in local and regional development. *Regional Studies*, 51(1), 46–57.

Prange, H. (2008). Explaining varieties of regional innovation policies in Europe. *European Urban and Regional Studies*, 15, 39–52.

Rodríguez-Pose, A. (2018). The revenge of the places that don't matter (and what to do about it). *Cambridge Journal of Regions, Economy and Society*, 11(1), 189–209.

Rodrik, D. (2018). Populism and the economics of globalization. *Journal of International Business Policy*, 18, 1–22.

Sabel, C., and Zeitlin, J. (2012). Experimentalist governance. In: Levi-Faur, D. (ed.) *The Oxford Handbook of Governance.* Oxford: Oxford University Press, 169–83.

Schot, J. and Steinmueller, W.E. (2018). Three frames for innovation policy: R&D, systems of innovation and transformative change. *Research Policy*, 47(9), 1554–67.

Shearmur, R., Carrincazeaux, C., and Doloreux, D. (2016). The geographies of innovations: beyond one-size-fits-all. In: Shearmur, R., Carrincazeaux, C. and Doloreux, D. (eds) *Handbook on the Geographies of Innovation.* Cheltenham, UK and Northampton, MA, USA: Edward Elgar Publishing, 1–16.

Smith, B.R., and Stevens, C.E. (2010). Different types of social entrepreneurship: The role of geography and embeddedness on the measurement and scaling of social value. *Entrepreneurship and Regional Development*, 22(6), 575–98.

Stöhr, W. (1980). *Development from Below: The Bottom-up and Periphery-inward Development Paradigm*. IIR-Discussion Papers, 6. WU Vienna University of Economics and Business, Vienna.

Tödtling, F., and Trippl, M. (2005). One size fits all? Towards a differentiated regional innovation policy. *Research Policy*, 34(1), 1203–19.

Tödtling, F., and Trippl, M. (2018). Regional innovation policies for new path development: Beyond neo-liberal and traditional systemic views. *European Planning Studies*, 26(9), 1779–95.

Uyarra, E., Ribeiro, B., and Dale-Clough, L. (2019). Exploring the normative turn in regional innovation policy: Responsibility and the quest for public value. *European Planning Studies*, 27(12), 2359–75.

Williams, D.R. (2014). Making sense of 'place': Reflections on pluralism and positionality in place research. *Landscape and Urban Planning*, 131, 74–82.

World Bank (2009). *World Development Report 2009: Reshaping Economic Geography*. Washington DC: World Bank.

3. Policy learning in regions: the potential of co-generative research methodologies to help responsible innovation

Ainhoa Arrona, James Karlsen and Miren Larrea

1. INTRODUCTION

Due to an increasing awareness of the major challenges that societies face in terms of economic, social and environmental sustainability, regions are urged to broaden the scope and aims of their policy actions for innovation and development. Concepts such as transformative innovation policies (Steward, 2012) and responsible innovation (Owen et al., 2013) are now entering the academic and policy scenes and providing frameworks for thinking about the social and environmental implications of innovation. These concepts also provide a perspective on the potential of innovation and innovation policies to help develop responses to various social challenges.

Reframing regional innovation policies in these terms to include broader societal goals requires policy learning, which is one of several mechanisms for explaining policy changes and evolution. 'Policy learning' refers to the use of knowledge in policy development (and, more concretely, to policymakers' learning processes within the policy process), which is rooted in a variety of sources, such as their own and others' experiences, data, and research inputs, and materializes in specific transformations.

Policy learning is one frame that can help in understanding why and how policies change. Such learning is commonly used in the regional development field to explain how regional development and innovation policies evolve. Scholars have developed theoretical and empirical works to set out how policy learning occurs in regions and to systematize different sources, types and outputs of learning, as well as examining which capacities a region needs for different types of learning (Borrás, 2011; González-López, 2019).

In our view, two dimensions related to policy learning require further exploration, especially in light of new rationales for rethinking innovation: policy learning for responsible innovation and researchers' roles in such learning. Responsible innovation requires a change in the rationale of innovation policies; that is, it requires a paradigmatic change. Paradigmatic change, as previous studies have shown, requires social learning, a type of learning that produces a change in the hierarchies of the rationales and goals that shape policies. Although policies tend to develop in an evolutionary way and require time, in our view, approaches that actively seek to make deep changes in policies and practices can contribute to the adoption of a responsible innovation framework.

One question that immediately arises when addressing this issue is: what is researchers' responsibility in the regional innovation policy field regarding social learning and responsible innovation? Although the role of research and researchers in policy learning within regions has not received much attention and has seldom been studied, we believe the topic requires further attention to improve our understanding of how research can increase its impact within regional policies. While the scarce impact of research in policy can be explained by putting more weight and responsibility on researchers (since the stereotype is that they do not understand the policy world) or on policymakers (since they are purported to lack the capacity to absorb research), several scholarly voices in the field – including ours – have raised awareness of the need to better understand the interaction between the two.

With this aim, and based on a co-generative learning spirit, this chapter provides insights gained from four in-depth interviews conducted with policymakers in the Basque Country. The interviewees express their views on the interaction between research and policy, on the usefulness of research, and on their own capacities in policy learning. The finding of this chapter is that paradigmatic change will require new forms of social research that integrate dialogue and deliberation. Based on the experience of the authors in facilitating (Karlsen and Larrea, 2014a, 2018) and analysing (Arrona, 2017) action research (AR) processes, we consider that the regional innovation policy field can potentially transform itself based on the field's principles, but by integrating dialogical and deliberative dimensions from fields such as AR. In this chapter we share an exploratory attempt at such a goal.

Our framework for exploring this idea is action research for territorial development (ARTD), which is an AR approach developed in the regional innovation policy field – more specifically, in the field's intersection with

AR. The ARTD framework proposes knowledge co-generation between policymakers and researchers as a specific form of policy learning. Indeed, even though co-generation as a research methodology is seldom used in the regional development and innovation field, we believe that regional innovation policy can have an impact in the development of responsible innovation by complementing existing research approaches using co-generative methods.

The remainder of this chapter is structured as follows. First, we provide a general theoretical background on policy learning that shows the diversity of perspectives on such learning, followed by a review of specific literature on policy learning in the field of regional innovation in which we address the challenge of responsible innovation. The next section covers regional policy learning, which is the concept that best fits with the approach to policy learning described in this chapter. We then present two sections on ARTD and the field's approach to policy learning. Bearing the previous material in mind, we then end the chapter with a discussion of how AR and other co-generative frameworks can contribute to the challenge of developing responsible innovation, and our conclusions.

2.   POLICY LEARNING: AN ELUSIVE CONCEPT WITH DIVERSE INTERPRETATIONS

Heclo (1974) was the first to introduce the concept of policy learning and the idea of knowledge as an explanatory factor of policy change, in opposition to conflict- and power-based theories (Bennett and Howlett, 1992; Grin and Loeber, 2007). Since that time, learning in public policy has become a key theme of analysis in diverse fields (see Goyal and Howlett, 2018) and a central factor in most policy process frameworks. Policy learning may even be considered as a lens and theory in the policy process (Dunlop and Radaelli, 2018).

Learning in public policy may be understood in different ways, depending on what such learning entails and what its outputs are (Dunlop and Radaelli, 2013; Dunlop et al., 2018; Freeman, 2006). For example, knowledge and learning can be seen as instrumental to the policy process, as an evolutionary and incremental process that depends on previous beliefs, or as a collective and interactive phenomenon that begins with practice and views policy as being emergent (Freeman, 2007).

Various scholars have sought to systematize the vast work on policy learning. One of the most-cited attempts is that of Bennett and Howlett (1992), who identified different ways of understanding and using the concept in previous works, based on learning agents (state officials, policy networks or policy communities), the content of the learning (process-related issues, instruments or ideas) and the results of the learning (organizational change, changes in programmes or paradigm change). Thus, the change produced by learning depends on the object of learning and whether the learning occurs among a bounded set of actors or in the wider community.

Several developments and changes have occurred since Bennett and Howlett's (1992) seminal work. Among these changes, a shift has occurred from individual-focused learning to a collective conception of learning and a widening of the scope of learning agents (Grin and Loeber, 2007). A wider and more diverse body of work now exists with different underlying assumptions and approaches to learning and policy – such as rationalist, institutional and constructivist (Freeman, 2007) – as well as various approaches to learning that are linked to different uses and relationships with governance, such as instrumental, gaining power, legitimacy and democracy (Gilardi and Radaelli, 2012).

How we understand and approach learning has various implications, because the mechanisms, logics and benefits vary accordingly (Dunlop and Radaelli, 2013, 2018). For example, whereas an instrumental type of knowledge – that of solving concrete problems – can be produced by teaching, a conceptual reflexive type of learning involves deliberation.

Learning in general, and policy learning in particular, is also widely considered a key aspect in regional development and innovation. The relevance of tacit knowledge and interactive learning in fostering regional development is fundamental within place-based approaches and regional innovation policies (Dotti, 2014; Laranja et al., 2008; Moulaert and Sekia, 2003; Uyarra, 2007; Uyarra and Flanagan, 2010). Learning is also vital for innovation policymaking (Aranguren et al., 2017; Chaminade and Edquist, 2010; Flanagan and Uyarra, 2016; Koschatzky and Kroll, 2007; Mazzucato, 2016; Nauwelaers and Wintjes, 2002) and has emerged as an axis of innovation policy governance (Borrás, 2009; OECD, 2005).

Studies on policy learning in the regional development and innovation field have provided insights on, among other things, policy change in regions, mechanisms and sources of policy learning, and the organizational capacities required for different types of learning in the innovation field (e.g. Borrás, 2011; González-López, 2019; Nauwelaers and Wintjes, 2008). Policy learning, however, is usually focused on an instrumental type of learning (an updating of beliefs that occurs through trial and error or through others' experience), which centres on analytical capacities fostered through peer reviews, monitoring exercises, benchmarking and personal mobility (e.g. Borrás, 2011; Nauwelaers and Wintjes, 2008). As we argue in the next section, the adoption of rationales such as responsible innovation, which implies changing the logics of regional innovation policies, requires going beyond such types of instrumental learning and adopting a more reflexive approach to learning that is (1) based on practice, (2) occurs in interactions and (3) addresses underlying assumptions. Following Freeman (2006, p. 369), it is 'the way we think about learning which determines how well we do it'.

3. POLICY LEARNING IN THE REGIONAL INNOVATION FIELD: CHALLENGES OF RESPONSIBLE INNOVATION

In this chapter we want to focus on the need for innovation policy to face large-scale societal challenges. This debate has entered the field through the concept of responsible innovation (among others), which requires an overcoming of the instrumental dimension of policy learning. For this reason, we present in this section the concept of social learning as a type of policy learning that overcomes the instrumental dimension and AR as an approach to social learning.

We borrow a definition of 'responsible innovation' from the field of responsible research and innovation (RRI) as a 'transparent, interactive process by which societal actors and innovators become mutually responsive to each other with a view to the (ethical) acceptability, sustainability and societal desirability of the innovation process and its marketable products in order to allow a proper embedding of scientific and technological advances in our society' (Von Schomberg, 2011, p. 50).

RRI has gained currency as a key term in the policy learning literature (Bardone and Lind, 2016; Fisher, 2018; Rip, 2014). Scholars have proposed several different approaches and definitions of the concept (Stilgoe et al., 2013; Von Schomberg, 2013; Rip, 2014). The common aim of RRI is to guide research and innovation practice towards societal acceptability while fostering and shaping technological innovation. RRI is an attempt to reach a broader vision of research and innovation as a public good (Bardone and Lind, 2016; Felt, 2014). According to Bardone and Lind (2016, pp. 2–3), RRI is based on four pillars. The first is that research is a resource for society in order to address 'grand challenges' of our time, where some challenges are also created by the research fields themselves. The second pillar is participation, or the importance of engaging the citizenry and all other concerned parties (such as stakeholders). The third is a shift from outcomes to processes: research and innovation are inherently open-ended types of pursuit, which implies that the path and the possible outcomes cannot be predicted before the process is started. This is therefore a more realistic approach to the challenges that can arise during a given process. The fourth and final pillar is reflexivity, where broader issues concerning underlying elements, such as purposes, motivations, potential impacts and assumptions – but also the unavoidable fact of our ignorance and finitude – inevitably characterize individuals and institutions.

Bardone and Lind (2016) conceptualize responsibility as care, which is a promising approach that builds on the process pillar. This approach emphasizes the relationship between theory and practice. The concept can be interpreted as practical wisdom and refers to those situations where we as humans take action (i.e. where we apply knowledge in action). The idea of care, in particular, hints at the fact that RRI cannot be devoid of the very act of taking care of the process to which research and innovation belong (Burget et al., 2017). Nor does the idea distinguish the institutional from the personal, and it requires that individuals engage with personal responsibility for their own actions at the same time as reinforcing institutional responsibility for setting policy and providing redress (Wilford, 2018). This situation implies engagement, and engagement cannot be fully formalized, since it relies on personal commitment (Bardone and Lind, 2016) and responsibility in action. This idea connects RRI and responsibility as care to AR and responsibility in policymaking processes, especially for paradigmatic change. In order to make such changes, both researchers' and policymakers' values must be explicit in the policymaking process.

The main challenge with the practice of RRI is that the field has not managed to reach its ambitions. In practice, RRI has often ended up as mere tick-boxing activities of filling in research proposal forms or, in somewhat futile participatory activities, as ends in themselves (Bogner and Torgersen, 2018). The following two comments from the policymakers interviewed for this chapter both describe a situation in which people are aware not only of the relevance of the concept but also of the concept's low level of actual transformation of policymaking:

> The way the concept of responsible innovation has reached us is still insufficient. It's a new concept that we probably haven't internalized enough yet, though we are aware that it is relevant for the future and that we should consider it.

> As for responsible innovation, we have to think of it in terms of the future, but the answers are not evident . . .. Today we don't integrate it into our policymaking – we don't know how.

The policymakers were also open to considering research as part of the strategy to integrate responsible innovation into their policy process:

[Elected politicians and civil servants] need spaces for reflection that aren't necessarily linked to direct actions, but help them to think, to get out of our daily routines.

We don't have reference frameworks . . . we would need someone to present us with a menu of different options to decide what's the right combination.

Fitjar et al. (2019) pose the need to adapt the RRI concept to the regional scale and they take a step forward in this direction since they propose a framework that integrates RRI within the main regional innovation policy framework, namely, research and innovation for smart specialization. We share their interpretation that adopting a responsible innovation perspective puts divergent voices and interests, as well as the power dimension, conflicts, tacit assumptions and normative values, at the centre of the innovation policymaking. We bear these features in mind when we rethink how we approach policy learning and social research for policy learning and change.

4.   REGIONAL POLICY LEARNING: TOWARDS RESPONSIBLE INNOVATION

Adopting a framework such as responsible innovation in practice, which requires us to reflect and act on the effects of innovation in economic, social and environmental terms, implies questioning existing policies and practices and prioritizing some goals over others. Doing so thus implies questioning the underlying assumptions behind existing policy action and even addressing the power dimension involved in any transformation (Loeber et al., 2007). In other words, a change such as that required for rethinking regional policy action in order to face social challenges requires us to foster a type of learning that, as previously stated, is reflexive and involves deliberation (Freeman 2006, 2007; Gilardi and Radaelli, 2012; Dunlop and Radaelli, 2013) and affects and changes policy goals and practices.

An interesting concept for thinking about these terms is Benz and Fürst's (2002) concept of regional policy learning, which is 'a special case of policy learning: it is a process of collective learning geared to a strategy of regional development with those actors participating who contribute to regional development' (p. 22). Regional policy learning is a collective process of learning rooted in the territory, where both individual and collective learning occurs that affects the cognitive dimensions and structures of actors' interests, thus leading to structural changes and the reallocation of resources. Such learning involves a process that goes beyond instrumental learning and affects policy goals and the actors involved.

Research and policy approaches that are based on fostering multi-actor collaboration and social learning could indeed be a source for regional policy learning. The literature on consensus building, collaborative planning and social learning has already shown that collaboration and facilitated dialogues that explicitly address underlying assumptions and conflicting views, promote a review of actors' rationales and reflect on their role in policy practice may promote deep and long-term capacity building and system changes (Ansell and Gash, 2008; Fischer and Mandell, 2012; Grin and Van de Graaf, 1996; Innes and Booher, 2010; Loeber et al., 2007). ARTD is a research approach that aims to foster this type of learning for regional development and innovation. We thus propose an exploration of the potential of AR as an approach that can help integrate responsibility within policy learning.

5.   ARTD: A METHODOLOGY FOR SOCIAL LEARNING

ARTD has been interpreted both as a strategy for territorial development (Karlsen and Larrea, 2014a) and as a methodology for research (Karlsen and Larrea, 2018). In this chapter we focus on ARTD as a methodology for research that can be used for policy learning and, more specifically, regional policy learning. ARTD emerged at the intersection of the regional innovation policy field with AR and has been applied by a trans-local research community in the Basque Country (Spain), Agder (Norway), and Rafaela and Tierra del Fuego (Argentina).

The methodological core of ARTD is its proposal of dialogical processes between policymakers and researchers in order to co-generate knowledge in the context of policy processes. The participants are usually elected politicians and civil servants, but other territorial actors with a stake in the specific policy process (such as firms, vocational training centres and the like) participate as well. The learning process is oriented towards a policy problem that is agreed on by all participants. Researchers facilitate reflection processes in which they contribute their field, process and experiential knowledge; the policymakers do the same. After the reflection process, policymakers make specific decisions followed by actions. The process continues cyclically, continuously defining new problems.

One of the core concepts in ARTD is collective knowing, a learned pattern of collective action that can be interpreted as the capability of territorial actors to solve problems together. Thus, through ongoing cycles of reflection and action for solving concrete problems, the use of ARTD generates a collective capability that is embedded in the territory. We can appreciate some features of ARTD in the words of policymakers who have experienced the process:

> I think that in processes like this, there is learning that goes beyond the process
> ... in our case, we're learning a lot of things to apply in other projects – for example, the facilitation work.

Collective knowing is developed through interactions in the long term; the following comment refers to this approach as well:

> I think that it's important that there is a permanence of people [researchers and policymakers] in the learning process. This doesn't mean that projects or scenarios should be the same, but the people should remain ... we understand each other – our limitations, interests and priorities – and we know what we can ask for; that habit brings about learning.

ARTD's approach to policy learning (Karlsen and Larrea, 2014b) is rooted in praxis and in a co-generative (and thus non-linear) view of the interaction between research and policy, as well as in the need to address ideological positions in learning and policy processes.

Praxis is interpreted in ARTD as a specific type of relationship between theory and practice in which concepts and frameworks are continuously tested in practice, either to make them more robust (if they help solve problems) or to discard them (if they do not). The framework focuses on the concept of praxis in order to distinguish between linear modes and co-generative modes of policy learning. In the linear mode, policymakers first reflect on what they are going to do; next, they decide on and plan the entire process before beginning any action; finally, they implement what they have already decided on.

The following comments on this type of approach were made by the policymakers we interviewed. They recognize that the way to integrate knowledge from research in their policy processes has traditionally been linear, and they doubt the effectiveness of that approach:

> [Research outputs] can always have a value, but the risk is they might not be so linked to the needs, and then the usability is limited. I wouldn't give up on them, and we keep that path, because we're used to that. But, yes, there is a risk that those research works will have little impact.

> If you write a report for me, in the best cases I'll read it and make my own conclusions, but without a chance for interaction and feedback, it will end up being just paper.

One of the interviewees missed research outputs having a more explicit goal in terms of policy learning:

> These projects [i.e. regarding the linear approach to research] don't have an established goal in terms of our learning: we fund the agents' scientific goals, but there are no specific goals in terms of the territory.

However, the same policymaker recognized that policymakers often lack the mechanisms to learn from the research outputs they have access to in linear ways:

> We don't have a systematic evaluation of the recommendations that research reports and papers make, which reduces the chances for us to innovate.

Another policymaker underlined the limitations to learning:

> Our life cycle is usually a term. Priorities . . . change. The reports come to you, and . . . a term change [often occurs] at that point . . . thus it's not only an issue of the research side but also an issue of our reality.

ARTD was originally defined to complement this type of approach in regional innovation policy. ARTD proposes an alternative to the traditional linear approaches of policymaking through integrating research in policy in the form of praxis – cyclical (i.e. non-linear) processes in which reflections and actions continuously happen that transform the interpretations of the situation that policymakers and researchers had at the beginning of the process.

The policymakers we interviewed had experience of ARTD processes as well as of linear approaches. They pointed out some advantages of ARTD:

> Action research is important because you construct the work process while extracting outputs, modifying, intervening . . . you learn things that were obvious, that you hadn't seen before.

> [C]onclusions are better . . . and the results are more actionable . . . participants share the problem [and] the diagnosis, and that's an important value . . . it's important to be part of something bigger that transcends our ego.

> When a policymaker confronts a problem alone, the recommendation is already decided beforehand; in a participatory process it's not like that. Someone will make you think about something else, which is valuable.

The value of ARTD as a process of knowledge generation in the context of application can be perceived in the following comment as well:

> You understand problems not because of what you've read, but because of how you contextualize, and you contextualize from your own experience. That's the [key] to learning or not.

The interviewees also saw problems and disadvantages:

> The main problem in participatory policy-learning processes is urgency. Co-generative and participatory processes have different timing . . . I need to be a participant to understand, but without taking up too much time.

However, the framework does not exclusively address praxis, which is generally considered necessary but insufficient. Transformations derived from policy learning are categorized as social transformations and have to do with paradigm change. In these cases, policy learning requires integrating an ideological debate that is often avoided in innovation policy processes. Praxis in a context in which the ideological debate is omitted and the problems are addressed exclusively at the technical level can help to improve the efficiency of the programmes but will hardly achieve social change. Our interpretation of ideology and politics in this section has nothing to do with political parties or partisan positions. The ideology is derived from the position that each actor occupies in society, the territory or the world as well as the perspective that this position gives on the problems that are being addressed. The political dimension has to do with the consideration that, from this perspective, each actor has a different interpretation of what is desirable for the territory and will use power to make what is desirable happen. From this perspective, all territorial actors, including researchers, have ideological and political positions.

The policymakers also referred to power during the interviews:

> When you start working in collaboration, you're sharing your power. And that needs to be learned. Even though you might have made the political decision to collaborate, you need to learn . . . with researchers, for example, one thing we have learned is to make conflicts explicit.

Policymakers also shared their perspective on the role of researchers in policy learning. Regarding policymakers' experience in co-generative policy learning in ARTD, one said:

> [Researchers] help us better diagnose the problem . . . then they go back to their world and bring inputs, reflections and references from around the world . . . which we've applied and have had results. Even more so, researchers don't come to us with a recipe, but we implement things together.

6. AN ANALYTICAL FRAMEWORK FOR POLICY LEARNING IN ARTD

Following the previous introduction to ARTD as an approach to policy learning from the perspective of both researchers and policymakers, we now present an analytical framework developed as part of ARTD that summarizes the different strategies for policy learning depending on how praxis and various ideological positions are approached.

The combination of different positions creates four possible approaches to policy learning (Table 3.1). Option IV, social learning, represents the collective learning of the actors who make social change possible. We consider that social learning thus defined is the type of learning that can contribute to regional policy learning and responsible innovation.

Table 3.1   Contribution of research in policy learning

	Implicit political/ ideological positions	Explicit political/ ideological positions
Linear approach from theory to practice	I. Recipe book for policy	III. Political discourse
Non-linear approach to theory and practice	II. Improvement of programme efficiency	IV. Social learning

Source: Karlsen and Larrea (2014b).

By way of an introduction to the discussion later in this chapter, we provide a brief description of each approach below.

I.   Recipe Book for Policy

Sometimes the contribution that research makes to policy encounters difficulties when moving from reflection to action. When the reflection does not include explicit ideological positions, the possibilities for social change diminish. In these cases, the results of research can be transformed into 'recipe books', which are compilations of normative recommendations for policies – that is, recommendations of what should be done that have already been thought out and that are apparently ready for implementation. Supplying solutions before implementation instead of constructing solutions with those who will be doing the implementing leads to recipes becoming difficult to use in practice. By not taking into consideration the political and ideological positions of those who are participating in the policy process, research cannot consider the potential conflicts that may arise, which then hinders the potential of policy learning for social change.

II.   Improvement of Programme Efficiency

When working on policies through praxis, but without explicitly addressing ideological and political positions, people often make improvements to the efficiency of programmes, which helps to do what they have already done, only making better use of the available resources. But this strategy is not enough for the challenges (such as responsible innovation) that regions face today, which require paradigm change. Paradigm change requires people to address the existing conflicts due to ideological and political differences.

III.   Political Discourse

When people explicitly address ideological and political positions, but without praxis, the processes end up shaping political discourse. This type of speech helps the transformation of policy by marking a horizon for change and then legitimizing that change. Such speech is insufficient for transformation to occur, however. ARTD integrates the ideological and political dimensions in the process of dialogue, not only through discourse but also through the expressions of the ideology perceptible in habits rooted in practice. Therefore, the ideology is not made explicit exclusively in large-scale discourses; it also occurs in small-scale actions.

IV.   Social Learning

When praxis and the explicit ideological and political dimension converge, possibilities emerge for a policy-learning process with an impact on the societal challenges faced today and embedded in the concept of responsible innovation set out in this chapter.

7.   DISCUSSION: GENERATING FAVOURABLE CONDITIONS FOR CO-GENERATIVE POLICY LEARNING

We began this chapter with an overview of policy learning, with a focus more specifically on policy learning in the regional innovation field and the concept of regional policy learning. In doing so, we addressed responsible innovation as one of the main challenges that the innovation policy field faces today. We have argued that this concept poses the need to overcome policy-learning processes that are focused on technical problem solving in order to address paradigm change.

In the second section of this chapter, we proposed action research, more specifically ARTD, a branch of AR developed in the context of the regional innovation policy field, as a possible strategy for policy learning that integrates not only praxis but also the ideological discussion at the core of praxis. We combined our voices as authors with the voices of policymakers who have participated with us in ARTD processes in order to better share the different perspectives involved in policy learning in ARTD.

It is now time to address the question that guides this discussion section: are policymakers and researchers in the regional innovation policy field ready to complement their actual approaches to policy learning with approaches based on AR or other co-generative approaches?

In the introduction to this chapter, we advanced two potential arguments for the poor impact of research on policy, and thus on policy learning. When we analyse research–policy dynamics, we can frame the problem differently, generally by rooting the problem on the researcher side, on the policymaker side or in the interaction between the two (Stone et al., 2001). As Stone et al. (2001, pp. 3–4) show, the problem of the lack of influence of research in policy can be defined in part because of 'the ignorance of politicians about the existence of policy relevant research, or the incapacity of over-stretched bureaucrats to absorb research', which, in our view, is an underlying idea that is present in many works in the regional development and innovation literature. But the problem can also be defined as poor policy comprehension of researchers concerning both the policy process and how research might be relevant to this process; this is an issue that several regional innovation scholars, including ourselves, have pointed out as being relevant (e.g. Arrona and Zabala-Iturriagagoitia, 2019; Flanagan and Uyarra, 2016; Karlsen and Larrea, 2014a; Uyarra et al., 2017). In our view, these problems are significant, and co-generative approaches such as ARTD can bring these two communities together to generate better conditions for regional policy learning that will lead to responsible innovation. In order to combine our own voices with those of policymakers who have experience of co-generative policy-learning processes, we have constructed the discussion below based on comments extracted from the interviews.

Although researchers in the regional innovation policy field often interact with policymakers, co-generative research methodologies are still scarce, and sometimes a feeling of disconnection exists between the two communities.

> Generally speaking, researchers are used to working in a certain way, and you feel comfortable in your bubble, and among your papers.

Academia and criteria for excellence do not favour co-generative research, as co-generated knowing (such as knowledge in action) is more difficult to share in traditional academic formats. The policymakers we interviewed perceived that researchers might feel uncomfortable if they were brought out of their usual ways of approaching research and into co-generative methodologies.

> In the social sciences (competitiveness, political management, economics, etc.) without a doubt [co-generation] should be that way. . ..I guess it feels limiting . . . because in the other world [traditional research] they're freer . . .. But I think the future should be like that [i.e. co-generative]: research should constantly enrich the work of public institutions.

We consider that the paradigmatic changes required by societal challenges and responsible innovation do not affect policymakers exclusively; they also affect researchers. Part of paradigmatic change points to more horizontal, participatory and democratic knowledge-creation processes, which in turn affect research methodologies. In this context, the policymakers we interviewed considered that the connection between policymakers and researchers should be examined:

> I believe . . . that research and policymaking should align. Maybe it's a dream, but it's very thought provoking.

> Policymakers are far from research, and researchers are far from policy. The solution is not that either of them sticks to the other; there should be successive approaching moves.

AR and co-generative research processes are, of course, not the only alternatives to more democratic knowledge-production processes, but they can serve as a test bed in the field of regional innovation policies. One interviewee proposed these types of research processes as a meeting point for researchers and policymakers:

> When there are new problems, new challenges, programmes related to change . . . you need co-generation, at different stages of the process: at design, at implementation and also at evaluation. And that way, different agents would learn: government, private agents, universities . . ..

Following the previously presented idea of the need for absorptive capacity to understand the logics of the other community, we discussed with various policymakers what we refer to as the arrogance of both policy and research. In both cases, this refers to a sense of superiority derived from the feeling of having the 'right knowledge', which was not accessible to the other community. The participants recognized this phenomenon, saying that 'policymakers' arrogance comes from public legitimation, but society doesn't legitimate us to do anything we want'. As another policymaker stated:

> I would tell researchers that through our public policy we're continuously experimenting, and what researchers lack is the recognition that in our everyday activities, we're constructing knowledge. Sometimes it seems that knowledge only comes from the university.

One solution that an interviewee proposed to overcome the distance created by the lack of absorptive capacity on both sides was not one where the two communities would completely adapt to the other; as this interviewee said, 'We all have a partial perspective; we should meet each other midway.'

Some of the interviewees saw the need to generate absorptive capacity to work with researchers in co-generative processes, but they recognized that it can be difficult to overcome the assumption that any time used in co-generative processes could be wasted time:

> We all have needs [of absorptive capacity], and policymakers [do] also . . . [but] we have a short-term view, and thus we have difficulties engaging in such [co-generative] methodologies, because people might think of them as a waste of time. And maybe, to a great extent, there's no capacity to see that this type of learning goes beyond . . . short-term results.

Some of the difficulties in engaging with co-generative policy-learning processes are thus the inimical conditions created by requirements in the academic world and the daily pressures in the policy world to make short-term decisions. We also noted the recognition that policymakers must be aware of their need to learn in order to become involved in policy learning:

> Before absorptive capacity comes the [recognition of] the need to learn . . .. [Politicians] have to change . . . and they have to be aware that they have to change. . . .If they feel that need, capacity will come afterwards.

ARTD should not necessarily be interpreted as an alternative to other research methods. Due to its dialogic nature, ARTD can be a good strategy for developing absorptive capacity, both in policymaking and research communities, concerning how to work together. This situation benefits not only further AR-based policy-learning processes but also any policy-learning process that involves policymakers and researchers in search of responsible innovation.

8.   CONCLUSIONS

This chapter has addressed policy learning in the framework of the innovation policy field. After providing a general framework on this concept, we have focused on the development of a central idea. Innovation policy today faces a challenge in integrating sustainability and responsibility so that policy will be oriented towards facing societal challenges in a way that is socially desirable. This challenge affects policymakers, since they must rethink the goals of innovation policy and experiment with new ways of policymaking that will ensure inclusiveness in order to negotiate such goals. As we have argued in this chapter, the incorporation of learning approaches that include reflexivity seems to be key for achieving the change of rationale involved in new ways such as this.

However, the challenge equally affects researchers, who are often encouraged through the concept of RRI to develop research that is socially beneficial. Instead of thinking along two parallel and separate lines, this chapter has addressed the responsibility dimension that RRI poses by looking at social researchers' contributions to the concrete challenge of adopting responsible innovation within regional innovation policies. In our view, researchers can play an active role – and thus develop socially beneficial research – in promoting social learning that will help policymakers adopt responsible innovation in practice. Specifically, this chapter has proposed AR as one possible strategy to do so and has illustrated, using the words of policymakers, the learning – and change – that co-generation can promote.

Nevertheless, researchers' more direct involvement in policy practice challenges the traditional practices of researchers and policymakers alike and the ways in which they interact. Throughout this chapter, we have attempted to provide insights into these challenges so that we can gain an understanding of how to improve these interactions and promote learning. In our view, understanding and improving how regions can learn, and how regional innovation policies can adapt to building responses that will be responsible, inclusive and sustainable, should include a reflection of how the research and policy worlds can better interact in this collective challenge.

REFERENCES

Ansell, C., and Gash, A. (2008). Collaborative governance in theory and practice. *Journal of Public Administration Research and Theory*, 18(4), 543–71.

Aranguren, M.J., Magro, E., and Wilson, J.R. (2017). Regional competitiveness policies in an era of smart specialization strategies, in R. Huggins and

P. Thompson (eds), *Handbook of Regions and Competitiveness*, Cheltenham, UK and Northampton, MA, USA: Edward Elgar Publishing, pp. 543–63.

Arrona, A. (2017). *Can interpretive policy analysis contribute to a critical scholarship on regional innovation policy studies?* Orkestra working paper series in territorial competitiveness no. 2017-R01, vol. 1.

Arrona, A., and Zabala-Iturriagagoitia, J.M. (2019). On the study and practice of regional innovation policy: The potential of interpretive policy analysis. *Innovation*, 32(1), 148–63.

Bardone, E., and Lind, M. (2016). Towards a phronetic space for responsible research (and innovation). *Life Sciences, Society and Policy*, 12(5), 1–18.

Bennett, C.J., and Howlett, M. (1992). The lessons of learning: Reconciling theories of policy learning and policy change. *Policy Sciences*, 25(3), 275–94.

Benz, A., and Fürst, D. (2002). Policy learning in regional networks. *European Urban and Regional Studies*, 9(1), 21–35.

Bogner, A., and Torgersen, H. (2018). Precaution, responsible innovation and beyond: In search of a sustainable agricultural biotechnology policy. *Frontiers in Plant Science*, 9 (1884), 1–10.

Borrás, S. (2009). *The widening and deepening of innovation policy: What conditions provide for effective governance?* CIRCLE working paper 2009/2, Lund University.

Borrás, S. (2011). Policy learning and organizational capacities in innovation policies. *Science and Public Policy*, 38(9), 725–34.

Burget, M., Bardone, E., and Pedaste, M. (2017). Definitions and conceptual dimensions of responsible research and innovation: A literature review. *Science and Engineering Ethics*, 23(1), 1–19.

Chaminade, C., and Edquist, C. (2010). Rationales for public policy intervention in the innovation process: Systems of innovation approach, in R.E. Smits, S. Kuhlmann and P. Shapira (eds), *The Theory and Practice of Innovation Policy: An International Handbook*, Cheltenham, UK and Northampton, MA, USA: Edward Elgar Publishing, pp. 95–119.

Dotti, N.F. (2014). *Literature review on territorial innovation models, geography of research and policy innovations*, GREATPI working paper no. 1, Brussels.

Dunlop, C.A., and Radaelli, C.M. (2013). Systematising policy learning: From monolith to dimensions. *Political Studies*, 61(3), 599–619.

Dunlop, C.A., and Radaelli, C.M. (2018). Does policy learning meet the standards of an analytical framework of the policy process? *Policy Studies Journal*, 46(S1), S48–S68.

Dunlop, C.A., Radaelli, C.M., and Trein, P. (eds) (2018). *Learning in Public Policy: Analysis, Modes and Outcomes*, London: Palgrave Macmillan UK.

Felt, U. (2014). Within, across and beyond: Reconsidering the role of social sciences and humanities in Europe. *Science as Culture*, 23(3), 384–96.

Fischer, F. and Mandell, A. (2012). Transformative learning in planning and policy deliberation: Probing social meaning and tacit assumptions, in F. Fischer and Herbert Gotweiss (eds), *The Argumentative Turn Revisited*, Durham, NC: Duke University Press, pp. 343–70.

Fisher, E. (2018). Ends of responsible innovation. *Journal of Responsible Innovation*, 5(3), 253–56.

Fitjar, R.D., Benneworth, P., and Asheim, B.T. (2019). Towards regional responsible research and innovation? Integrating RRI and RIS3 in European innovation policy. *Science and Public Policy*, 46(5), 772–83.

Flanagan, K., and Uyarra, E. (2016). Four dangers in innovation policy studies – and how to avoid them. *Industry and Innovation*, 23(2), 177–88.
Freeman, R. (2006). Learning in public policy, in M. Moran, M. Rein and R.E. Goodin (eds), *The Oxford Handbook of Public Policy*, Oxford, UK: Oxford University Press, pp. 367–88.
Freeman, R. (2007). Epistemological bricolage: How practitioners make sense of learning. *Administration & Society*, 39(4), 476–96.
Gilardi, F., and Radaelli, C.M. (2012). Governance and learning, in D. Levi-Faur (ed.), *Oxford Handbook of Governance*, Oxford, UK: Oxford University Press, pp. 155–68.
González-López, M. (2019). Understanding policy learning in regional innovation policies: Lessons from the Galician case. *Innovation: The European Journal of Social Science Research*, 32(1), 104–18.
Goyal, N., and Howlett, M. (2018). Lessons learned and not learned: Bibliometric analysis of policy learning, in C.A. Dunlop, C.M. Radaelli and P. Trein (eds), *Learning in Public Policy: Analysis, Modes and Outcomes*, London: Palgrave Macmillan UK, pp. 27–49.
Grin, J., and Loeber, A. (2007). Theories of policy learning: Agency, structure, and change, in F. Fischer, G.J. Miller and M.S. Sidney (eds), *Handbook of Public Policy Analysis*, London: Taylor & Francis, pp. 201–19.
Grin, J., and Van de Graaf, H. (1996). Implementation as communicative action: An interpretive understanding of interactions between policy actors and target groups. *Policy Sciences*, 29, 291–319.
Heclo, H. (1974). *Modern Social Politics in Britain and Sweden: From Relief to Income Maintenance*. New York, NY: Yale University Press.
Innes, J.E., and Booher, D.E. (2010). *Planning with Complexity: An Introduction to Collaborative Rationality for Public Policy*, New York, NY: Routledge.
Karlsen, J., and Larrea, M. (2014a). *Territorial Development and Action Research: Innovation through Dialogue*, Farnham, UK: Gower.
Karlsen, J., and Larrea, M. (2014b). The contribution of action research to policy learning: The case of Gipuzkoa Sarean, *International Journal of Action Research*, 10(2), 129–55.
Karlsen, J., and Larrea, M. (2018). Regional innovation system as a framework for the co-generation of policy: An action research approach, in A. Isaksen, R. Martin and M. Tripple (eds), *New Avenues for Regional Innovation Systems: Theoretical Advances, Empirical Cases and Policy Lessons*, Cham, Switzerland: Springer, pp. 257–64.
Koschatzky, K., and Kroll, H. (2007). Which side of the coin? The regional governance of science and innovation. *Regional Studies*, 41(8), 1115–27.
Laranja, M., Uyarra, E., and Flanagan, K. (2008). Policies for science, technology and innovation: Translating rationales into regional policies in a multi-level setting. *Research Policy*, 37(5), 823–35.
Loeber, A., van Mierlo, B., Grin, J., and Leeuwis, C. (2007). The practical value of theory: Conceptualising learning in the pursuit of a sustainable development, in A.E.J. Wals (ed.), *Social Learning towards a Sustainable World: Principles, Perspectives, and Praxis*, Wageningen, the Netherlands: Wageningen Academic Publishers, pp. 83–97.
Mazzucato, M. (2016). From market fixing to market-creating: A new framework for innovation policy. *Industry and Innovation*, 23(2), 140–56.

Moulaert, F., and Sekia, F. (2003). Territorial innovation models: A critical survey. *Regional Studies*, 37(3), 289–302.

Nauwelaers, C., and Wintjes, R. (2002). Innovating SMEs and regions: The need for policy intelligence and interactive policies. *Technology Analysis & Strategic Management*, 14(2), 201–15.

Nauwelaers, C., and Wintjes, R. (2008). Innovation policy, innovation in policy: Policy learning within and across systems and clusters, in C. Nauwelaers and R. Wintjes (eds), *Innovation Policy in Europe: Measurement and Strategy*, Cheltenham, UK and Northampton, MA, USA: Edward Elgar Publishing, pp. 225–68.

OECD (2005). *Governance of innovation systems, vol. 1: synthesis report.* Paris: Organisation for Economic Cooperation and Development.

Owen, R.J., Bessant, J.R., and Heintz, M. (eds) (2013). *Responsible Innovation*, vol. 104. Chichester, UK: Wiley.

Rip, A. (2014). The past and future of RRI. *Life Sciences, Society and Policy*, 10(17), 1–15.

Steward, F. (2012). Transformative innovation policy to meet the challenge of climate change. *Technology, Analysis & Strategic Management*, 24(4), 331–43.

Stilgoe, J., Owen, R., and Macnaghten, P. (2013). Developing a framework for responsible innovation. *Research Policy*, 42, 1568–80.

Stone, D., Maxwell, S., and Keating, M. (2001). 'Bridging research and policy', presented at Bridging Research and Policy workshop, Warwick University, 16–17 July. Accessed 24 May 2019 at http://www2.warwick.ac.uk/fac/soc/pais/research/researchcentres/csgr/research/keytopic/other/bridging.pdf.

Uyarra, E. (2007). Key dilemmas of regional innovation policies. *Innovation: The European Journal of Social Science Research*, 20(3), 243–61.

Uyarra, E., and Flanagan, K. (2010). From regional systems of innovation to regions as innovation policy spaces. *Environment and Planning C: Government and Policy*, 28(4), 681–95.

Uyarra, E., Flanagan, K., Magro, E., Wilson, J.R., and Sotarauta, M. (2017). Understanding regional innovation policy dynamics: Actors, agency and learning, *Environment and Planning C: Politics and Space*, 35(4), 559–68.

Von Schomberg, R. (2011). Prospects for technology assessment in a framework of responsible research and innovation, in M. Dusseldorp and R. Beecroft (eds), *Technikfolgen Abschätzen Lehren: Bildungspotenziale Transdisziplinärer Methode*, Wiesbaden, Germany: Springer VS, pp. 39–61.

Von Schomberg, R. (2013). A vision of responsible innovation, in R. Owen, M. Heintz and J. Bessant (eds), *Responsible Innovation: Managing the Responsible Emergence of Science and Innovation in Society*, London: Wiley, pp. 51–74.

Wilford, S. (2018). First line steps in requirements identification for guidelines development in responsible research and innovation (RRI). *Systemic Practice and Action Research*, 31, 539–56.

4. Regional autonomy and innovation policy

Elisabeth Baier and Andrea Zenker

1. INTRODUCTION

Regional innovation policy is determined by numerous rationales and philosophies at different governance levels. It is influenced by supra-national and national framework conditions, regional responsibilities, and European Union (EU) policy making alike. In a very broad sense, national innovation policies contribute to shaping the framework conditions for innovation activities within a national territory, while regional innovation policy can focus on the specific conditions in sub-national territories. Regional innovation policy can thus more decidedly address regional strengths and weaknesses as well as territorial opportunities through region-specific tailored approaches. This may, for instance, concern specific industrial structures – in terms of business types, sectors, competitive advantages – or further context conditions that influence innovation activities. The latter category comprises science and research, skills, education and training, innovation funding, intermediary structures such as technology transfer, the creation of an encouraging climate for founders, and the support of business networks and clusters. It can be assumed that – in addition to a framing policy on the national scale – a targeted focus on regional actors and activities can better refer to the specific conditions in the territories considered and has the capacity to boost territory-based innovation processes.

The regionalisation of innovation policy has been discussed intensely over the last two decades (Fritsch and Stephan 2005; Koschatzky 2000; Perry and May 2007; Prange 2008; Reger 1998; Tödtling and Trippl 2005). However, whether regional innovation policy can unfold its full potential, relies inter alia upon varying degrees in decision-making power, budgetary responsibility, and region-specific technological and institutional trajectories. Thus, the degree of regional autonomy related to regional innovation policy making is worth considering in greater detail.[1]

This holds in particular since, in the current EU programming period, innovation and research has become one of the key priorities of the

European Regional Development Fund (ERDF), and the access to this funding depends on the implementation of regional innovation strategies, as one of the ex-ante conditionalities (European Commission 2014).[2] The regionalisation of innovation policy becomes even more refined with the community-led local development approach. This approach focuses on the development of sub-regional areas. It should be led by local action groups that are composed of representatives of local public and private socio-economic interests that develop multi-sectoral area-based local development strategies considering in particular local needs and potentials.[3] For many regions, EU structural funding constitutes a significant share of the regional budgetary resources. Financial allocations for Cohesion Funds and European Regional Development funds amount to €351.8bn in the current funding period.[4] Although in some countries – such as Germany – other sources of funding may eclipse the budgetary volume of structural funding itself, it remains a valid proxy for budgetary power for the majority of European regions where this is not the case. In large parts of Eastern and Southern Europe, European structural funding still constitutes the prominent, in part nearly exclusive, source of funding for regional innovation policy.[5]

EU budgets assigned to the research and innovation priority axis in the ERDF require the fulfilment of certain ex-ante conditionalities such as regional research and innovation strategies. Taking this together, it could be assumed that regions with higher levels of autonomy might be better positioned for designing and implementing territory-specific innovation supporting strategies and policies.

In this regard Oates (2011) found, firstly, that lower levels of government have more and better information about what people need and, secondly, that measures of fiscal centralisation are significantly negatively correlated with levels of per capita real income. Transferring this finding to the topic of regional autonomy and innovation policy making, it would imply that decision makers on the regional level are more knowledgeable about innovation activities and innovation actors in the regional innovation system and their needs and also that certain budgetary power on the regional level could lead to better economic and innovation outcomes.

Taking account of these and more recent developments, in this chapter we enlarge the discussion on regional autonomy and innovation policy by implementing a dynamic approach. Given that the degree of regional autonomy varies notably among European countries and even within the regions of a country (Baier et al. 2013), we reason that a higher degree of regional autonomy is able to promote and deliver tailored approaches. In order to be able to investigate this relationship in greater detail, we need an operationalisation of the idea of regional autonomy. This raises certain questions. How can the notion of regional autonomy be conceptualised? Which indicators can be proposed in order to operationalise regional autonomy in a comparative perspective across Europe? Which factors contribute to changes in the degree of regional autonomy over time?

We are unable to answer these questions in full, but we have intended to provide insight into the degree of regional autonomy across Europe. This might be helpful for further analyses of innovation policies and the monitoring of its effectiveness in European regions. Additionally, our insights might trigger a discussion on regional innovation policy and governance, in particular the aspect of autonomy especially in comparative analyses. With this in mind, we hope to contribute to a better understanding of regional innovation policy rationales and their implementation.

We attempt to address this topic in different ways. Firstly, we discuss the topic of regional autonomy, referring to the most recent theoretical contributions in the innovation systems framework and decentralisation processes in this respect. Secondly, we look at the situation in an empirical manner and see what conclusions can be derived for regional policy making by taking a dynamic approach. We especially take into consideration the national constitutional settings. Along these lines, the following section is devoted to the conceptual framework of this contribution. It focuses on regional autonomy and its rationales, and relates them to innovation in a territorial context, including the concept of regional innovation systems. The third section introduces our empirical approach to the measurement of regional autonomy. It is followed by section 4, which displays the results of our analysis, while the final section concludes our contribution by summarising and reflecting on the main results.

2. REGIONAL AUTONOMY, DEVOLUTION AND DECENTRALISATION: A CONCEPTUAL APPROACH FOR ANALYSING REGIONAL INNOVATION POLICY

Aspects of regional autonomy and decentralisation, in particular fiscal decentralisation and autonomy, have been addressed in other contexts such as regional social expenditures and the provision of services (Herrero-Alcalde and Tránchez-Martín 2017), reduction of income differences, and the contribution to convergence in different policy settings (Kyriacou et al. 2015) or economic growth (Ezcurra and Rodríguez-Pose 2013). At the time of writing, their application to regional innovation policy making has not been discussed extensively.

Concerning the term "regional or territorial autonomy", Suksi (2012) notes a lack of terminological clarity. Before proceeding, it seems worthwhile to discuss in detail the notion of regional autonomy. The discussion of autonomy has philosophical roots and is originally attributed to individual persons (Christman 2003). The concept incorporates the notion that an individual's behaviour is based on reasons and intentions and the individual is free to behave accordingly. This implies that the individual is responsible and accountable for him/herself and his/her actions.

Thus, autonomy describes the state of being self-governed. This is inherently different from the meaning of independence. According to Dahl (1982, p. 16), independence in a political sense means "not to be under the control of another". Thus, we understand autonomy in the sense of having room for manoeuvre within a hierarchical structure. Concerning the notion of territorial or regional autonomy, this can be translated to regional self-government within a certain constitutional setting. According to this translation, legal autonomy defines the boundaries of decision making within a superordinate system (such as the nation state) while being accountable and responsible for decision making and the outcomes rendered by law or by the constitution.

Elazar (1991) and Marks et al. (2008) distinguish between self-rule and shared rule as the two central components for regional authority. In this reference frame, self-rule consists of the scope of policy for which a regional government is responsible (policy scope), the extent to which the region controls its financial resources (fiscal authority) and the extent to which a region is endowed with representative institutions (representation). Shared rule is understood as the extent to which a region co-determines the authoritative decisions of the central government (role in central government).

This might lead to regional self-government and a certain leeway for regional forms of organisation. Cooperation and division of work between different governance levels is generally defined in the constitution, which also specifies the different responsibilities and scope of action of the different levels. However, in order to be fully operational, policy on the regional level needs not only the legal and human resource power, but also financial resources in order to shape regional ecosystems and innovation activities to progress. Thus, we operationalise and use the term regional autonomy in the following way, based on former considerations (Baier et al. 2013) and the reflections above. Regional autonomy is higher, if the given territorial entity (1) has general political competence to take independent decisions and can be held responsible for these decisions (2) has relevant influence on budgetary decisions and (3) has factual room for action.

Summarising, regional autonomy characterises the state of self-govern-ment for a certain territorial entity on a sub-national level at a certain point in time. It is interrelated with regional governance, which can be contextualised from different disciplinary perspectives. It implies a territorial component including territorial hierarchy (e.g. communes and municipalities – counties – region) from a geographical perspective, and from an economics perspective it can be related to an understanding of market mechanisms and the allocation of resources as well as market failures. From a political science perspective, it can be related to debates on the balancing of and bargaining about political power, and from an administrative perspective it conveys the administrative and process-oriented elements of governing. Thus regional governance is a broad concept depending on a number of different factors, ranging from the territorial endowment, institutional framework conditions and differing social practices to direct and dynamic responses from within the logic of the political system itself (Scott 1998).

Whichever perspective is taken, regional governance remains first and foremost embedded in the respective national context in addition to the influence from superior policy levels. For example, most regional innova-tion promoting activities are embedded (at least to a certain degree) in national and supra-national science, technology and innovation policy frameworks, a fact that has given rise to a broad and ongoing multi-level governance discourse in regional innovation policy research (Crespy et al. 2007; Uyarra 2007; Uyarra and Flanagan 2010, 2017).

Since the degree of regional autonomy may evolve over time, it becomes additionally important to take a dynamic approach and to look closer at the processes that lead to perceptible changes in this respect. As an example, European Member States have restructured their governance system during the past decades to promote the devolution of state functions to sub-national levels (Loughlin 2007). This is also related to the fact that the regional level across the EU has increased in importance during the past decades, in terms of both authority and expenditure (including the management of public expenditures and EU Structural Funds, cf. Charron et al. 2014).

Devolution processes are by no means homogenous across Europe and often depend on national idiosyncrasies that have their roots in the consti-tutional and administrative history of the countries. Thus, European coun-tries are on different trajectories determined by historical backgrounds and path dependency, institutional transformation, and consolidation of regional autonomy (Rodríguez-Pose and Bwire 2003). As a result, differ-ent types of regionalisation continue to co-exist in Europe (Yoder 2007) with regard to the functions and competences that are devolved to the sub-national level in general and in innovation policy making in particular. Additionally, there are asymmetries between the degree of devolution to different regions within one nation and the degree of interaction of the regions with the European level.

Although devolution and decentralisation are to a certain extent related, they are not wholly congruent. Decentralisation is often decided top-down and can be understood as a strategy for the transfer of powers from central government to lower levels in a political–administrative and territorial hierarchy (Agrawal 1999; Bresser-Pereira 2004). Devolution is usually a response to demands for more local or regional autonomy, to which government officials in the central government accede (Bresser-Pereira 2004). Thus, it can be triggered top-down, even from the supra-national level, or it can have its roots in bottom-up movements. Bresser-Pereira (2004) concludes that decentralisation is a public management strategy, but devolution is a political decision with managerial consequences. Devolution strongly embraces the transfer of governance responsibility for specified functions to sub-national levels, either publicly or privately owned, that are somewhat out of the direct control of the central government (Ferguson and Chandrasekharan 2005).

As regards the evolvement of regional autonomy, devolution and decentralisation can be understood as triggering factors for the transformative process that lead from a certain degree of regional autonomy at one point in time to another. Figure 4.1 gives a schematic overview of the dynamic approach. In Europe, devolution and decentralisation processes are initiated inter alia by requirements coming from the EU level. A major share of funding (such as from the ERDF or the Cohesion Fund) targets regions with specific territorial characteristics (such as remote, mountainous or sparsely populated areas) and with different development states that relate to the gross national income per inhabitant in order to ensure further social and economic convergence. Due to the fact that the funding has to be administered, Managing Authorities have been installed at lower levels – either on a national level or on a regional level.

More specifically focusing on innovation, the regional level gained

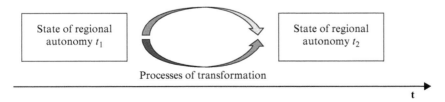

Source: Own elaboration.

Figure 4.1   Dynamic perspective on processes of transformation

attention in innovation analyses and policy design during the last decades. Various arguments emphasise the benefits of considering innovation in its (territorial) context: the mere recognition that cooperation not only promotes but is increasingly indispensable for the success of innovations points at the importance of proximity (see, e.g., Boschma 2005 or Balland et al. 2014) for innovation and development. Given the high complexity of innovation processes, it can be assumed that barriers with respect to languages, mentalities and habits or opportunities for personal exchanges are lower when partners are characterised by higher degrees of proximity. In addition, knowledge flows (especially the flow of tacit knowledge, cf. Polanyi 1997) can be more easily realised in situations of higher (geographical) proximity (Asheim and Coenen 2005). Territorially specific knowledge is held by local and regional actors (see, e.g., the concept of "sticky knowledge" in Morgan 2004 or Asheim and Isaksen 2002), and common legal and mental frameworks facilitate networking and trust building (see also the discussion on social capital in the 1990s, e.g. Putnam 1995). These factors enable developing bottom-up processes in territories.

The territorial dimension in the context of EU policies – specifically cohesion and development policies – received increased attention through the "place-based approach" put forward by Barca (2009). Its focus is on the strategic development of territories, based on their (local) potentials in order to strengthen development and cohesion. The approach claims to go beyond decentralising public functions and argues in favour of responsibilities for designing and implementing policies on "different levels of government and special-purpose local institutions (private associations, joint local authority bodies, cooperation across national borders, public–private partnerships and so on)" (Barca 2009, p. 41). In line with the concept of shared rule (Elazar 1991; Marks et al. 2008), Barca (2009) proposes to implement a division of work and of responsibilities in which higher-level authorities shape the general frame for using EU funds, while lower levels are asked to implement this in a context-specific tailored way in their territories (ibid.; see also OECD 2009 and the "new paradigm of regional policy" in support of building innovative regions, as well as Koschatzky and Stahlecker 2010).

This rationale of territorial innovation and of shared responsibilities is a crucial aspect of cohesion policy in the programming period 2014–2020. Countries and regions have developed Smart Specialisation Strategies as an ex-ante conditionality (European Commission 2014) for accessing the European Structural Investment Funds (ESIFs). Territorial and research- and innovation-related aspects are jointly considered for stimulating innovativeness and industrial transition especially in less-developed regions (see, e.g., Foray et al. 2018).[6]

Summarising, the regional dimension in innovation policy design and implementation is undisputed. But how can innovation in a territorial context be analysed, especially in its interrelated systemic perspective? A well-known framework for analysis is the concept of innovation systems, an approach that is discussed on the national and regional levels as well as from a sectoral and technological perspective (see, e.g., Lundvall 1992; Lundvall et al. 2002; Cooke 1992; Braczyk et al. 1998; Freeman 2000; Edquist 2000; Cooke et al. 1997; Malerba 2002; Markard and Truffer 2008; Bergek et al. 2008). On this basis, Kuhlmann and Arnold (2001) developed a heuristic of a national innovation system that includes the two main sub-systems of (1) industry and (2) education and research. Revisiting the insights from innovation research over the last two or three decades, the necessity to enlarge the classical innovation systems framework by pointing to a wider range of actors, institutions and innovation modes relevant for the innovation landscape has become increasingly obvious (Warnke et al. 2016). In their revision of the innovation system concept, Warnke et al. (2016) took recent innovation phenomena such as user innovation, social innovation, collaborative innovation, the emergence of new innovation intermediaries, venture philanthropy, social or relational capital and non-research and development (R&D)-intensive industries into account. This led to a new innovation system heuristic (Figure 4.2) that intends to provide a conceptual framework for policy makers, researchers and further interested parties to analyse innovation processes in a systemic perspective. It shows that innovation supply and demand is at the core of innovation (inner triangle, dashed line), while innovation input (star-shaped dotted line) conceptualises the support of innovation activities. These activities are embedded in a general context (star-shaped broken line) that determines the specific conditions in which innovation takes place.

Examples for actors are given for each category. The cloud design and the dotted lines intend to indicate that the actors and actor groups are by no means self-contained but interact with the other elements and evolve over time. The elements of innovation systems are not considered as "closed systems"; they are open and interact with their environment. These interactions bring in additional knowledge, actors and activities (Warnke et al. 2016). Thus, the system itself changes over time, which also holds for the general context conditions such as the policy framework.

Figure 4.2 emphasises the role of policy as one important framework condition that contributes to the framing of innovation processes. Research, technology and innovation policies are at the core when it comes to shaping the context for innovation, but Figure 4.2 also shows that various further policies have an impact on innovation activities. Additionally,

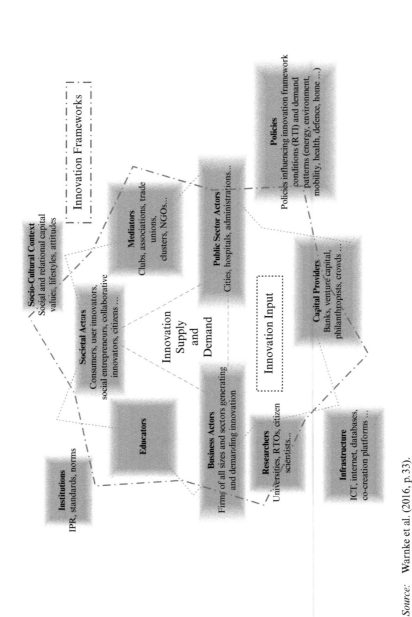

Source: Warnke et al. (2016, p. 33).

Figure 4.2   The revised innovation system analytical framework

policies towards the Grand Challenges[7] are expected to have a significant impact on innovation and innovation strategies.

Considering the advantages of sub-national innovation policies in the innovation systems conceptual framework leads us to conclude that a certain room for manoeuvre is needed for regional innovation policy in order to implement a tailored territory-specific approach. This does not mean that superordinate levels – mostly the national level – do not have a role to play, but, on the contrary, that well-coordinated multi-level governance and multi-level actor approaches support a favourable regional context for innovation and to promote innovation actors and their innovation-related activities. Summarising, it can be expected that the opportunity for autonomous regional action within a context of multi-level governance supports a territory-specific approach to innovation policy that draws on regional competences, network building capabilities, proximity and trust.

3. OPERATIONALISATION: INDICATORS OF REGIONAL AUTONOMY

In order to develop a comprehensive set of indicators, suitable to describe the present state of the degree of autonomy in European regions, it is necessary to adhere to a reference framework that allows for a better understanding of the task, since measuring regional autonomy involves various dimensions. With respect to the operationalisation of regional autonomy in the field of innovation policy making, we refer mostly to the elements of regional self-rule, since we are strongly interested in the leeway of regional policy making.

Referring to the revised innovation system framework (see Figure 4.2) and, as indicated above, regional autonomy and its operationalisation concerning innovation policy focuses on the "policy cloud" of the innovation framework level (Figure 4.2, Innovation Frameworks part). Embedded in our conceptual approach as outlined in section 2, we assume that (1) innovation policy has a pertinent impact on shaping the framework conditions for innovation in a given territory, (2) territory-specific innovation support tailored to regional innovation activities can promote specific strengths and competitive advantages within these territories, and (3) degrees of freedom for designing and implementing regional policies are enhanced through opportunities for autonomous action.

In an earlier study, Baier et al. (2013) proposed a set of indicators, which we now update and revise. Comparing the results from the first data collection phase (end of 2012) with the results from the current data collection phase (May 2019) enables us to consider regional autonomy in a dynamic perspective. The operationalisation of the regional autonomy in the European regions includes the set of indicators and variables as displayed in Table 4.1. The construction of the indicators is based on a qualitative assessment of constitutions, regional strategies and management setting in the light of the ERDF contribution, which will be explained in detail in the next section.

Table 4.1   Indicators and variables for regional autonomy

Indicators	Variables
General regional autonomy	Analyses of the framework conditions set by the constitution
Regional competences with regard to innovation policy	Analyses of the framework conditions set by the constitutions and practicalities in regional innovation policy making in the Member States as well as Smart Specialisation Strategies on the regional level
Regional influence on Structural Fund allocations (ERDF)	• National or regional affiliation of the responsible Managing Authority for ERDF contribution • Availability of ERDF Operational Programmes on the regional level

Source: Own elaboration.

The first indicator, "General regional autonomy", is based on a review of the constitutions of the European Member States with specific attention to the degree of power regions are granted in their national contexts. In conducting this review, specific attention was paid to electoral laws and the existence of a regional representation on the sub-national level. In terms of ranking we used a 5-point scale, where the value 1 was assigned to regions in a fully centralised country without a regional legislative body; 2 to regions in a dominantly centralised context with, for instance, centrally appointed regional representatives; 3 to a shared central/regional structure (centrally appointed representatives plus regionally elected representatives); 4 to dominantly regionalised contexts with regionally elected representatives; and 5 to regions with regionally elected governments that have wideranging competencies and also representations in other countries and/or operate in proximity to European institutions. Where the distribution of responsibilities between the national state and the regional level is homogenous within a country, this results in identical ratings for all regions of one nation. In some cases, however, individual regions have a special status in their national context (e.g. in Italy, Spain, the UK, cf. also Charron et al. 2014), so that different parts of one country are assigned different rankings.

We keep this indicator for the revised indicator system for regional autonomy, as it sets the general framework conditions as regards innovation policy making. Next, we update our analysis from 2012.

When updating this indicator, we would expect to see only minor changes. The constitution is the major legal reference document of a country, describing the formal system of primary principles and laws that regulate the government of a country and the interplay of its institutions on a general level. Often the most fundamental principles are absolute and certain articles may not be amended under any circumstances.

The second indicator, "Regional competences with regard to innovation policy", was derived in a similar way, namely from a focused review of EU Member States' constitutions plus complementary sources concerning the organisation of innovation policy making in the different countries. In contrast to the first variable, a particular focus was put on competences and legislative powers in innovation-related policy making, that is, in the fields of research, innovation, technology or education policies. Hence, this aspect explicitly reflects the fact whether regions can decide autonomously on innovation-related policy issues or whether much of this competence remains on the central level. In contrast to the variable that represents "general regional autonomy", this variable was expressed on a 3-point scale, with 1 indicating full centralisation of Research, Technological Development and Innovation (RTDI) policies, that is, neither legislative nor administrative competences for such policies on the regional level; 2 indicating dominantly centralised RTDI policy governance, that is, most legislative competences remain at the national level except in some areas; and 3 indicating a wide range of regional competencies in RTDI policies.

Besides the fact that the variable is strongly determined by framework conditions that refer to the constitutions of the member countries, it is likewise influenced by EU requirements. Compared with our earlier investigation, we would expect to see some changes in the values of this variable.

To complement the two formerly mentioned indicators, the third indicator gives an explicit view of the regional influence on Structural Fund allocations and vice versa. It is mainly directed towards the ERDF, which aims to strengthen economic and social cohesion in the EU by correcting imbalances between its regions, depending on the category of region as regards the state of development. Thus, the indicator "Regional influence on structural fund allocations (ERDF)" is a composite of two separate variables (by calculating their average), reflecting distinct yet connected aspects of the complex process of structural fund allocations in which regions are involved. It is operationalised by taking an administrative and a programming perspective.

The administrative perspective illustrates whether the plans for structural funding are managed regionally and if the communication between the authorities and the recipients of funding happens at that level. In some cases, responsibilities are shared among a number of different agencies at the national level and a number of regional administrations. In general, EU regional policy "is implemented by national and regional bodies in partnership with the European Commission."[8] The implementation of EU policies includes selecting, monitoring and evaluating projects, based on Partnership Agreements and Operational Programmes. Managing Authorities in EU Member States and regions play a crucial role in this process.[9]

Thus, the variable contains information about the Managing Authorities in the EU Member States. For the construction of the variable and in order to investigate any changes compared with our previous analysis, we compared the affiliation of the responsible Managing Authority – either on the national or the regional level or both – of the funding period 2007–2013 and the funding period 2014–2020.[10] To give a clear attribution of these intermediate forms, a 5-point scale is used. According to the logic of the scales developed for the first indicator, all countries in which just regional authorities were involved received a score of 5, whereas all countries in which just national authorities were involved received a score of 1. Intermediate configurations were assigned scores between those extremes.[11]

In addition to the administrative perspective, the programming perspective reflects to what extent the Operational Programmes are developed for the regional level. In accordance with the administrative perspective, we likewise considered the two different funding periods. Even in cases where one national agency officially administers all the programmes, it can still interact and cooperate intensively with public and private representatives of the regions as well as with regional policy makers to adapt its plans to regional needs and characteristics. As with the administrative dimension, there are few countries in which Operational Programmes are either developed purely for the national or exclusively for the regional level. Additionally, the programming dimension takes into account whether regional Operational Programmes were available in all or in a limited number of selected regions. If all regions have their own Operational Programmes, the score, as per the logic of the previous scales, will be 5; if only a limited number of regions have Operational Programmes, the score will be 3; and the score will be 1 if a country has no regional Operational Programmes at all.[12]

We expect to see some changes in the values for the different Member States, due to different conditionalities for the allocation of EU funding as well as previous experiences with the management of structural funding in a multi-level setting. This indicator incorporates elements of regional self-rule and shared rule with the national and supra-national levels.

4. EMPIRICAL RESULTS: REGIONAL AUTONOMY AND INNOVATION POLICY AT THE REGIONAL LEVEL

Table 4.2 presents the findings from our analysis of documents, strategies and further information and displays values according to the three main indicators for each of the 28 Member States, also differentiated by year and thus partly integrating the results of our analysis from 2012. If the degree of regional autonomy differs for single regions within one country, these deviations are indicated with reference to the regions concerned. Depending on the country-specific constitutional backgrounds, our analysis relates to one specific regional level per country, as mentioned above.

Our recent analysis shows that European countries differ in their governance structures with respect to innovation policy. This confirms the findings of our previous paper (Baier et al. 2013) and mirrors not only country-specific organisational and administrative structures, and different rationales of innovation policy, but also different framework conditions (e.g. size) and traditions. While some countries laid down federal structures with wide-ranging competencies for the regional level in their constitutions, others have a rather centralist tradition and have only recently introduced regional administrative structures in order to comply with the conditions of the ESIF.

Table 4.2 shows that a number of countries can be described as rather centralised with regard to the indicators that we selected for our analysis. These countries do not foresee a regional governance level in their constitution and do not define innovation policy competencies at a sub-national regional level.[13] This group of countries covers Portugal (with the exception of the Autonomous Regions), Luxembourg, Estonia, Latvia, Lithuania, Malta, Ireland, Cyprus and Slovenia. Not surprisingly, most of these are smaller countries in which further regionalisation might not have positive effects for innovation and economic development. In these cases, scaling down competencies to a lower territorial level could even result in a fragmentation of the innovation system.

On the other side of the spectrum, Europe has a range of countries with large degrees of regional autonomy, both concerning administrative governance granted by the constitution and with respect to innovation policy competence. Here, the regional level is granted extensive political and

Table 4.2   Indicators of regional autonomy over time

Member State	General regional autonomy	Regional competences with regard to innovation policy	Regional influence on structural fund allocations (ERDF)	Year
Austria	5	2	4.5	2012
	4	2	1	2019
Belgium	5	3	5	2012
	5	3	5	2019
Bulgaria	1	1	1	2012
	2	1	1	2019
Croatia	–	–	–	2012
	2	1	1	2019
Cyprus	1	1	1	2012
	1	1	1	2019
Czechia	4	2	3	2012
	4	2	1.5	2019
Denmark	2	1	1	2012
(except Greenland, Faroe Islands)	2	1	1	2019
Estonia	1	1	1	2012
	1	1	1	2019
Finland (except Aland)	2	2	4	2012
	2	3	1	2019
Finland (Aland)	4	2	4	2012
	4	3	1	2019
France	3	2	5	2012
	3	3	4.5	2019
France (more autonomous)	4	2	5	2012
	4	3	4.5	2019
Germany	5	3	4.5	2012
	5	3	5	2019
Greece	3	1	2.5	2012
	3	2	4.5	2019
Hungary	2	1	2.5	2012
	3	1	3	2019
Ireland	1	1	5	2012
	1	1	5	2019
Italy (except Trentino, South Tyrol)	4	2	4	2012
	4	2	4	2019
Italy (Trentino, South Tyrol)	5	3	4	2012
	5	3	4	2019

Table 4.2   (continued)

Member State	General regional autonomy	Regional competences with regard to innovation policy	Regional influence on structural fund allocations (ERDF)	Year
Latvia	1	1	1	2012
	1	1	1	2019
Lithuania	1	1	1	2012
	2	1	1	2019
Luxembourg	1	1	1	2012
	1	1	1	2019
Malta	1	1	1	2012
	1	1	1	2019
the Netherlands	2	2	5	2012
	3	2	4.5	2019
Poland	3	2	5	2012
	3	2	4	2019
Portugal (except Madeira, Azores)	1	1	5	2012
	1	1	4.5	2019
Portugal (Madeira, Azores)	3	1	5	2012
	3	1	4.5	2019
Romania	1	1	1	2012
	2	2	1	2019
Slovakia	3	1	2.5	2012
	3	1	1	2019
Slovenia	1	1	1	2012
	1	1	1	2019
Spain (except autonomous regions, cities)	3	2	3	2012
	3	2	3	2019
Spain (autonomous regions, cities)	4/5	2	3	2012
	4/5	2	3	2019
Sweden	2	1	3	2012
	2	1	3	2019
UK (England)	1	1	5	2012
	1	2	3.5	2019
UK (devolved)	5	3	5	2012
	5	3	3.5	2019

Source: Own elaboration based on national constitutions, country-specific information and strategies, and information from the European Commission.

executive power – these countries tend to have a federal structure. Regions have their own constitutions in addition to the constitution of the nation state and high degrees of autonomy with respect to innovation policy. In these cases, national bodies generally shape the general framework conditions for research, technological development and innovation, and the regions design and implement tailored innovation policies that correspond to the territory-specific strengths, weaknesses, development goals and visions. Examples for this group of countries are Belgium, some parts of the United Kingdom and of Italy, as well as Germany.

The intermediate group is characterised by governance structures that combine national and regional competencies. Regions have certain legislative competencies and government bodies. Often, elected regional representatives and a representative of the central government are responsible for governing the region (examples are France and Poland; in the Netherlands, the King's Commissioner is part of the provincial government, while in Greece, a Secretary-General represents the national government on the sub-national level). This national–regional organisation may result in diverging competencies for innovation policy, as some examples show. For instance, while innovation policy is under the auspices of the national governments in Hungary and Slovakia, French regions are responsible for designing and implementing their strategies for economic development and innovation.

In addition, there are intermediate situations in some countries, such as where the regional level is laid down in the constitution, but innovation policy competence is not (fully) carried out on the regional level. Allocation of administrative tasks in Czechia, for example, follows the rationale of dualistic structure. Czech regions fulfil regional self-government tasks and tasks of state administration (if foreseen by law). Concerning innovation and smart specialisation, most of the 14 regions elaborated innovation strategies, and regional input was considered in the national Smart Specialisation Strategy. The regions do not have regional Smart Specialisation Strategies, but regional documents are annexed to the national strategy. Bulgaria's governance is dominantly centralised and follows the rationale of national specialisation and high concentration of ESIF. Bulgarian regions developed their regional innovation strategies in the previous programming period. Following the rationale of the national strategy, regions did not develop regional Smart Specialisation Strategies, but the national strategy takes into account the regional level. The constitutions of both Czechia and Bulgaria are comparatively recent and date from the beginning of the 1990s (with amendments in the 2000s). The regional policy of the European Union uses the system of territorial units on the sub-national scale – in this respect, both Czechia and Bulgaria have a more recent tradition of EU regional policy than "older" (and federally organised) Member States.

A further peculiarity of some European regions is their internal differentiation of governance structures as regards innovation policy making. Regions of these countries may be characterised by different degrees of autonomy based on our indicators. This is the case in Finland, France, Italy, Portugal, Spain and the United Kingdom, as shown in Table 4.2. We summarised the values assigned to the three indicators and derived five categories, which are described in the legend of the map of Figure 4.3. The result is a map displaying the heterogeneous pattern of governance

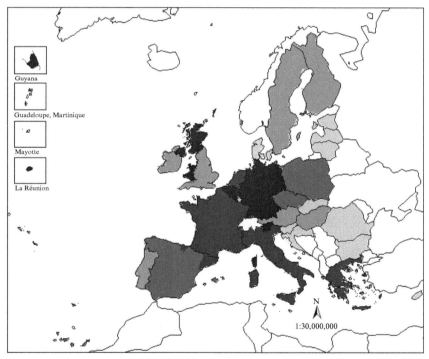

Legend: Regional autonomy of regional innovation policy in Europe 2019 (total index):

☐ low; values 3–5 ■ substantial; values 9.0001–11

■ limited; values 5.0001–7 ■ high; 11.0001+

■ medium; values 7.0001–9

Source: Own analysis and elaboration; © EuroGeographics for the administrative boundaries; map produced with Esri ArcMap 10.4.

Figure 4.3 Map of regional autonomy, 2019

structures and innovation policy competencies across Europe with an explicit recognition of the differences within single countries.

In addition to looking at the different groups of regions as regards the state of regional autonomy today, we aimed at an investigation of the transformation processes, discussing noticeable changes between 2012 and 2019 and detecting underlying development trends.

We expected to see only minor changes in the indicator "General regional autonomy", since it is strongly determined by the constitution of a country, within which amendments take place only sporadically. Comparing the values between 2012 and 2019, our expectation was confirmed. We could hardly find evidence for a noticeable change. The indicator is stable over time, since amendments to the constitution are rare for most of the European Member States and the framework conditions set by the constitution do not change a lot.

With respect to the other two indicators, "Regional competences with regard to innovation policy" and "Regional influence on structural fund allocations (ERDF)", we expected to see more transformations. This holds in particular for the third indicator. By looking at the empirical evidence, we are able to identify a number of countries, such as Austria, Czechia, Finland, Greece and Hungary, that reveal perceptible changes in the values of the variables, albeit in different directions. In some countries we identify a shift from the regional to the national level (e.g. Austria, Czechia, Finland) in the administrative handling of Structural Funding. Other countries (e.g. Greece) reveal opposed development trends. It can be assumed that these observable changes are triggered by the supra-national level, mainly due to adjustments in ex-ante conditionalities or administrative requirements. This is complemented by processes of policy learning coming from evaluations and benchmarking.

Illustrative examples for the transformation processes come from Austria and Greece. In the funding period 2007–2013 Austria had nine ERDF programmes and nine regional Managing Authorities, one for each Bundesland and one on the national level. The number of ERDF programmes and the number of Managing Authorities was reduced to one respectively for the funding period 2014–2020. The reduction of the number of ERDF programmes took place in the framework of the Austrian ERDF Reform Agenda. This reduction was driven by efficiency aspects, namely the decrease of overhead costs.[14] Austria is thus an example of a country with efficiency-based centralisation of its administration. Quite contrary are the developments in Greece. Here the number of Operational Programmes in the ERDF allocation increased and a larger share of decision making and management competences was delegated to the regions in order to make optimal use of ESIF for the period 2014–2020.[15] In order to support national and regional Managing Authorities, the "Technical Assistance" axis included support for national and regional units by reinforcing systems and processes of management and coordination or upgrading the managerial and delivery capacity of the beneficiaries. Thus, the rationale behind the changes between the two programming periods can be found in the optimisation of administrative and management processes.

The indicator "Regional competences with regard to innovation policy" reveals only minor changes when we compare the values for the years 2012 and 2019. These changes apply to the three countries of Romania, the UK and Greece and point in the same direction, indicating a tendency towards greater regional autonomy. These changes can be attributed to processes of transformation in a political power dimension and a management dimension, since the regions in these countries nowadays develop their own innovation strategies. In consequence, regional innovation policy making gained more independence from the national level. These developments can by and large be traced back to policy changes on the supra-national level and the implementation of the smart specialisation concept.

These findings show that processes of transformation were mainly triggered by policies and administrative requirements on the supra-national level and incorporate a shift in the hierarchical power relationships between the nation state and its regions, and management consequences on the operational level, as well as a resource dimension by proactively leveraging efficiency potentials.

Except for the indicator "General regional autonomy", the regional level tends to have gained in importance in our measurement approach. As regards the latter two indicators, "Regional competences with regard to innovation policy" and "Regional influence on structural fund allocations (ERDF)", changes in the regional autonomy in the field of innovation policy making are increasingly triggered by framework conditions that are set by the EU.

This does not come as a surprise, since the indicator "Regional influence on structural funds allocations (ERDF)" explicitly relates to and targets EU policy making. However, concerning the indicator "Regional competences with regard to innovation policy", it seems noteworthy that the regional level increased in importance in regional innovation policy making.

5. CONCLUSIONS

The objective of this chapter was to contribute to the understanding of the interrelatedness of regional autonomy and regional innovation policy making in a theoretical and empirical way. Firstly, we framed regional autonomy by distinguishing between self-rule and shared rule and incorporating the idea into the revised innovation systems framework, which served a major theoretical reference scheme. In addition, we applied a dynamic approach in order to understand underlying transformation processes concerning the state of regional autonomy. Secondly, we aimed to understand regional autonomy in an empirical respect by proposing a set of indicators and variables suitable for measuring the degree of regional autonomy in the European Member States, with reference to the role of EU funding and national constitutional settings. The operationalisation refers to three central aspects for an empirical description of regional autonomy, which are relevant for regional innovation policy: general regional autonomy as foreseen by the constitution, autonomy understood as room for manoeuvre with regard to regional innovation policy making and regional influence on the allocation of European structural funding.

The results showed that the degree of regional autonomy differs across the European Member States and in some cases even between the regions within one country. Regional decision-making power and the degrees of freedom for designing and implementing regional innovation policy is, however, a dynamic process that develops against different backgrounds and in different directions. The advancements in the degree of regional autonomy, observed between 2012 and 2019, are based on comparatively recent developments, which are mainly triggered by regional cohesion and economic development policy in the EU. Even in those cases where the degree of regional autonomy is large, exclusive regional self-rule remains an exception. This shows that innovation policy at the regional level underlies various influences from the national or the supra-national level. This is congruent with the conceptual approach of regional innovation systems, which are understood to be embedded in superior contexts and frameworks.

The topic of regional autonomy, and in particular a dynamic approach to regional autonomy in connection with regional innovation policy making, raises new questions and provides ample scope for future research either in the form of quantitative analyses (e.g. in order to relate the performance of a region as regards innovation capabilities to the varying degrees of regional autonomy) or as qualitative analyses in the form of case studies (e.g. in order to get deeper insights into the complexity of the relationship of the different actors). In particular, a better understanding of shifts in innovation policy making and its consequences might contribute to policy learning and might lead to a more efficient and target-oriented policy design. In addition, enriching the current indicator set – for instance through including details concerning the origins of regional innovation policy budgets in the form of quantitative indicators – could enhance options for interpreting regional innovation policy governance and rationales.

Summarising, we conclude that different models are pursued in the different Member States concerning the state of regional autonomy. It would be interesting to see how regional innovation policy making further evolves, especially in countries with similar characteristics such as size or administrative structure. In addition, and acknowledging that our approach is based on desk research and document analysis, adding expert knowledge from individual countries could contribute to a more refined analysis. This could be particularly interesting in countries where development trends between 2012 and 2019 became apparent, for example in Austria and Greece. Overall, broadening the approach presented here could contribute to enhancing the knowledge base with respect to the topic of regional autonomy and innovation policy, on the conceptual and the policy-oriented dimensions alike.

ACKNOWLEDGEMENTS

We would like to thank the members of the EURIPER project whose comments have helped us to make this contribution more pertinent. In addition, we wish to thank Professor Dr. Knut Koschatzky for valuable comments on a previous version of this chapter, which helped us to express our thoughts in a more concise manner.

NOTES

1. In our understanding, regional innovation policy supports innovation in a region through a specific set of measures and instruments tailored to regional needs. It is shaped by regional actors who have the legitimacy, budgetary means and certain degrees of freedom to design and implement innovation-supporting policy by adjusting bottom-up and top-down impulses for the promotion of innovation.
2. Cf. https://ec.europa.eu/regional_policy/sources/docgener/informat/2014/eac_guidance_esif_part2_en.pdf. All webpages supplied in these notes were accessed in May or June 2019.
3. For further information, see, for example, https://ec.europa.eu/regional_policy/sources/docgener/informat/2014/community_en.pdf.
4. See https://ec.europa.eu/regional_policy/en/funding/available-budget/. The total budget

for European Structural and Investment Funds (ESIF) for the 2014–2020 period amounts to €644.97bn, from which the Cohesion Fund accounts for 11.6% and ERDF for 43.3%. From this total budget, "Competitiveness of SMEs" (Small and Medium-sized Enterprises) and "Research & Innovation" rank among the first five positions in terms of total budget. The range of the ESIF regional policy budget – including Cohesion and European Regional Development funds – is from €63.4bn (Poland) to €19.5m (Luxembourg). Cf. https://cohesiondata.ec.europa.eu/overview and https://cohe siondata.ec.europa.eu/dataset/ESIF-Regional-Policy-budget-by-country-2014-2020/fi ft-a67j.

5. Between 2014 and 2016, European structural investments funds are expected to account for approximately 14% of total public investment on average, and even to reach up to 70% in some Member States. Cf. https://ec.europa.eu/regional_policy/en/policy/what/investment-policy/esif-contribution/.

6. Cf. also https://ec.europa.eu/regional_policy/sources/docgener/informat/2014/smart_spec ialisation_en.pdf.

7. While the current Horizon 2020 framework programme for research covered seven main Societal Challenges (1. Health, demographic change and wellbeing; 2. Food security, sustainable agriculture and forestry, marine and maritime and inland water research and the bioeconomy; 3. Secure, clean and efficient energy; 4. Smart, green and integrated transport; 5. Climate action, environment, resource efficiency and raw materials; 6. Europe in a changing world – inclusive, innovative and reflective societies; and 7. Secure societies – protecting freedom and security of Europe and its citizens), the upcoming Horizon Europe programme targets five main Global Challenges (1. Health; 2. Inclusive and secure society; 3. Digital and industry; 4. Climate, energy and mobility; and 5. Food and natural resources), cf. https://ec.europa.eu/programmes/horizon2020/ en/h2020-section/societal-challenges and https://www.researchconnect.eu/funding-views/ horizon-europe/.

8. Cf. https://ec.europa.eu/regional_policy/en/policy/how/stages-step-by-step/.

9. Cf. https://ec.europa.eu/regional_policy/en/policy/how/stages-step-by-step/ and European Commission, Directorate-General for Regional and Urban Policy (2015).

10. The information for this variable was compiled from the European Commission regional policy web page. Cf. https://ec.europa.eu/regional_policy/en/atlas/managing-authorities /?search=1&keywords=&periodId=3&countryCode=AT&typeId=INT.

11. Here we deviate from the scale we used in Baier et al. (2013).

12. The information for this variable was compiled from the European Commission regional policy web page. Cf. https://ec.europa.eu/regional_policy/en/atlas/programmes/.

13. That is, referring to a governance level between the national state and the local level – local self-government for matters at this territorial level is usually laid down in the constitutions.

14. Cf. http://europa.eu/rapid/press-release_IP-14-1174_en.htm.

15. Cf. https://ec.europa.eu/info/sites/info/files/partnership-agreement-greece-summary-may 2014_en.pdf.

REFERENCES

Agrawal, A. (1999). Accountability in decentralization: A framework with South Asian and West African cases, *The Journal of Developing Areas*, 33(4), 473–502.

Asheim, B.T., and Coenen, L. (2005). Knowledge bases and regional innovation systems: Comparing Nordic clusters, *Research Policy*, 34(8), 1173–90.

Asheim, B.T., and Isaksen, A. (2002). Regional innovation systems: The integration of local "sticky" and global "ubiquitous" knowledge, *The Journal of Technology Transfer*, 27(1), 77–86.

Baier, E., Kroll, H., and Zenker, A. (2013). *Regional autonomy with regard to innovation policy: A differentiated illustration of the European status quo*, Working Papers Firms and Region Nr. R3/2013, Karlsruhe.

Balland, P.A., Boschma, R., and Frenken, K. (2014). Proximity and innovation: From statics to dynamics, *Regional Studies*, 49(6), 1–14.

Barca, F. (2009). *An agenda for a reformed cohesion policy: A place-based approach to meeting European Union challenges and expectations*. Independent report prepared at the request of Danuta Hübner, Commissioner for Regional Policy, accessed 12 June 2019, at ec.europa.eu/regional_policy/archive/policy/future/pdf/report_barca_v0306.pdf.

Bergek, A., Jacobsson, S., Carlsson, B., Lindmark, S., and Rickne, A. (2008). Analyzing the functional dynamics of technological innovation systems: A scheme of analysis, *Research Policy*, 37(3), 407–29.

Boschma, R. (2005). Proximity and innovation: A critical assessment, *Research Policy*, 39(1), 61–74.

Braczyk, H.J., Cooke, P., and Heidenreich, M. (eds) (1998). *Regional Innovation Systems: The Role of Governances in a Globalized World*, London: UCL Press.

Bresser-Pereira, L.C. (2004). *Democracy and Public Management Reform: Building the Republican State*, Oxford: Oxford University Press.

Charron, N., Dijkstra, L., and Lapuente, V. (2014). Regional governance matters: Quality of government within European Union member states, *Regional Studies*, 17(4), 68–90.

Christman, J. (2003). Autonomy in moral and political philosophy, *Stanford Encyclopedia of Philosophy*, accessed 18 November 2019, at https://plato.stanford.edu/entries/autonomy-moral/.

Cooke, P. (1992). Regional innovation systems: Competitive regulation in the New Europe, *Geoforum*, 23(3), 365–82.

Cooke, P., Gomez Uranga, M., and Etxebarria, G. (1997). Regional innovation systems: Institutional and organisational dimensions, *Research Policy*, 26, 475–91.

Crespy, C., Héraud, J.A., and Perry, B. (2007). Multi-level governance, regions and science in France: Between competition and equality, *Regional Studies*, 41(8), 1069–84.

Dahl, R. (1982). *Dilemmas of Pluralist Democracy*, New Haven, CT: Yale University Press.

Edquist, C. (2000). Systems of innovation approaches: Their emergence and characteristics, in C. Edquist and M.D. McKelvey (eds), *Systems of Innovation: Growth, Competitiveness and Employment*, Cheltenham, UK and Northampton, MA, USA: Edward Elgar Publishing, pp. 3–37.

Elazar, D.J. (1991). *Federal Systems of the World: A Handbook of Federal, Confederal and Autonomy Arrangements*, Harlow, UK: Longman Group.

European Commission (2014). *Guidance on ex ante conditionalities for the European Structural and Investment Funds: Part II*, accessed 14 June 2019, at ec.europa.eu/regional_policy/sources/docgener/informat/2014/eac_guidance_esif_part2_en.pdf.

European Commission, Directorate-General for Regional and Urban Policy (2015). *European Structural and Investment Funds 2014–2020: Official texts and commentaries*, accessed 27 May 2019, at https://ec.europa.eu/regional_policy/sources/docgener/guides/blue_book/blueguide_en.pdf.

Ezcurra, R., and Rodríguez-Pose, A. (2013). Political decentralization, economic growth and regional disparities in the OECD, *Regional Studies*, 47(3), 388–401.

Ferguson, I., and Chandrasekharan, C. (2005). Paths and pitfalls of decentralisation for sustainable forest management: Experiences of the Asia-Pacific region, in C.J. Pierce Colfer and D. Capistrano (eds), *The Politics of Decentralisation: Forests, Power and People*, London: Earthscan, pp. 63–85.

Foray, D., Morgan, K., and Radosevic, S. (2018). *The role of smart specialization in the EU research and innovation policy landscape*, accessed 14 June 2019, at ec.europa.eu/regional_policy/sources/docgener/brochure/smart/role_smartspeciali sation_ri.pdf.

Freeman, C. (2000). The National System of Innovation in historical perspective, in C. Edquist and M.D. McKelvey (eds), *Systems of Innovation: Growth, Competitiveness and Employment*, Cheltenham, UK and Northampton, MA, USA: Edward Elgar Publishing, pp. 41–60.

Fritsch, M., and Stephan, A. (2005). Regionalization of innovation policy: Introduction to the special issue, *Research Policy*, 34(8), 1123–27.

Herrero-Alcalde, A., and Tránchez-Martín J.M. (2017). Demographic, political, institutional and financial determinants of regional social expenditure: The case of Spain, *Regional Studies*, 51(6), 920–32.

Koschatzky, K. (2000). *The regionalisation of innovation policy in Germany: Theoretical foundations and recent experience*, Working Papers Firms and Region Nr. R1/2000, Karlsruhe.

Koschatzky, K., and Stahlecker, T. (2010). *Cohesion policy in the light of place-based innovation support: New approaches in multi-actors, decentralised regional settings with bottom-up strategies?*, accessed 12 June 2019, at www.isi.fraunhofer.de/content/dam/isi/dokumente/ccp/unternehmen-region/2010/ap_r1_2010.pdf.

Kuhlmann, S., and Arnold, E. (2001). *RCN in the Norwegian Research and Innovation System*, Background report no. 12 in the evaluation of the Research Council of Norway, Karlsruhe, Brighton, accessed 14 June 2019, at ris.utwente.nl/ws/files/15070352/RCN_in_the_Norwegian_Research_and_Innovation_Syste_1_.pdf.

Kyriacou, A.P., Muinelo-Gallo, L., and Roca-Sagalés, O. (2015). Fiscal decentralisation and regional disparities: The importance of good governance, *Papers in Regional Science*, 9(1), 89–108.

Loughlin, J. (2007). Reconfiguring the state: Trends in territorial governance in European states, *Regional and Federal Studies*, 17(4), 385–403.

Lundvall, B.Å. (1992). Introduction, in B.Å. Lundvall (ed.), *National Systems of Innovation: Towards a Theory of Innovation and Interactive Learning*, London: Pinter Publishers, pp. 1–19.

Lundvall, B.Å., Johnson, B., Andersen, E.S., and Dalum, B. (2002). National systems of production, innovation and competence building, *Research Policy*, 31(2), 213–31.

Malerba, F. (2002). Sectoral systems of innovation and production, *Research Policy*, 31, 247–64.

Markard, J., and Truffer, B. (2008). Technological innovation systems and the multi-level perspective: Towards an integrated framework, *Research Policy*, 37(4), 596–615.

Marks, G., Hooghe, L., and Schakel, A. (2008). Measuring regional authority, *Regional and Federal Studies*, 18, 111–21.

Morgan, K. (2004). The exaggerated death of geography: Learning, proximity and territorial innovation systems, *Journal of Economic Geography*, 4(1), 3–21.

Oates, W.E. (2011). *Fiscal Federalism.* Cheltenham, UK and Northampton, MA, USA: Edward Elgar Publishing.

OECD (2009). *Investing for growth: Building innovative regions. Conclusions of the meeting of the Territorial Development Policy Committee (TDPC) at ministerial level, 31 March 2009*, accessed 14 June 2019, at www.oecd.org/cfe/regional-policy/TDPC%202009%20Ministerial%20Conclusions.pdf.

Perry, B., and May, T. (2007). Governance, science policy and regions: An introduction, *Regional Studies*, 41(8), 1039–50.

Polanyi, M. (1997). The tacit dimension, in L. Prusak (ed.), *Knowledge in Organizations: Resources for the Knowledge-based Economy*, Boston, Oxford and Johannesburg: Butterworth-Heinemann, pp. 135–46.

Prange, H. (2008). Explaining varieties of regional innovation policies in Europe, *European Urban and Regional Studies*, 15(1), 39–52.

Putnam, R.D. (1995). Bowling Alone: America's Declining Social Capital, *Journal of Democracy*, 6(1), 65–78.

Reger, G. (1998). Changes in the R&D strategies of transnational firms: Challenges for national technology and innovation policy, *STI Review*, 22, 243–76.

Rodríguez-Pose, A., and Bwire, A. (2003). The economic (in)efficiency of devolution, *Environment and Planning A: Economy and Space*, 36(11), 1907–28.

Scott, A.J. (1998). From Silicon Valley to Hollywood, in H.-J. Braczyk, P. Cooke and M. Heidenreich (eds), *Regional Innovation Systems: The Role of Governances in a Globalized World*, London: UCL Press, pp. 136–62.

Suksi, M. (2012). Sub-state governance through territorial autonomy: On the relationship between autonomy and federalism, in A.G. Gagnon and M. Keating (eds), *Political Autonomy and Divided Societies: Imagining Democratic Alternatives in Complex Settings*, Basingstoke: Palgrave Macmillan, pp. 60–79.

Tödtling, F., and Trippl, M. (2005). One size fits all: Towards a differentiated regional innovation policy approach, *Research Policy*, 34(8), 1203–19.

Uyarra, E. (2007). Key dilemmas of regional innovation policies, *Innovation*, 20(3), 243–61.

Uyarra, E., and Flanagan, K. (2010). Understanding the innovation impacts of public procurement, *European Planning Studies*, 18(1), 123–43.

Uyarra, E., and Flanagan, K. (2017). Understanding regional innovation policy dynamics: Actors, agency and learning, *Politics and Space*, 35(4), 559–68.

Warnke, P., Koschatzky, K., Dönitz, E., Zenker, A., Stahlecker, T., Som, O., Cuhls, K., and. Güth, S. (2016). *Opening up the innovation system framework towards new actors and institutions*, Karlsruhe, accessed 14 June 2019, at www.isi.fraunhofer.de/content/dam/isi/dokumente/ccp/innovation-systems-policy-analysis/2016/discussionpaper_49_2016.pdf.

Yoder, J.A. (2007). Leading the way to regionalization in post-communist Europe: An examination of the process and outcomes of regional reform in Poland, *East European Politics and Societies*, 21(3), 424–46.

5. EU regional development policy, from regional convergence to development through innovation

Cristina Ares

1. INTRODUCTION

The European Regional Development Policy (ERDP) is the part of the European Community (EC) / European Union (EU) Cohesion Policy that is focused on regional development. Frequently, the EU Cohesion Policy altogether is also called European Regional Policy.

The European regional economic system is "a result of varying national economies reflecting different institutional and historical economic processes, which have been subsequently overlaid with the processes of European integration" (McCann, 2015, p. 44). The reason for launching an EC ERDP was the willingness to compensate the less favoured regions for the costs of adaptation to the single market. To do this, a growing percentage of the scarce common budget was devoted to investing in reducing interregional disparities. Thus, from the very beginning of the integration process in the late 1950s, in contrast to most EC policies, the objectives of the ERDP were not only regulative or indeed distributive but also redistributive (Lowi, 1972).

However, the EU Cohesion Policy changed with the beginning of the new century. It did so especially at two key history-making moments, which were 1999, in preparation for the accession of ten new Member States mainly in Central and Eastern Europe from 2004 onwards, and 2013, when key adjustments for the period 2014–2020 were approved.

On both occasions, policy innovations were introduced aiming to invest EU funding better. Indeed, in 2013, ex ante conditions to receive funds and an enhanced focus on delivering results were put at the forefront. Moreover, variations in the underlying logic of the ERDP are related to the progressive substitution of the idea of helping the less favoured regions to converge, for the rationale of enhancing the competitiveness of the EU as a whole by means of regional development through innovation. In this sense, smart specialization strategies have become key instruments.

This chapter offers an overview of the evolution of the ERDP, and the state of the art by 2020.

2. APPEARANCE, CONSOLIDATION AND CHANGE OF THE ERDP

2.1 Appearance

As has already been pointed out, in the beginning, EC aids to the less developed regions were viewed as a necessary policy measure to make the single market succeed. In fact, the appearance of the ERDP is linked to a report authored by the Italian economist Tommaso Padoa-Schioppa (1987) that showed the risks posed by the single market, which is defined by the freedom of movement of goods, people, services and capital, to those territories and social groups with fewer resources.

Regional development understood as regional convergence has been a political objective of the EC/EU in the letter of the treaties from the outset of the integration process after the Second World War. In the preamble of the Treaty establishing the European Economic Community (EEC), signed in Rome on 25 March 1957 (entrance into force: 1 January 1958), the six founding Member States declared themselves to be "anxious to strengthen the unity of their economies and to ensure their harmonious development by reducing the differences existing between the various regions and the backwardness of the less favoured regions" (page 2, paragraph five).

In 1968, the Directorate-General for Regional Development (REGIO), that is, the department of the EC in charge of this policy, was created. The European Regional Development Fund (ERDF), which is its main instrument, was established in 1975, after the entrance into the EC of the United Kingdom along with Ireland and Denmark. Additionally, the Committee on Regional Development (REGI) of the European Parliament (EP) was set up in 1975 as well, four years before the first direct election to this chamber.

2.2 Consolidation of the ERDP

The adhesion of Greece (1981), Portugal and Spain (1986) brought qualitative and quantitative modifications to the policy-making of the ERDP. First, this policy was integrated into a broader one, the EC/EU Cohesion Policy, whose purpose is more extensively economic, social and territorial cohesion. Moreover, ever since its inception in the 1980s, Cohesion Policy had started to compete with the Common Agricultural Policy (CAP) for the EC/EU budget. Previously, agricultural expenses had consumed 80% of EC public resources.

Furthermore, in 1988, the European Council achieved an agreement for introducing changes in the EC budgetary processes. It set a multiannual frame, called financial perspectives, on the first occasion for five years and from 1993 onwards for periods of seven years. This mid-run scheme was introduced in order to ease planning and avoid permanent national quarrels over funding and policy priorities. It's worth noting that, because of this budgetary innovation, the main policy decisions, especially regarding policies that receive more funds from the EC/EU budget, such as cohesion, started to be bargained more in line with the long-term EC/EU strategic planning documents, such as the Lisbon Strategy or Europe 2020.

The first reform of the EEC Treaty, which was introduced by the Single European Act (SEA) (signature: 17 February 1986; entrance into force: 1 July 1987), added an entire chapter on economic and social cohesion. Later on, the Treaty of Maastricht (signature: 7 February 1992; entrance into force: 1 November 1993) incorporated a new financial instrument, the Cohesion Fund (CF), for delivering EC investments to entire states.

One of the key moments of the EU Cohesion Policy was the bargaining over the multiannual financial framework (MFF) for the period 2000–2006, in preparation for the adhesion of ten new Member States. Meeting in Berlin in 1999, the European Council reformed the financial instruments of Cohesion Policy to extend them to the candidate countries without increasing the budgetary level. The decision taken was trying to enhance the efficiency of EU cohesion funding.

It's also important to note that, from the entrance into force of the Treaty of Lisbon (1 December 2009), the EU MFF has taken the form of a regulation (formerly, it was just an institutional agreement), and this has to be approved under a special legislative procedure that requires the majority of all members of the EP (including those absent or not voting) and the unanimity of the states in the Council of the EU. Although the extension of the ordinary legislative procedure to this decision has been consciously avoided so far, the shift of the MFF from an institutional agreement to an EU law implies a noticeable empowering of the EP. Additionally, the Lisbon Treaty enhanced the EP on regional development also because it moved the approval of the general regulation of the EU Cohesion Policy's financial instruments, the European Structural and Investment Funds (ESIF), from the assent procedure to the ordinary legislative procedure. Moreover, it was this last EU Treaty's reform that formally recognized the concept of "territorial" cohesion. This also strengthened positive action in favour of the outermost regions.

Lastly, even though Cohesion Policy was originally the only openly EU redistributive policy, at least before the empowerment of the EP by the Lisbon Treaty, the predominance of an intergovernmental bargaining logic undermined the capacity of influence of the European Commission in shaping its priorities along with its redistributive objectives.

In concrete, from the reforms of cohesion policy in 1993 to the last ones of 2013 there was a consolidation of national governments' control of structural fund expenditure to the detriment of the Commission's policy preferences (Bache, 1998; Allen, 2010). The prospect of enlargements (1995, 2004/2009) was obviously one of the major driving forces. From 2013, this could be changing to a certain extent because of the EP's new powers and the enhanced competition for funding between policy areas.

2.3 The Shifting Rationale of the ERDP

At least rhetorically, the rationale of the ERDP has suffered a noticeable evolution over time since the 1999 Berlin European Council, as can be seen in Table 5.1. This has followed two lines: investing EU funding better and putting the focus on the competitiveness of the EU as a whole instead of on regional development convergence across Europe by means of strengthening the economies of the less developed regions.

In summary, the compensation logic started to be, at least rhetorically, replaced by a new logic based on competitiveness and growth. This is

Table 5.1   The shifting rationale of the ERDP

Periods	Rationale
1958–1987, 1988–1992 and 1993–1999	Regional and national compensation, solidarity
	Development of the less favoured regions, regional convergence
2000–2006	Effectiveness
	Growth, jobs and innovation in line with the EU's priorities set out in the "Lisbon Strategy"
2007–2013	EU investments profitability, results
	Growth, jobs and innovation in line with the EU's priorities set out in the "Lisbon Strategy"
2014–2020	EU investments profitability, results
	Goals of the Europe 2020 Strategy: smart, sustainable and inclusive growth
	Innovation-driven regional development

Source: Own elaboration.

focused on concentrating the limited capacity of the EU to invest in those regions that can demonstrate that they have enough aptitude to get profit from its funds.

The Great Recession consolidated this reorientation by opening a debate on the percentage of structural funding that should be invested outside the less favoured regions. Notwithstanding this, in practice, also in the period 2014–2020, most of the EU budget for cohesion continues to go to the less developed regions, as will be detailed later on.

The programming period 2014–2020 introduced quite a lot of policy novelties to promote effective delivery in line with the EU's Budget Focused on Results (BFOR) initiative. The rationale behind the requirements to qualify for receiving EU money, the follow-up criteria and the requests for evaluating all programmes' results strengthened in 2013 was executing European Structural and Investment funding effectively. Besides, the purpose was much more ambitious. It included fostering the implementation of key EU legislation and supporting wider EU policy objectives, such as action on climate change. Moreover, conditionality was used to force the fulfilment of national recommendations and to activate country-specific policy reforms (European Commission, 2017e, p. 12).

3.   THE POLITICS OF CHANGE IN THE ERDP: OBJECTIVES, BUDGET, FUNDS AND CATEGORIES OF REGIONS

3.1   Structural Objectives

At its inception, the EC/EU Cohesion Policy had a complex scheme of differentiated objectives explained by the intergovernmental logic of bargaining on the allocation of the structural common budget. Nevertheless, the objectives of the funds were simplified for the periods 2007–2013 and, more deeply, 2014–2020. From 2007 onwards, community initiatives disappeared as a differentiated policy instrument, and EU funding started to be more strictly linked to the general strategic documents, the Lisbon Agenda and Europe 2020, and the MFFs of each of the programming periods.

Table 5.2 covers the evolution of regional structural fund objectives and initiatives. Then, it excludes the cohesion objective for states with a gross domestic product (GDP) of less than 90% of the EU average, whose specific financial instrument is the CF from 1993.

Table 5.3 expands the information on community initiatives.

Table 5.2   Structural fund regional objectives and initiatives*

Financial perspective	Objectives	Initiatives
1988–1992	Objective 1: regions where the GDP per capita is less than 75% of the EU average (ERDF, ESF, EAGGF-Guidance) Objective 2: regions affected by industrial decline, where the unemployment level is above the EU average (ERDF, ESF) Objective 3: combats long-term unemployment (ESF) Objective 4: facilitates adaptation of workers to industrial change (ESF) Objective 5a: assists agriculture and forestry (EAGGF-Guidance) Objective 5b: assists the development of rural areas, mainly via diversification (ERDF, ESF, and EAGGF)	ADAPT; EMPLOYMENT; INTERREG; KONVER; LEADER; PESCA; RECHAR; REGIS; RESIDER; RETEX; SME; URBAN (ERDF, ESF, EAGGF-Guidance)
1993–1999	Objective 1: regions where the GDP per capita is less than 75% of the EU average (ERDF, ESF, EAGGF-Guidance) Objective 2: regions affected by industrial decline, where the unemployment level is above the EU average (ERDF, ESF) Objective 3 combined with Objective 4: to facilitate the integration of young people Objective 5a (EAGGF-Guidance) and 5b (ERDF, ESF and EAGGF) Objective 6 for sparsely populated Nordic areas (ERDF, ESF and EAGGF-Guidance), introduced after the 1995 enlargement	ADAPT; EMPLOYMENT; INTERREG; KONVER; LEADER; PESCA; RECHAR; REGIS; RESIDER; RETEX; SME; URBAN (ERDF, ESF, EAGGF-Guidance)
2000–2006	Objective 1: as before, but with stricter application of eligibility criteria + previously eligible for Objective 6 + phasing out for those regions eligible before 2000 for Objective 1 Objective 2: regions facing major change in the industrial services and fisheries sectors, rural areas in serious decline, and disadvantaged urban areas (ERDF, ESF and EAGGF-Guidance) Objective 3: regions not covered by other objectives with a focus on modernizing education, training and employment	EQUAL; INTERREG; LEADER (ERDF, ESF, EAGGF-Guidance)

97

Table 5.2 (continued)

Financial perspective	Objectives	Initiatives
2007–2013	Convergence: to support growth and job creation in states using the cohesion criteria, and regions using the Objective 1 criteria + phasing out for those states and regions that would have remained eligible if the cohesion threshold had been set at 90% of the EU15 average GDP per capita and the regional threshold at 75% of the EU15 average GDP per capita and not that of the EU25 (CF, ERDF and ESF), 81.5%** Competitiveness and employment: all regions not covered by the Convergence Objective + phasing out for those regions that qualified for Objective 1 in the former period but whose GDP per capita now exceeds 75% of the EU15 average GDP per capita (ERDF and ESF), 15.9%** European territorial cooperation (formerly INTERREG) for cross-border cooperation for NUTS3 regions that have maritime, national or EU borders, for transnational cooperation for 13 Commission-identified EU regional cooperation zones between NUTS3 regions, and for interregional cooperation and the establishment of networks and the exchange of experience (ERDF), 2.5%**	—
2014–2020	Investment in Growth and Jobs (CF, ERDF and ESF), 96.33%** (313.2 billion euro) European territorial cooperation (ERDF), 2.75%** (11.7 billion euros)	—

Notes:

*   Associated financial instruments in brackets. Acronyms: CF, Cohesion Fund; EAGGF, European Agricultural Guidance and Guarantee Fund; ESF, European Social Fund; ERDF, European Regional Development Fund.

** Budget as percentage of structural funds in the period.

Source: Own elaboration adapted from Allen (2010, p.234).

Table 5.3   Community initiatives, 1988–2006

Initiative	Financial perspective	Purpose
ADAPT	1988–1999	Adaptation of the workforce to industrial change
EMPLOYMENT	1988–1999	Integration into working life of women, young people and the disadvantaged
EQUAL	2000–2006	Transnational cooperation to combat all forms of discrimination in the labour market
INTERREG	1988–2006	Cross-border, transnational and interregional cooperation*
KONVER	1988–1999	Adaptation to industrial change in defence-industry dependent regions
LEADER	1988–2006	Rural development
PESCA	1988–1999	Restructuring the fisheries sector
RECHAR	1988–1999	Adaptation to industrial change in coal-dependent areas
REGIS	1988–1999	Support for the most remote regions
RESIDER	1988–1999	Adaptation to industrial change in steel-dependent regions
RETEX	1988–1999	Adaptation to industrial change in textile-dependent regions
SME	1988–1999	Small and medium-size enterprises in disadvantaged areas
URBAN	1988–1999	Urban policy

Note: *   From 2007 onwards, cross-border, transnational and interregional cooperation are covered under the objective "European territorial cooperation".

Source: Own elaboration adapted from Allen (2010, p. 240).

3.2   Cohesion Policy Funding

The increasing importance of the EC/EU Cohesion Policy from the mid-1980s is reflected in the figures of structural fund expenditures as percentage of the common budget. These are shown in Table 5.4, along with the numbers of absolute structural EC/EU expenses.

Table 5.5 shows the distribution of EU cohesion resources between funds in 2014–2020.

3.3   The European Structural and Investment Fund (ESIF) in 2014–2020

In the programming period 2014–2020, the expression European Structural and Investment Fund (ESIF) is used in reference to five tools: the European

Table 5.4   Structural funding

Periods	EU structural funding	As percentage of the EC/EU budget
1988–1992	ECU 64 billion	17.2
1993–1999	ECU 168 billion (more than double the former period)	32.2
2000–2006	213 billion euros for the EU15 and 22 billion euros for the new members during 2004–2006	34.8
2007–2013	347 billion euros	36.7
2014–2020	371 billion euros (454 for all ESIFs, including the European Agricultural Fund for Rural Development (EAFRD) and the European Maritime and Fisheries Fund (EMFF)	34

Source: Own elaboration based on institutional documents, and Allen (2010, p. 233).

Table 5.5   Allocation of resources between ESI Funds (2014–2020)

Fund*	Billion euros	Percentage
ERDF	199	43.2
ESF	84	18.2
EAFRD	99.3	21.6
EMFF	5.8	1.2
YEI	8.9	1.9
CF	63.3	13.7

Note: *   Acronyms: ERDF, European Regional Development Fund; ESF, European Social Fund; EAFRD, European Agricultural Fund for Rural Development; EMFF, European Maritime and Fisheries Fund; YEI, Youth Employment Initiative; CF, Cohesion Fund.

Source: Institutional documents.

Regional Development Fund (ERDF), the European Social Fund (ESF), the Cohesion Fund (CF), the European Agricultural Fund for Rural Development (EAFRD) and the European Maritime and Fisheries Fund (EMFF).

Among these tools, the ERDF, which appeared in 1975, is the one focused on regional balanced development. As shown in Table 5.6, in the current MFF, there are three main categories of regions: less developed regions (those with a GDP per capita below 75% of the average GDP), transition regions (between 75% and 90%) and more developed regions

Table 5.6   Distribution of structural budget between categories of regions, 2014–2020

Category	Billion euros	Percentage	Budget
Less developed regions GDP per capita less than 75% of the average GDP of the EU27*	164	52.45	162.6 billion
Transition regions GDP is between 75% and 90% of the average GDP	32	10.24	39 billion
More developed regions whose GDP per capita is above 90% of the average GDP	49	15.67	53.1 billion
Outermost and sparsely populated northern regions (extra allocation)	1.4	0.44	0.9 billion
States (Cohesion Fund)	66.4	21.19	68.7 billion

Note: *   Calculated from EU figures for the period 2007–2009.

Source: 2013 Regulation of the ESIF and other institutional documents.

(above 90%). Furthermore, there are other types of regions that receive a special treatment under the framework of Cohesion Policy and indeed other EU policies too. These are the northern sparsely populated regions (Art. 2 of Protocol 6 to the 1994 Act of Accession), the outermost regions and the border regions.

The nine outermost regions, which are Guadeloupe, French Guiana, Martinique, Mayotte, Reunion Island and Saint-Martin (France), Canary Islands (Spain), and the Azores and Madeira (Portugal), have been considered special in the treaties since 1999 and particularly from the entrance into force of the Treaty of Lisbon (December 2009), which recognized their right to be beneficiaries of special measures not only within the framework of the EU Cohesion Policy but also regarding agriculture or competition (Art. 349 TFEU [Treaty on the Functioning of the European Union]).

The special status of outermost regions is based on their remoteness, insularity and distinctive vulnerability, for instance in terms of climate change. These characteristic features could be posing extra barriers to their development. In its 2017 Communication titled "A stronger and renewed strategic partnership with the EU's outermost regions", the EC presented a new approach to augment the effectivity of EU funding in these regions by appointing new paths towards growth and job creation. The solution proposed is a reinforced partnership between the EU, national and regional actors to improve their coordination. The motto is a "new governance based on a strong partnership" (European Commission, 2017c, p. 2). What's more, Annex I of this Communication contains a broad list of actions to foster the development of the outermost regions, including a budgetary provision of 4 million euros in the Horizon 2020 programme for the period 2018–2020. This intends to expand the regions' capacities to take part in the EU Research and Innovation Policy.

Regarding border regions, it is worth saying that for decades INTERREG programmes have made a noticeable contribution to bringing authorities and citizens in general closer together across the EU. Indeed, their execution continues to advance on the ground. This represents, for instance, 2,800 firms more involved in cooperation on research and innovation across borders (European Commission, 2017e, p. 14).

As a final point, the European Commission published also in 2017 a Communication on boosting growth and cohesion in EU border regions that suggests several concrete proposals to enhance the economic, social and territorial potential of these spaces (European Commission, 2017b).

4. GOVERNING EC/EU STRUCTURAL FUNDING: POLICY PRINCIPLES AND REGIONAL CAPACITY

4.1 Policy Principles

From its early days, the EC/EU Cohesion Policy has been ruled by the following four principles: concentration, programming, additionality and partnership. Regarding the concentration of resources, in the period 2014–2020, 70% of these still go to the poorest regions and countries. Programming means that this policy doesn't provide funds for single actions, but it delivers money for multiannual programmes that are consistent with the EU objectives and priorities previously defined in strategic documents, such as the Lisbon Strategy or Europe 2020. Additionality implies that the EU investment cannot replace national ones; it just supplements them. Partnership sets an obligation to involve regional and local actors along all stages of the EU policy-making process from design to evaluation. It aims to adapt EU policy decisions to regional and local realities and preferences.

The introduction of this last principle of partnership was related to the role of regional as well as local actors in the EC/EU policy-making, indeed beyond Cohesion Policy. The concept of multilevel governance was first developed and applied in this policy field in order to analyse direct connections between subnational institutions, both public and private, and

Table 5.7   Types of multilevel governance

Type I	Type II
General-purpose jurisdictions	Task-specific jurisdictions
Nonintersecting memberships	Intersecting memberships
Jurisdictions at a limited number of levels	No limit to the number of jurisdictional levels
Systemwide architecture	Flexible designs

Source: Marks and Hooghe (2003, p. 236).

European ones, especially the EC since the earliest stages of the EU policy process.

Two types of multilevel governance were conceptually distinguished, although they can coexist in practice (Table 5.7). In Type I multilevel governance, authority comes from democratic elections, and executive and legislative bodies, whereas it is more flexible in Type II, where public decisions are taken with the aim of achieving Pareto optimal solutions in order to solve problems.

The notion of multilevel governance has been broadly criticized, first of all, because of its poor democratic credentials, particularly in Type II, but also for heuristic reasons (Ares, 2010a, 2010b; Bache, 1999; Bache and Bristow, 2003; Christiansen, 1997; Jeffery, 2000; Keating and Wilson, 2014; Neshkova, 2010; Tatham, 2014; van Hecke et al., 2016).

Regarding some of the critiques that are more directly related to Cohesion Policy, to start with, multilevel governance has tended to confuse between access to the European level of decision-making and real capacity to have an impact on EU policy decisions. Moreover, many regions have encountered serious barriers not only to influence but actually to be involved in EU policy-making, including within the domain of regional development policy, despite the fact that this should be the easiest setting because of the principle of partnership (Callanan and Tatham, 2014; Jeffery, 2000; Heinelt and Niederhafner, 2008).

Furthermore, there is no evidence of association between partnership and regionalization within Member States; on the contrary, there are data about re-centralization trends that have taken place during the last decades in various decentralized EU countries (Bolgherini, 2014; Máiz et al., 2010; Oliveira and Breda-Vázquez, 2012; Peters and Pierre, 2004; Tatham, 2016).

Apart from the impact of different pre-existing domestic factors as well as the strategies of national governments to avoid the necessity for subnational reinforcement, it is worth acknowledging that "the Commission's role in promoting multi-level governance has not been consistent across time or across responsible directorates"; moreover, sometimes it has promoted centralization (Bache et al., 2011, p. 139).

At the same time, the extension, the rationale and the "regionalization" of the policy design of national regional development policies are very diverse. In certain cases, individual regional needs and preferences are considered at times of fixing national investment priorities but in others they are just established according to a central plan. For some Member States, lagging regions and in general the less favoured ones are a true concern, whereas in others the distribution of funding for regional development is more balanced. Finally, although this is explicitly forbidden, sometimes the EU Cohesion Policy is the most important instrument of the national regional policy.

4.2   Monitoring and Promoting Regional Capacity

The EU is increasingly focused on regional capacity because there are plenty of data that may be used to probe the relationship between institutional strength and economic performance.

"Administrative capacity" could be defined as the capabilities for management, programming, monitoring and evaluation (*ex-ante, in itinere* and *ex-post*) (Milio, 2010, pp. 32–43). This is an operational understanding oriented towards problem-solving.

For Milio (2010), management, programming, monitoring and evaluation are related to each other by their outcomes. None of them separately can guarantee administrative capacity, but their conjoint effects reduce the gap of implementation associated with poor regional capacity.

Moving beyond the conceptual framework, this author describes a model of political behaviour that has a positive impact on the regional administrative machinery. This improves regional policy outputs and outcomes, and it explains their various degrees of administrative fitness. The political factors considered in the model are political interference, political stability and political accountability.

Political interference is understood as an invasive, disruptive political action towards the administrative domain. The positive model is characterized by a clear distinction between political and administrative responsibilities that favours good management. "Weak management", on the contrary, is "the lack of horizontal coordination and clarity of role among personnel" (Milio, 2010, p. 48).

Political stability is operationally defined as a maximum of two cabinets during a legislature. This is linked to the continuity of the programming process and follow-through on implementation. "Low programming" is understood as "incoherence in strategy and late approval" (Milio, 2010, p. 48).

Finally, political accountability means that external organizations or individuals have the capacity to assess policy decisions and administrative and financial actions. Milio (2010) expects political accountability to influence both monitoring and evaluation because it implies more fair information available at any point in time. Monitoring systems in place and a culture of evaluation are positive for making use of funds.

Bovaird and Löffler (2003, p. 322) list ten attributes of "good governance": citizen engagement, transparency, accountability, social inclusion (gender, ethnicity, age, religion, etc.), ethical and honest behaviour, equity (fair procedures and due process), the ability to compete in a global environment, the capacity to work effectively in partnership, sustainability, and respect for the rule of law. This is a broader definition that goes beyond "administrative capacity". It could be expected that the importance of these ten elements vary between regions and over time.

The EC's DG REGIO funded directly the first round of the European Quality of Government Index (EQI). This is a dataset delivered by Charron, Dijkstra and Lapuente (2014 and 2015) and Charron and Lapuente (2018) that provides survey data on governance and corruption at the EU regional level (Table 5.8).

Quality of governance is here defined as the "capacity to implement policies in an impartial, non-corrupt, and efficient way" (Charron and Lapuente, 2018, p. 23). Both perceptions and experiences of public services' quality and fraud are measured. It is worth noting that this is the first dataset on the quality of government at the subnational level.

After the publication of the EQI's third round in 2018, assessment of trends could be done. As Charron and Lapuente underline (2018, pp. 23–4), there is no convergence in regional capacity across Europe, which is a result consistent with previous studies, such as Farole et al. (2011). Moreover, there is also a meaningful difference between regions that remain equal in terms of capacity to implement policies over time and regions with a shifting EQI. In the second group, there are regions that have improved their capacities since 2010, most of them from Eastern countries, which is an encouraging result, and regions with a declining EQI, which is in contrast disturbing, such as numerous regions in Italy, Greece and Spain. Notwithstanding, there are also Southern regions that show better capacities in 2017, for instance Navarra in Spain or the majority of the Portuguese regions.

Figure 5.1 presents the EQI's results in 2010 and 2017.

Member States have been adopting measures to improve regional institutional capacity where necessary, for instance by means of networks of knowledge and good practice sharing, e-learning, or compulsory training (European Commission, 2017e). Other examples or tools used to match abilities with needs and execute ESI funding more effectively have been the

Table 5.8   Dimensions of the regional quality of government index

Dimensions	Questions (Options in brackets)
Rule of law	• How would you rate the quality of the police force in your area? (Low/high, 0–10) • The police force gives special advantages to certain people in my area (Agree/disagree, 0–10) • All citizens are treated equally by the police force in my area (Agree, rather agree, rather disagree, or disagree, 1–4) • Corruption is prevalent in the police force in my area (Agree/disagree, 0–10)
Government effectiveness	• How would you rate the quality of public education in your area? (Low/high, 0–10) • How would you rate the quality of the public healthcare system in your area? (Low/high, 0–10) • Certain people are given special advantages in the public education system in my area (Agree/disagree, 0–10) • Certain people are given special advantages in the public healthcare system in my area (Agree/disagree, 0–10) • All citizens are treated equally in the public education system in my area (Agree, rather agree, rather disagree, or disagree, 1–4) • All citizens are treated equally in the public healthcare system in my area (Agree, rather agree, rather disagree, or disagree, 1–4)
Voice and accountability	• In your opinion, if corruption by a public employee or politician were to occur in your area, how likely is it that such corruption would be exposed by the local mass media? (Unlikely/likely, 0–10) • Please respond to the following: Elections in my area are honest and clean from corruption (Agree/disagree, 0–10)
Corruption	• Corruption is prevalent in my area's local public school system (Agree/disagree, 0–10) • Corruption is prevalent in the public healthcare system in my area (Agree/disagree, 0–10) • In the past 12 months have you or anyone living in your household paid a bribe in any form to: Health or medical services? (Yes/no) • In your opinion, how often do you think other citizens in your area use bribery to obtain public services? (Never/very often, 0–10)

Source: Own elaboration following Charron et al. (2014, pp. 83–4).

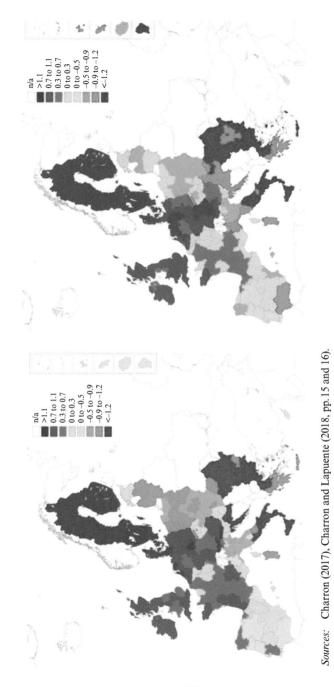

Sources: Charron (2017), Charron and Lapuente (2018, pp. 15 and 16).

Figure 5.1   EQI in 2010 (first round), left, and 2017 (third round), right

rationalization of funds' management, the recruitment of additional staff, dedicated contact points and informational events.

In addition to efforts made at national level, the EC has been helping with crucial aspects directly as well, by means of peer learning and exchange, state aid, public procurement, the smart specialization platform, and special aid for low-income and low-growth regions (European Commission, 2017e, p. 14).

Moreover, the Commission is contributing to identify barriers to EU investments' profitability in the less favoured regions. In its 2017 *Lagging regions report*, it enumerates five reasons why some territories are not attaining the projected rate of growth. These are: macroeconomic disparities; lower productivity, employment rates and educational accomplishment; reduced investment, both public and private; poor institutional quality and immature innovation schemes; and relevant demographic decline and particularly the out-migration of the younger and more skilled age groups (European Commission, 2017a, pp. iv–v).

In the same document, the Commission offers some recommendations for overcoming obstacles to regional development. These are: further investments in education and infrastructure, better links between cities and their surroundings, smart specialization strategies, more funds for improving quality of institutions and regional administrative capacities, and more emphasis on identifying the necessary conditions for investment (conditionalities) by reinforcing the connection between the national annual investments and Cohesion Policy.

5. CONCLUSIONS

This overview of the ERDP has underlined the main change in the rationale of the policy, which consists of abandoning the compensation logic and the objective of helping the less favoured regions to converge with the most advanced parts of the EC/EU, in favour of investing more common structural budget in those territories where more results can be achieved, with the purpose of enhancing the competitiveness of the whole EU.

Besides this, other current trends in the EU Cohesion Policy are related to the convenience of putting more emphasis on contextual factors, mainly the most specific barriers to growth and employment identified within each region. This concerns mostly lagging regions, where EU funding represents a great part of their public investment.

Summing up, the ERDP has moved towards more comprehensive and well-timed strategies for regional development, in the direction of more integrated approaches, and "from a one-size-fits-all policy to regionally differentiated investments and policy responses" (European Commission, 2017a, p. 49).

Disparities between regions were relevant in the policy discussions that contributed to the Europe 2020 strategy, which orientated EU policies towards the promotion of smart, sustainable and inclusive growth (European Commission, 2010). Many EU regions "remain largely unconnected with the major trans-Europe transport networks, and the connectivity of these regions is likely to remain very low for the foreseeable future" (McCann, 2015, p. 33). Indeed, adapting EU Cohesion Policy to the peculiarities of the EU regional reality, "with high frequency interactions of people, knowledge, goods and services taking place between a group of small and medium-scale urban centres, rather than hinterland-core interactions being dominated by a single large urban centre" (McCann, 2015, p. 30) merits more attention in the next programming period, 2021–2027.

Additionally, more place-sensitive policies may "represent the best method to both stem and reverse the rise of anti-establishment voting, which is threatening not only European integration but also the very economic, social and political stability which has overseen the longest period of relative peace and prosperity the continent has witnessed in its long history" (Dijkstra et al., 2018, p. 20).

The seventh *Report on economic, social and territorial cohesion* enumerated smart specialization as one of the three most relevant measures that were incorporated in the period 2014–2020 to improve the quality of investments, along with the ex-ante conditionality and the enhanced emphasis put on results (European Commission, 2017d, p. 16). Currently smart specialization is viewed as the most complete European industrial and decentralized innovation policy.

The smart specialization approach to EU Cohesion Policy design and implementation has been effective in terms of involvement of diverse stakeholders, although it possesses challenges regarding transparency and citizen participation in the politics of regional development. This should be compensated from 2021 onwards at least by the empowerment of regional and local representatives in policy and investment prioritizing.

REFERENCES

General References

Allen, D. (2010). The Structural Funds and Cohesion Policy, in H. Wallace, M.A. Pollack and A.R. Young (eds), *Policy-making in the European Union*, Oxford: Oxford University Press, pp. 229–52.

Ares, C. (2010a). A vueltas con la "gobernanza multinivel". *Revista Española de Ciencia Política*, 22, 119–33.
Ares, C. (2010b). *La participación de las regiones en el sistema político de la Unión Europea*, Valencia: Tirant lo Blanch.
Bache, I. (1998). *The politics of European Union Regional Policy: Multi-level governance or flexible gatekeeping?* Sheffield: Sheffield Academic Press.
Bache, I. (1999). The extended gatekeeper: Central government and the implementation of the EC regional policy in the UK. *Journal of European Public Policy*, 6, 28–45.
Bache, I., and Bristow, G. (2003). Devolution and the gatekeeping role of the core executive: The struggle for European funds. *British Journal of Politics and International Relations*, 5, 405–27.
Bache, I., Andreou, G., Atanasova, G., and Tomsic, D. (2011). Europeanization and multi-level governance in south-east Europe: The domestic impact of EU cohesion policy and pre-accession aid. *Journal of European Public Policy*, 18 (1), 122–41.
Bolgherini, S. (2014). Can austerity lead to recentralisation? Italian local government during the economic crisis. *South European Society and Politics*, 19 (2), 193–214.
Bovaird, T., and Löffler, E. (2003). Evaluating the quality of public governance: Indicators, models and methodologies. *International Review of Administrative Sciences*, 69, 313–28.
Callanan, M., and Tatham, M. (2014). Territorial interest representation in the European Union: Actors, objectives and strategies. *Journal of European Public Policy*, 21 (2), 188–210.
Charron, N. (2017). *European Quality of Government Index (EQI) microdata* [dataset]. http://doi.org/10.1080/00343404.2013.770141.
Charron, N., and Lapuente, V. (2018). *Quality of government in EU regions: Spatial and temporal patterns*. Working Paper Series, Gothenburg: The Quality of Government Institute.
Charron, N., Dijkstra L., and Lapuente, V. (2014). Regional governance matters: Quality of government within European Union member states. *Regional Studies*, 48 (1), 68–90.
Charron, N., Dijkstra, L., and Lapuente, V. (2015). Mapping the regional divide in Europe: A measure for assessing quality of government in 2006 European regions. *Social Indicators Research*, 122 (2), 315–46.
Christiansen, T. (1997). Reconstructing European space: From territorial politics to multilevel governance, in K.E. Jorgensen (ed.), *Reflective approaches to European governance*, London: Macmillan Press, pp. 51–68.
Dijkstra, L., Poelman, H., and Rodríguez-Pose, A. (2018). *The geography of EU discontent*. Working Papers by the Directorate-General for Regional Policy, 12, Luxembourg: Publications Office of the European Union.
European Commission (2010). *Communication from the Commission. Europe 2020. A strategy for smart, sustainable and inclusive growth* [COM (2010) 2020].
European Commission (2017a). *Commission staff working document, Competitiveness in low-income and low-growth regions. The lagging regions report* [SWD (2017) 132 final].
European Commission (2017b). *Communication from the Commission to the Council and the European Parliament, "Boosting growth and cohesion in EU border regions"* [COM (2017) 534 final].

European Commission (2017c). *Communication from the Commission to the European Parliament, the Council, the European Economic and Social Committee, the Committee of the Regions and the European Investment Bank, "A stronger and renewed strategic partnership with the EU's outermost regions"* [COM/2017/0623 final].

European Commission (2017d). *My region, my Europe, our future. Seventh report on economic, social and territorial cohesion* [COM (2017) 583 final].

European Commission (2017e). *Report from the Commission to the European Parliament, the Council, the European Economic and Social Committee and the Committee of the Regions, "Strategic report 2017 on the implementation of the European Structural and Investment Funds"* [COM (2017) 755 final].

Farole, T., Rodríguez-Pose, A., and Storper, M. (2011). Cohesion policy in the European Union: Growth, geography, institutions. *Journal of Common Market Studies*, 49 (5), 1089–1111.

Heinelt, H., and Niederhafner, S. (2008). Cities and organized interest intermediation in the EU multi-level system. *European Urban and Regional Studies*, 15, 173–87.

Jeffery, C. (2000). Sub-national mobilization and European integration: Does it make any difference? *Journal of Common Market Studies*, 38, 1–23.

Keating, M., and Wilson, A. (2014). Regions with regionalism? The rescaling of interest groups in six European states. *European Journal of Political Research*, 53, 840–57.

Lowi, T.J. (1972). Four systems of policy politics and choice. *Public Administration Review*, 32 (4), 298–310.

McCann, P. (2015). *The regional and urban policy of the European Union: Cohesion, results-orientation and smart specialisation*, Cheltenham, UK and Northampton, MA, USA: Edward Elgar Publishing.

Máiz, R., Caamaño, F., and Azpiarte, M. (2010). The hidden counterpoint of Spanish federalism: Recentralization and resymmetrization in Spain (1978–2008). *Regional and Federal Studies*, 20 (1), 63–82.

Marks, G., and Hooghe, L. (2003). Unravelling the central state, but how? Types of multi-level governance. *American Political Science Review*, 97 (2), 233–43.

Milio, S. (ed.) (2010). *From policy to implementation in the European Union: The challenge of a multi-level governance system*, London: I.B. Tauris Publishers.

Neshkova, M.I. (2010). The impact of subnational interests on supranational regulation. *Journal of European Public Policy*, 17 (8), 1193–1211.

Oliveira, C., and Breda-Vázquez, I. (2012). Europeanisation of territorial policies in Portugal and Italy: A cross-national comparison. *Policy & Politics*, 40 (1), 89–105.

Padoa-Schioppa, T. (1987). *Efficacité, stabilité, équité*, Paris: Economica.

Peters, B.G., and Pierre, J. (2004). Multi-level governance and democracy: A Faustian bargain?, in I. Bache and M. Flinders (eds), *Multi-level governance*, Oxford: Oxford University Press, pp. 75–89.

Tatham, M. (2014). Same game but more players? Subnational lobbying in an enlarged Union. *Regional and Federal Studies*, 24 (3), 341–61.

Tatham, M. (2016). *With, without, or against the state? How European regions play the Brussels game*, Oxford: Oxford University Press.

Van Hecke, M., Bursens, P., and Beyers, J. (2016). You'll never lobby alone: Explaining the participation of sub-national authorities in the European Commission's open consultation. *Journal of Common Market Studies*, 54 (6), 1433–48.

Main Regulations on ERDP Instruments for the Period 2014–2020

Council Regulation (EU, Euratom) No 1311/2013 of 2 December 2013 laying down the multiannual financial framework for the years 2014–2020.

Regulation (EU) No 1299/2013 of the European Parliament and of the Council of 17 December 2013 on specific provisions for the support from the European Regional Development Fund to the European territorial cooperation goal.

Regulation (EU) No 1301/2013 of the European Parliament and of the Council of 17 December 2013 on the European Regional Development Fund and on specific provisions concerning the Investment for growth and jobs goal and repealing Regulation (EC) No 1080/2006.

Regulation (EU) No 1302/2013 of the European Parliament and of the Council of 17 December 2013 amending Regulation (EC) No 1082/2006 on a European grouping of territorial cooperation (EGTC) as regards the clarification, simplification and improvement of the establishment and functioning of such groupings.

Regulation (EU) No 1303/2013 of the European Parliament and of the Council of 17 December 2013 laying down common provisions on the European Regional Development Fund, the European Social Fund, the Cohesion Fund, the European Agricultural Fund for Rural Development and the European Maritime and Fisheries Fund and laying down general provisions on the European Regional Development Fund, the European Social Fund, the Cohesion Fund and the European Maritime and Fisheries Fund and repealing Council Regulation (EC) No 1083/2006.

Institutional Links

Committee of the Regions (CoR), https://cor.europa.eu/en, last accessed on 18 November 2019.

European Commission's Directorate-General for Regional Development (REGIO), http://ec.europa.eu/regional_policy/en/, last accessed on 18 November 2019.

European Parliament's Committee on Regional Development (REGI), http://www.europarl.europa.eu/committees/en/regi/home.html, last accessed on 18 November 2019.

European Quality of Government Index 2017, http://ec.europa.eu/regional_policy/en/information/maps/quality_of_governance, last accessed on 18 November 2019.

6. An overview of the European Union innovation policy from the regional perspective

María del Carmen Sánchez-Carreira

1. INTRODUCTION

The innovative capacity of a given territory is a main driver for its long-term growth and development. Therefore, a combination of policies from different levels of government seeks to improve the innovation environment and capabilities. The different levels of government (European Union [EU], national, regional or local) can design and implement policies that affect innovation, both directly and indirectly.

This chapter discusses the foundation and evolution of the EU innovation policy over time, focusing on its key moments, rationales, objectives, tools and trends; and emphasising the regional perspective. The EU innovation policy has traditionally focused on research, according to the linear model of innovation. However, innovation has been gradually introduced. Among other actions and tools, Framework Programmes (FPs) and Structural Funds (SFs) have been involved in this introduction.

Innovation policies are characterised by a multilevel model, because powers to implement policies are distributed among different levels of governments. Regions have increasingly become relevant actors. Nevertheless, the EU innovation policy, and mainly FPs, have hardly considered the territorial dimension, the economic development or the innovation level of the regions. Several attempts to include some cohesion element in the EU innovation policy have been made over time, through different tools, including SFs.

This chapter is made up of four sections. The first section deals with the foundation and evolution of the EU innovation policy, the key moments and rationales. The second section tackles the main tools of the EU innovation policy. The third section addresses the regional perspective of the EU innovation policy, focusing on the links between EU innovation policies and regional cohesion, from the background to the current Smart

Specialisation (SS) strategies. The last section presents the main conclusions and implications from the analysis.

2. THE FOUNDATION AND EVOLUTION OF THE EU INNOVATION POLICY

2.1   The Context of the EU Innovation Policy

Innovation is a crucial factor triggering economic development and growth. Therefore, policies that foster innovation are supported from different theoretical perspectives. The specific characteristics of innovation (uncertainty, indivisibility, lack of appropriability, externalities, public goods, etc.) argue for public intervention to boost innovation, based on different reasons depending on the theoretical perspective (Arrow, 1962; Dasgupta and Stoneman, 1987; Lundvall and Borrás, 2005; Vence, 2007; Foray, 2009; Fagerberg, 2017). The neoclassical perspective, based on the existence of market failures, justifies public intervention to generate incentives, whereas the evolutionist perspective, focused on systemic failures, underlines interrelations among the actors and elements that compose the innovation system.

Innovation policy should be understood in a broad sense, including scientific and technology policies, and industrial policy. Thus, it can be defined as any public intervention aimed at improving and encouraging the productive system (Rothwell, 1983; Lundvall and Borrás, 2005; Vence, 2007) or as encompassing all policies that have an impact on innovation (Fagerberg, 2017). In a narrower perspective, it refers to policies that attempt to affect innovation (Edquist, 2004), focusing on direct policies. Either way, innovation policy is an overarching policy, which means that "it is not a single policy, but an entire set of policies and instruments" (Reillon, 2016, p. 30).

Based on the traditional importance of the linear model of innovation, innovation policy evolves from scientific to technological policy and later to innovation policy. Therefore, the focus moves from research and production of new knowledge to technologies and sectors, and later to innovation, attempting to improve competitiveness and economic performance (Lundvall and Borrás, 2005). This shift towards a systemic and interactive model of innovation results in different and more complex policies, underlining the interactions among the different agents involved in innovation (see this volume, Chapter 1).

The three original treaties of the European Economic Community (EEC) refer to research. Thus, the European Coal and Steel Community

(ECSC) and European Atomic Energy Community (Euratom) treaties include research in the specific fields covered. The Treaty of Rome leads to different research programmes prioritising advanced technologies (European Commission, 2016).

Within the EU framework, four different levels of government can design and implement innovation policies: local, regional, national and EU. This complex organisation requires coordination among the different levels of government (Kaiser and Prange, 2004; Barca, 2009; OECD, 2011; Uyarra et al., 2007; Baier et al., 2013).

The foundations for the EU innovation policy are found in articles 179 to 189 of the Treaty on the Functioning of the EU. The EU has different competences on innovation, from making recommendations to the Member States (MS) or setting monitoring and benchmarking activities to having full competences. The gradual inclusion of research and development (R&D) and innovation policy in the EU treaties allows innovation to become a shared competence. However, this option has never been used yet. The EU innovation policy aims at supporting MS and regions in the development and implementation of an up-to-date and efficient innovation policy (Reillon, 2016). The intervention of the EU on innovation is based on the subsidiarity principle, which means supplementing national and regional actions, and consistency between national and EU policies (Reillon, 2017).

The Department of the European Commission (EC) in charge of the policy on research, science and innovation is the Directorate-General for Research and Innovation (DG RTD). However, due to the cross-cutting nature of innovation, other departments manage some innovation issues, including the Directorate-General for Enterprise and Industry.

In complete contrast to many other EU policies, which are implemented and/or executed from the national and/or regional governments, most EU innovation actions are directly implemented by the EC. They tend to consist of funding for research and innovation, in addition to regional and national budgets.

As well as the EU and national powers, the role of regions is significant (Landabaso, 2000; Fernández et al., 2007; Fernández et al., 2010; De Brujin and Lagendijk, 2005; Tödtling and Trippl, 2005). However, the EU regional innovation policies differ concerning the level of competences, budgets, resources and capabilities, as well as their focus and main instruments (see this volume, Chapters 2 and 4, and the case studies in Chapters 9 to 12). Three different levels can be identified in regional innovation policies: EU actions with regional focus; national actions with regional focus; and innovation policies specific to each region.

2.2   Key Moments and Rationales in the EU Innovation Policy

Further to the founding treaties mentioned above, another important moment in the EU innovation policy is the mid-1980s, for a focus on research. Research and technological development were included in Title VI of the Single European Act, becoming a formal community policy. The policy aims at strengthening the scientific and technological basis of European industry to become more competitive worldwide, bearing in mind the existing innovation gap with the USA and Japan. The Treaty of Maastricht included Title XV (Research and Technological Development), extending the scope to cover all research activities, from basic research to any field concerning EU goals, becoming a horizontal policy. After this, the Treaty of Lisbon included research as a shared competence (Guzzetti, 1995; Reillon, 2015, 2017).

Another relevant moment is the launching of the First FP of Research and Technological Development in 1984. Multiannual programmes such as this are the main basis of the EU research and innovation policy and they have continued until the present day. Nevertheless, there have been other previous EU initiatives concerning research.

Within the context of the linear model of innovation and the importance of science push, several international research organisations have been created since 1950 and mainly in the 1970s. They are the European Organization for Nuclear Research (CERN, 1954), the European Southern Observatory (ESO, 1962), Airbus (1972), the European Molecular Biology Laboratory (EMBL, 1974), the European Science Foundation (ESF, 1974) and the European Space Agency (ESA, 1975) (Borrás, 2003; Lundvall and Borrás, 2005; Reillon, 2017).

Moreover, COST (Cooperation in Science and Technology) is an intergovernmental programme established in 1971 to support transnational cooperation in several scientific areas. It was the precursor of the advanced multidisciplinary research, EU FPs and Eureka that started in 1985, focused on collaboration networks for firms, including non-EU countries.

Several programmes fund research besides FPs. These programmes tend to be sectorial (environment – LIFE; energy – COMMET, THERMIE, VALOREM; information and communications technology – ESPRIT, RACE; industry technologies –BRITE) or focused on small and medium-sized enterprises (SMEs) (SPRINT) or peripheral regions (STRIDE). The STAR programme attempts to promote access of SMEs of peripheral regions to telecommunications. And the VALUE programme addresses the dissemination and utilisation of the results of scientific and technical research (Vence, 1998; Rossi, 2005; Reillon, 2017).

The EU focus on innovation is recent. Thus, the EU has explicitly included innovation policies since the mid-1990s. Two key moments have been the Green Paper on Innovation, published in 1995, and the First Action Plan for Innovation in Europe, launched in 1996 (Rossi, 2005). The Green Paper aims at identifying the factors that affect the EU innovation, proposing measures to increase the EU's innovation capacity (European Commission, 1995). The Plan attempts to foster innovation culture, establish a favourable framework for innovation, and improve articulation between research and innovation (European Commission, 1996).

Two main EU strategies comprise highlights, so far, of the twenty-first century. The first is the Lisbon Strategy, approved in 2000, with the aim of the EU's becoming the world's most competitive and dynamic knowledge-based economy, capable of sustainable economic growth with more and better jobs and greater social cohesion. The Barcelona Summit, held in 2002, set up the goal of achieving 3% of gross domestic product (GDP) allocated to R&D expenditures by 2010, being two-thirds executed by the private sector. This goal was ambitious, but the resources were limited. Therefore, the interim report shows limited progress (Kok, 2004), which resulted in a revision of the strategy in 2005. One of the recommendations was to use cohesion policy instruments to advance the Lisbon Strategy, which was duly implemented for the 2007–2013 programming period.

Within the context of the Lisbon Strategy, the European Research Area (ERA) was created in 2001, as a European internal market for research. In the area, researchers, technology and knowledge can circulate freely. The ERA also aims at gathering and coordinating EU research, to increase its impact. Other relevant moments have been the creation of the European Research Council in 2007 to support frontier research across all fields, and of the European Institute of Innovation & Technology (EIT) in 2008 to contribute to the sustainable economic growth and industrial competitiveness, strengthening the EU's innovation capacity. The EIT was the first EU initiative to foster and integrate higher education, research, firms and other agents involved in the innovation process, supporting knowledge and innovation communities (KIC) in key issues.

A second strategy worth noting is the Innovation Union, one of the seven flagship initiatives of the Europe 2020 Strategy for Smart, Sustainable and Inclusive Growth. Approved in 2010, it aimed at improving conditions and access to finance for research and innovation in the EU, to ensure that innovative ideas could be turned into products and services that create growth and jobs (European Commission, 2010, 2013). The Innovation Union set the target of investing 3% of the GDP in R&D. It may be considered the EU's first comprehensive innovation strategy, because it encompassed the whole process, from research to commercialisation, and it involved all agents. In this sense, its work is continued through the European Innovation Partnerships, a new initiative that fosters cooperation along the whole innovation chain, joining relevant public and private actors at different levels (EU, national and regional) across policy areas and industrial sectors to meet specific societal challenges.

3.   MAIN TOOLS OF THE EU INNOVATION POLICY

The EU innovation policy consists of different tools, underlining the FPs. Other relevant tools are the SFs, other funds for research and innovation, and other actions.

3.1   The FPs

The main tool of the EU to foster innovation and mainly research has been the multiannual R&D FPs, which set the thematic priority areas for science and technology in a certain period. Since the Treaty of Maastricht, the FPs have been not only a programming tool, but also a financial tool (Guzzetti, 1995; Vence, 1998; Reillon, 2017).

The first FP was launched in 1984 and focused on biotechnology, telecommunications and industrial fields. The FPs continued until the Seventh FP (2007–2013) (European Commission, 2016), when the programmes were substituted by Horizon 2020 (2014–2020). They focused on funding research and projects, mainly in advanced technological areas, promoting cooperation among different disciplines, partners and countries.[1]

The Fourth FP (1994–1998) was the first one after the Maastricht Treaty and it joined the diverse fragmented R&D community actuations to improve efficiency and coordination. It acted under the subsidiarity principle, providing European added value, and it introduced targeted socioeconomic research. The Fifth FP (1998–2002) instigated a significant change, because it required that research serve society and citizens. The ERA also introduces changes in the goals and structure of the FPs (Vence, 1998; European Commission, 2016; Reillon, 2017).

The current EU FP for Research and Innovation is called Horizon 2020 (H2020). It was launched within the context of the Europe 2020 Strategy, addressing three main issues: excellent science, industrial leadership and tackling societal challenges. H2020 gathers the EU's research, development and innovation (RD&I) funding and attempts to simplify the procedures, reducing bureaucracy and time. Its scope is broad, because it provides funding from the idea to the market, covering research and innovation. It

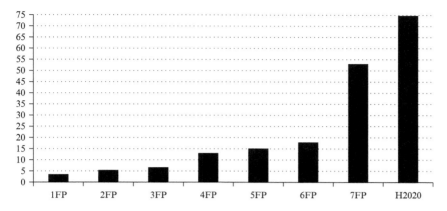

Source: Own elaboration based on Vence (1998), European Commission (2016), Reillon (2017), EUR-Lex (2019) and EC Information.

Figure 6.1   Evolution of the budget of the FPs (billion euros)

is not structured by thematic areas, but by challenges. The main challenges are social ones, such as health, clean energy and transport.

The evolution of the FPs (Figure 6.1, Table 6.1) shows an increasing budget, mainly from the Seventh FP. The larger budgets reveal the growing relevance of research and innovation for the EU. Thus, the EU allocated less than 2% of its budget to research in 1981, while nowadays this figure is roughly 7.5% (Reillon, 2017). Despite the main focus on research, more attention to innovation issues is notable. The increasing focus on the SMEs is another feature that is clear in the Seventh FP, complemented by the Competitiveness and Innovation Programme (Rodil, 2007).

Moreover, the range of topics has been broadened, shifting the focus from advanced scientific and technologic areas to societal changes (Table 6.1, Figure 6.2). However, the main areas funded by the FPs have been information and communications technology (ICT), energy, health, transport and space, environment, materials and processes, and agriculture (Guzzetti, 1995; Vence, 1998; Andrée, 2009; Reillon, 2017).

Another trend is the decreasing number of specific programmes attempting to reduce fragmentation. Nevertheless, the horizontal actions aimed at supporting the EU research and innovation capabilities have been expanded and diversified, from initial grants for transnational cooperative research projects to partnerships, as well as the bodies that manage them (Vence, 1998; Rodil, 2007; Reillon, 2017).

Table 6.2 shows other actions included in the FPs, which tend to be horizontal and broader, attempting to include all innovation aspects

Table 6.1   Summary information of Framework Programmes

Framework Programme	Period	Budget (€ billion)	Thematic priorities
First Framework Programme	1984–1987	3.27	Agriculture Industrial competitiveness Raw materials Energy Development aid Living conditions
Second Framework Programme	1987–1991	5.36	Quality of life (health and environment) ICT and services (including transport) Modernisation of industrial sectors Biological resources Energy Science and technology for development Marine resources
Third Framework Programme	1990–1994	6.60	ICT Energy Environment Quality of life Biotechnology
Fourth Framework Programme	1994–1998	13.12	ICT Industrial technologies Environment Life sciences Agriculture and fisheries Energy Transport Targeted socioeconomic research

Fifth Framework Programme	1998–2002	14.96	➢ Quality of life and management of living resources
			  – Health, food and biotechnologies
			  – Agriculture, fisheries and forestries
			➢ User-friendly information society
			  – ICT
			  – Future and emerging technologies
			➢ Competitive and sustainable growth
			  – Products, processes and organisation
			  – Materials and measures
			  – Transport and marine technologies
			  – Aeronautics

Table 6.1   (continued)

Framework Programme	Period	Budget (€ billion)	Thematic priorities
			➢ Energy, environment and sustainable development – Environment – Energy
Sixth Framework Programme	2002–2006	17.90	➢ Quality of life and management of living resources – Life sciences, genomics and biotechnologies – Food quality and safety ➢ User-friendly information society – Information society technologies – Nanotechnologies, materials and processes ➢ Competitive and sustainable growth – Transport – Aeronautics and space – Energy, environment and sustainable development – Citizens and governance in knowledge society
Seventh Framework Programme	2007–2013	53.20	Health Food, agriculture, fisheries and biotechnology ICT Nanotechnologies, materials and processes Space Transport and aeronautics Environment and climatic change Energy Socioeconomic sciences and the humanities Security
Horizon 2020	2014–2020	74.80	ICT Nanotechnologies, materials and processes Biotechnologies Space

Table 6.1   (continued)

Framework Programme	Period	Budget (€ billion)	Thematic priorities
			Health, demographic change and wellbeing
			Food, agriculture, forestry, water and marine
			Smart, green and integrated transport
			Climate action, environment and raw materials
			Secure, clean and efficient energy
			Inclusive, innovation and effective societies
			Secured societies
			Future and emerging technologies

Source: Own elaboration based on Vence (1998), European Commission (2016), Reillon (2017), EUR-Lex (2019) and EC information.

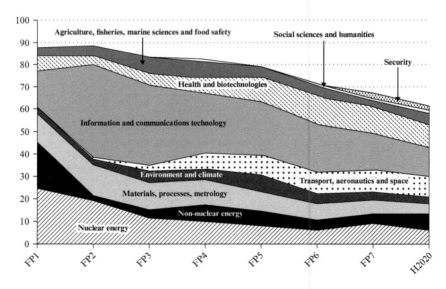

Source: Own elaboration based on EC information, EUR-Lex (2019), European Parliamentary Research Service and Reillon (2017).

Figure 6.2   Evolution of thematic activities of FPs

Table 6.2   Other actions included in the FPs

	FP1	FP2	FP3	FP4	FP5	FP6	FP7	FP8
Development and international cooperation		X	X	X	X		X	
Human resources (Training and mobility)	X	X	X	X	X	X	X	X
Innovation and SMEs, technology transfer, dissemination of results	X	X	X	X	X		X	
Research Infrastructures		X			X	X	X	X
Coordination and policy	X	X				X	X	
Science and Society						X	X	X
Joint Research Centres					X	X	X	X
European Institute of Innovation and Technology							X	X
Other actions*						X	X	X

Note: *   Other actions include Research Potential, Regions of Knowledge, Access to risk finance, and Spreading excellence and widening participation, among others.

Source: Own elaboration based on Vence (1998), Reillon (2017), EC information and EUR-Lex (2019).

(from initial support to international research cooperation, training and mobility, innovation and SMEs, societal challenges, access to risk finance, and different kinds of partnerships). As a result of the implementation of these new instruments, the relative weight of thematic priorities was reduced from 90% in the First FP to roughly 60% in the current H2020. However, the budget for each thematic priority rises, since the overall budget has been continuously increased. Concerning the horizontal actions, the most relevant focuses on "Human Resources". Other significant actions are "Innovation and SMEs, technology transfer, dissemination of results" and "Research Infrastructures". "International cooperation" was one of the main instruments for implementing the FPs. However, its importance has constantly decreased, because it stopped being a specific activity to be included in the thematic priorities (Reillon, 2017).

In addition to the calls of the FPs, there are other initiatives that receive budgets from them, managed by countries (Joint Programming Initiatives, Article 185 initiatives and ERA-NETs [European Research Area networks]) or industry (Joint Technology Initiatives). These initiatives attempt to bring together research efforts and enhance cooperation to achieve a higher funding scale to tackle social challenges and avoid fragmentation, which leads to a lower effectiveness (European Commission, 2008).

3.2 Other Funds for Research and Innovation

Another relevant tool of the innovation policy is the EU SFs,[2] which may contribute to fund research and innovation, and to develop and upgrade technological capabilities and skilled labour in less favoured regions (Fernández et al., 2007; Rodil, 2007; Fernández et al., 2010; Reillon, 2015). The relative weight of SFs differs by region, showing a trend to be more relevant in less developed regions, according to their allocation criteria.

In this sense, the Technological Fund is worth noting as an ERDF in the period 2007–2013. It was created to promote business RD&I in Spain, and mainly allocated to less developed regions. Its budget amounts to 3.3 billion euros. Moreover, the European Fund for Strategic Investment (EFSI) is one of the pillars of the Investment Plan for Europe, launched in 2015 during the financial crisis. This plan, called the Juncker Plan, aims at mobilising private investments, allocating roughly 41.1 billion euros to research and innovation.

Another tool, named Innovative Actions (IAs), aims at fostering regional innovative capacity in less favoured regions, under Article 10 of the ERDF. The IAs include Regional Technological Plans (RTPs), Regional Innovation Strategies (RIS), and Regional Innovation and Technology Transfer Strategies (RITTS) (Landabaso and Reid, 1999; Fernández et al. 2007; Fernández et al., 2010, Zabala-Iturriagagoitia et al., 2008). These actions will be discussed in the next section.

SFs and IAs are mainly focused on less developed regions. Therefore, there is a link between innovation and regional cohesion policies, an issue that will also be discussed in the next section. In fact, the EU cohesion policies increasingly include innovation (see this volume, Chapter 5).

Other relevant actions that link innovation and regions are the Regions of Knowledge and Research Potential programmes, as well as the Vanguard Initiative. The Regions of Knowledge Programme aimed at strengthening the research and innovation capabilities and potential of regions. It focused mainly on supporting and encouraging regional research-driven clusters, as well as enhancing cross-border regional cooperation in research. This programme was launched in 2003 as a pilot action, which later became a programme. The Research Potential Programme was set up in 2007 for less developed regions (convergence and outermost regions). It attempted to build links and collaboration among universities and to help researchers to participate in EU projects. These programmes did not fund research, but the development of strategies for regional innovation in the first programme, linking several regional partners (universities, research centres and enterprises) to strengthen the capacities and research potential; and staff exchanges, workshops, conferences and working groups, networking, advices, knowledge transfer, recruitment of researches and equipment in the second programme. The programmes highlight the relevance of supporting the local knowledge base, and the role of universities and research institutions in regional development.

Both programmes ended, but their basis and experience remain in the current SFs, Cohesion Policy (including SS) and H2020 (European Commission, 2014b). Moreover, the Vanguard Initiative for New Growth through Smart Specialisation launched in 2014 was driven by a group of European industrial regions,[3] with an agenda for influencing innovation and industrial policies. This regional network set a political commitment to engage in growth-oriented industrial collaborations, based on combined strengths linked to EU priorities, as well as mobilisation and alignment of resources based on SS and interregional cooperation principles. This initiative aims at fostering collaboration, co-creation and co-investment in projects across Europe, seeking the alignment of strategic investment and the development of industry-led and scalable projects, which contribute to the industrial renewal in Europe. The collaborative projects will be close to the market and emerge as a result of an interregional entrepreneurial discovery process among different players. The Vanguard Initiative seeks relevant knowledge and expertise to develop European value chains in priority areas, and to lead by example in developing interregional cooperation and multilevel governance for supporting clusters and regional eco-systems. It has developed pilot projects,[4] based on building synergies to enable world-class clusters and lead new industries. These have been implemented in a four-step approach: learn, connect, demonstrate and commercialise (Vanguard Initiative, 2014–2017).

Another tool makes use of other funds for research and innovation. Some of these funds are sectorial, such as in the fields of space (Copernicus, Galileo), nuclear energy (Euratom Research and Training Programme [RTP], International Thermonuclear Experimental Reactor [ITER]), and coal and steel production (the Research Fund for Coal and Steel). Moreover, other programmes are indirectly related to research and innovation. They do not fund research and innovation directly, but they have an impact on innovation (Reillon, 2015). These programmes are COSME (EU Programme for the Competitiveness of Enterprises and SMEs), Erasmus+ Programme, Third Health Programme, Life Programme and Connecting Europe Facility (CEF) Programme. Interreg Europe is also a community initiative funded by the ERDF since 1990 to enhance territorial cooperation, supporting cross-border, transnational and inter-regional actions. It aims at improving the implementation of regional development policies and programmes, sharing knowledge, experience and best practices, and focusing on four main topics: research and innovation, SMEs' competitiveness, low-carbon economy and environment, and resource efficiency. Finally, it is worth mentioning some EU initiatives focused on funding innovation, mainly under H2020.

3.3   Evolution and Recent Trends: A Brief Overview

The evolution of the EU innovation policy is described in the analysis of Borrás (2003) and Lundvall and Borrás (2005). These authors identify an initial focus on scientific policy in the 1960s, followed by a shift to technology policy and later to innovation policy. According to the classification of innovation policies followed by Fernández et al. (2007) and Fernández et al. (2010), the EU policy corresponds mainly with the first generation, focused on scientific and R&D activities, and based on the linear model of innovation. However, some measures suggest the emergence of a second generation of innovation policy, more focused on systems and infrastructures. Finally, the third generation of policies, focused on the creation of knowledge and learning processes, is not common in the EU innovation policy (see this volume, Chapters 1 and 3).

Concerning the recent trends in the EU innovation policy, there are four issues to highlight. Firstly, the Smart Specialisation Strategies (S3) seem a good tool for combining innovation and regional development. In fact, all regions need to have this tool as ex-ante conditionality to receive EU SFs to meet RD&I goals in the period 2014–2020. Secondly, some demand-side initiatives have increasingly been implemented, supported by the EU (Lead Markets Initiative, public procurement of innovation and pre-commercial procurement of innovation). Despite this trend, the traditional predominance of supply-side versus demand-side instruments remains. Thirdly, the new trends for the EU innovation policy may be linked with the policy goals stated by Commissioner Moedas in 2015: open innovation, open science and open to the world. Fourthly, the new programming period 2021–2027 is currently defining the funding and priorities. In this sense, the new FP (Ninth FP) will be named Horizon Europe and the proposed budget amounts to 97.6 billion euros. It will follow the path of H2020, despite presenting some new features. The main novelties will be the establishment of the European Innovation Council, aimed at identifying, funding and scaling up breakthrough and disruptive innovations from the lab to market applications, as well as setting new mission-oriented research, focusing on societal challenges and industrial competitiveness. The mission-oriented approach "can provide the means to focus on research, innovation and investments on solving critical problems, while spurring growth, jobs and resulting in positive spillovers across many sectors" (Mazzucato, 2018, p. 4). It also adopts a bottom-up approach. The missions are co-designed with citizens, stakeholders, the European Parliament and MS and attempt to achieve better communication and connect people to science (European Commission, 2018b; Mazzucato, 2018).

4. LINKING EU INNOVATION AND REGIONAL DEVELOPMENT POLICIES

4.1 Background

The process of European integration has been driven by growth and competitiveness aims. Although these objectives could be compatible with social and territorial cohesion, it seems difficult to achieve them simultaneously (Rodil et al., 2014). Thus, the development of innovative capabilities may enhance competitiveness, but it could negatively affect regional development and cohesion (Begg, 2008; Cornett and Sørensen, 2008; Rodríguez-Pose and Novak, 2013; Rodil et al., 2014; Foray et al., 2018a, 2018b).

Innovation is an activity dependent on spatial and social dimensions (Lundvall, 1992; Maskell and Malmberg, 1999; Gertler, 2001; Asheim and Isaksen, 2002; Rutten, 2016). Thus, it requires analysis of the relation between regional and innovation policies, and in particular the combination of cohesion and competitiveness goals, a challenging issue, because they seem contradictory goals (see this volume, Chapters 5, 7 and 8).

There is a two-way relationship between regional and innovation policies. On the one hand, innovation affects regional development, because it is a key factor for driving growth and competitiveness. On the other hand, innovation is determined by regional capabilities (human resources, productive structure, etc.), their innovative environment and absorption capacity. The regional analysis of the EU innovation policy should not be focused mainly on funds allocated to reduce disparities; it should also be mindful of regional effects of the EU policies (Vence, 1998; see this volume, Chapter 8).

Two EU-specific initiatives that attempted to balance the two goals were STRIDE and RIS. The STRIDE initiative, set in the period 1990–1993, aimed at promoting the research and technological development of the peripheral regions (Objectives 1 and 2 regions). This initiative, funded by SFs, was focused on three priorities: increasing the capacities for research; improving and encouraging the participation of institutions, research centres and businesses in international networks and research programmes; and developing links between research and industry. Most of these funds were not efficient concerning regional development, because they were mainly allocated to large RTD infrastructure projects, especially in the public sector. This fact accords with the linear model of innovation, as well as the limited absorption capacity of these regions and the lack of organisational and institutional competences (Landabaso and Reid, 1999; Morgan and Nauwelaers, 2003).

RTP and RIS[5] projects were launched in 1994 by the EC to support the definition and implementation of regional innovation policy. For two years they were pilot actions co-funded by the region, a status that allows regions to test innovation actions to promote innovation, mobilising their own social capital and focusing on SMEs. RIS were complemented with RITTS, focused on improving the efficiency of innovation infrastructures and policies (European Commission, 1997; Landabaso and Reid, 1999; Reillon, 2016).

Four pilot RTPs were funded during 1994–1996 (Wales,[6] United Kingdom; Lorraine, France; Limburg, the Netherlands; and Saxony, Germany, all of them Objective 2 regions). They were followed by RIS, RIS+ and RTT (Regional Technology Transfer) programmes in the period 1996–1999, accounting for a total of 66 programmes. The first four Objective 1 regions to implement the RIS were Norte (Portugal), Castile and León (Spain), Central Macedonia (Greece) and Abruzzo (Italy) (Landabaso and Reid, 1999; SOCINTEC, 2005). After these pilot actions, the ERDF funded IAs in the period 2000–2006 in three strategic areas: regional economies based on knowledge and innovation; the information society for regional development (eEurope Regio); and regional identity and sustainable development (SOCINTEC, 2005; Rossi, 2005).

These initiatives aimed at involving all regional innovation actors in the definition of local priorities (Landabaso and Reid, 1999; Morgan and Nauwelaers, 2003; Zabala-Iturriagagoitia et al., 2008; Andrée, 2009). In this way, RIS could be considered the basis of the current S3. In fact, it consisted of a method for designing and implementing regional innovation strategies, based on an interactive and systemic view of innovation. The process is similar, because it is based on a strategic and bottom-up approach, interaction with regional stakeholders, and assessment by the

EC and experts (Landabaso and Reid, 1999; Morgan and Nauwelaers, 2003). Moreover, there were three main phases in each RIS (Landabaso and Reid, 1999; Zabala-Iturriagagoitia et al., 2008): building consensus among the regional stakeholders; diagnosis (internal and external analysis of needs and capacities); and identification of projects according to the selected priorities and elaboration, design and implementation of a strategy, and its monitoring and evaluation.

More recently, the Vanguard Initiative for New Growth through Smart Specialisation has supported a broader application and visibility of SS principles, led by examples and aimed at enhancing EU competitiveness and growth. It also provides an evidence base to support the EC in the development of Smart Specialisation Platforms in key growth areas, such as Industrial Modernisation, Energy and Agri-food. This pioneering approach follows a bottom-up entrepreneurial discovery process on new growth and industrial renewal in European priority areas (Vanguard Initiative, 2014–2017).

Concerning the FPs, the main tool of the EU innovation policy, these have not considered the territorial dimension, the economic development, or the innovation level of countries or regions. They address directly to the beneficiaries, which are different kinds of partners, but no regions or countries. The selection is based on competitive calls and focused on scientific excellence criteria. However, several attempts to include some cohesion element in the FPs have been made over time, based on leveraging synergies between FPs and SFs (Corpakis, 2016; De Carli, 2017; Reillon, 2017). Thus, the Second FP introduced a criterion concerning greater cohesion, with the aim that all regions could benefit from funding and developing their research capacities. The Third and Fourth FPs attempted to include the cohesion criterion, according to the reports that evaluate the EU science and technology, which highlight the challenge of coordinating national policies and cohesion for less developed regions. The Third FP attempted to introduce a political commitment for cohesion reducing disparities between regions (Commission of the European Communities, 1988, 1989; Reillon, 2017). The Fourth FP underlined the need to strengthen research and structural policy, as well as the FPs and the SFs. However, the results were unsatisfactory, because excellence stands as the main criterion (Reillon, 2017).

Several studies (Vence et al., 2000; Boldrin and Canova, 2001; Vence and Rodil, 2003; Hudson, 2007; Reid, 2007; Rodil et al., 2014) highlight the spillover effects of FPs. The analysis of the participation of countries and regions in FPs and the raised funds shows a high concentration in developed areas, although it has levelled over time (Vence, 1998). Thus, the first three regions of each country account for 80% of the raised funds (European Commission, 1993; Commission of the European Communities, 1994; Vence, 1998). Moreover, most of these studies show a positive relationship between participation and returns with the level of R&D expenditure, at national and regional levels, as well as at agent level. This implies that the EU innovation policy has an important feedback effect on pre-existing regional disparities (see this volume, Chapters 7 and 8). Therefore, the uneven regional distribution of the EU innovation policy has effects not only in the short term, but also in the long term, as innovation is cumulative. In addition, there is feedback between the participation in RD&I activities and the building of regional innovation capacities and learning (Vence, 1998; Rodil, 2007) (see this volume, Chapters 8 and 3).

These studies refer to the challenging issue of combining two contradictory goals (excellence and cohesion). In this regard, within the context of revising the Lisbon Strategy, one recommendation has been to use cohesion policy instruments (see this volume, Chapter 5). Furthermore, one of the priorities of the Innovation Union Flagship Initiative is maximising social and territorial cohesion. As a result, the S3 arise as an ex-ante condition for using funds for research and innovation in the multiannual programme period 2014–2020.

The current FP, H2020, includes an instrument aimed at spreading excellence and widening participation. It addresses the causes of low participation in FPs (De Carli, 2017). Nevertheless, the resources for this action are limited, because it allocates less than 2% of the H2020 budget. The main actions of this programme are Teaming (Institution building), Twinning (Institutional networking) and ERA Chairs (Bringing excellence to institutions). These three actions are related to SS, mainly the first one, because the proposals should integrate within S3.

Moreover, the EU SFs aim at developing the innovation capacities of regions (Fernández et al., 2007; Rodil, 2007; Zabala-Iturriagagoitia et al., 2008; Fernández et al., 2010; Reillon, 2015, 2017; Pontikakis et al., 2018). About 25% of SFs (roughly 86 billion euros) was spent on R&D and innovation activities (European Commission, 2014a). Nowadays, four of the European Structural and Investment Funds (ESIFs) support research and innovation activities. In fact, between 50% and 80% of these funds should be allocated to at least two of the following four objectives: strengthening research, technological development and innovation; enhancing access to and the use of quality of ICT; enhancing the competitiveness of SMEs; and supporting the shift towards a low-carbon economy.

Despite the above-mentioned attempts to strengthen the links between innovation and cohesion policies, there is still much work to be done. Some previous experiences can help the EU to advance along this path, leveraging the potential of synergies between FPs and ESIFs. In this sense, the Seal of Excellence, launched in 2015, stands out as an example of synergies. It awards the projects submitted to the SME instrument of H2020 that deserve funding depending on selection criteria, but did not receive funding due to limited budget. This seal recognises the value of the proposal, supporting the search for alternative funding. Another example is the Stairway to Excellence, launched in 2014 as a pilot project to support regions and countries in implementing the S3, as well as developing and exploiting synergies between H2020 and ESIFs. The stairway was renewed and will be an important feature of the cohesion policy in the next pro-gramming period 2021–2027. Moreover, the complementarity between the FP and the Cohesion Fund should be improved (Reillon, 2017; European Commission, 2018a, 2018b; Pontikakis et al., 2018).

The next Horizon Europe will provide special support for MS lagging behind in research and innovation efforts. Moreover, it will attempt to leverage synergies with ESIFs and other European programmes, such as cohesion policy, and industrial and sectorial policies (Corpakis, 2016; De Carli, 2017; European Commission, 2017a, 2017b; Foray et al., 2018a, 2018b). In this sense, the EU Industrial Policy Strategy, launched in 2017, aims at improving business conditions for private innovation investment. Despite their positive effects, these synergies present some risks, such as the predominance of the excellence research goal versus cohesion and regional development (Corpakis, 2016; European Commission, 2017a; Foray et al., 2018a, 2018b).

4.2   The Smart Specialisation Strategies

The concept of SS is rooted in a report commissioned by the DG RTD to the Knowledge for Growth Expert Group in 2005, in the context of relaunching the Lisbon Strategy. This notes "the capacity of an economic system (a region for example) to generate new specialities through the discovery of new domains of opportunity and the local concentration and agglomeration of resources and competences in these domains" (Foray, 2014, p. 1).

SS refers to structural changes in economic systems in different forms, while S3 deals with those actions and measures (policies) that promote this kind of process. S3 policy should involve productive and institu-tional stakeholders that, from a bottom-up perspective, identify and develop potential domains for SS that governments could support. S3 are committed to concentrate and prioritise resources on few initiatives.

SS was not originally a spatial concept; its initial interests were science, technology and innovation. However, it was swiftly translated into regional policy[7] (McCann, 2015; see this volume, Chapters 1 and 2), when the EC

DG for Regional and Urban Policy embraced it. Its rationale was used as an enabling principle for investing SFs more efficiently (Foray, 2014).

S3 rationale fitted with the EU cohesion policy due to two reasons: it provided a policy prioritisation framework aligned with the Europe 2020 Strategy; and it followed a place-based logic (see this volume, Chapters 1 and 2), like the cohesion policy. Therefore, SS became a key pillar for the EU cohesion policy in the programming period 2014–2020. The EC decided that the design and implementation of a regional innovation smart specialisation strategy (RIS3) would be an ex-ante conditionality to receive SFs in the period 2014–2020.

The SS approach has become the main link, theoretical and practical, between the EU innovation and regional policies. The EC policy-making experience was important for adopting the SS concept. As indicated above, different initiatives funded by SFs, such as RIS or RITTS, have been implemented since the 1990s, aiming at establishing and strengthening regional innovation systems. Therefore, these previous experiences created the right conditions for the adoption of the SS approach by the EC.

The adoption of S3 has come together with a change, at least rhetorically, in the rationale of the cohesion policy towards promoting competitiveness and the effectiveness of investments. Nevertheless, this shift has not implied the exclusion of cohesion perspective, as in practice the main beneficiaries of cohesion funds continue to be lagged regions.

5. CONCLUSIONS

The innovative capacity of the EU countries and regions is a main driver of their long-term welfare. Therefore, different policies aim at improving the innovation environment and capabilities.

Concerning the EU innovation policy, there is a multilevel model, showing an increasing role of regions. The EU innovation policy can be considered unique, because most innovation actions are directly implemented by the EC.

The EU innovation policy has been traditionally focused on research and supply side. However, innovation has acquired growing relevance, mainly within the Lisbon Strategy and the Innovation Union Flagship. In this sense, there is a shift from the linear model of innovation to a systemic approach. Moreover, the innovation policy is increasingly focused on social challenges and demand side.

The FPs are the main tool of the EU innovation policy, although there are other tools, such as the SFs, which have increased the focus on research and innovation. The innovation policy, and mainly FPs, have not considered the territorial dimension or the development level. The selection is competitive and based on scientific criteria.

The relationship between the EU regional and innovation policies is challenging, due to the combination of conflicting goals, such as competitiveness and cohesion. However, several attempts to balance these two goals have been made over time, including some cohesion element in the innovation policy, as shown in STRIDE, RIS, ESIFs and even through the FPs. Despite the efforts, the results are still limited.

Since the 2000s the regional EU policy, also known as cohesion policy, has gradually shifted its rationale, at least rhetorically, from regional compensation and solidarity towards enhancing development and competitiveness through innovation and investments profitability. The regional policy is now conceived as an innovation-driven policy; therefore, innovation and research has become one of the key priorities of the ERDF. In this scenario, SS has emerged as a theoretical and practical basis for the EU regional policy, and as the main link between the EU regional and innovation policies. It involves a bottom-up and place-based approach to regional and innovation policies. Moreover, there is a considerable potential for leveraging synergies between cohesion policy and innovation policy. In fact, the EC proposes the coordination of funds (FPs, ESIFs and CFs), and also among different policies, including industrial policies. However, the existing synergies are not enough, and they face challenges. For example, they could involve risks to regional development, if they focus on excellence and competitiveness.

NOTES

1. Countries that are not EU Member States can benefit from the FPs, whether they contribute to fund them or they participate in them (but usually these countries do not receive funds if they do not fund the FPs).
2. These are mainly the European Regional Development Fund (ERDF), but also the European Social Fund (ESF), the Cohesion Fund (CF), the European Agricultural Fund for Rural Development (EAFRD), and the European Maritime and Fisheries Fund (EMFF).
3. The political leaders of ten European industrial regions gathered in November 2013 in Brussels to engage in a joint effort for the industrial future of Europe. New regions have been included in this initiative, accounting for 35 regions in July 2019. The political goal is to recognise the important role played by regions in promoting new industry-based growth.
4. The five pilot projects implemented are focused on advanced manufacturing for energy applications in harsh environments, bioeconomy, efficient and sustainable manufacturing, high performance production through 3D printing, and new nano-enabled products.
5. This initiative was named Regional Technology Plans in the first period 1994–1996. Afterwards, it was renamed Regional Innovation Strategies and aimed at encouraging regions to adopt a broad definition of innovation.
6. In this context, it is worth considering the contributions of the Welsh Development

Agency in the discussions about Regional Technology Strategies launched by the Directorate-General for Regional Policies in a workshop held in Brussels in June 1991, and of the Welsh academics Cooke and Morgan (Cooke and Morgan 1994; see also Landabaso and Reid, 1999).
7. When translating the logic of SS into spatial and economic geography terms, McCann (2015, pp. 174–5) indicates that it refers to concepts coming mainly from evolutionary economic geography, like relatedness, embeddedness and connectivity.

REFERENCES

Andrée, D. (2009). *Priority-setting in the European Research Framework Programme.* Stockholm: Vinnova.

Arrow, K. (1962). Economic welfare and the allocation of resources for innovation. In R. Nelson (ed.), *The Rate and Direction of Inventive Activity: Economic and Social Factors* (pp. 609–25). Princeton, NJ: Princeton University Press.

Asheim, B.T., and Isaksen, A. (2002). Regional Innovation Systems: The integration of local "sticky" and global ubiquitous knowledge. *Journal of Technology Transfer*, 27, 77–86.

Baier, E., Kroll, H., and Zenker, A. (2013). *Regional autonomy with regard to innovation policy: A differentiated illustration of the European status quo.* Working Paper Firms and Region Nr. R3/2013. Karlsruhe: Fraunhofer ISI.

Barca, F. (2009). *An agenda for a reformed cohesion policy: A place-based approach to meeting European Union challenges and expectations.* Independent Report prepared at the request of Danuta Hübner, Commissioner for Regional Policy. Brussels: European Commission.

Begg, I. (2008). Structural policy and economic convergence. *CESifo Forum*, 9(1), 3–9.

Boldrin, L., and Canova, F. (2001). Inequality and convergence in Europe's regions: Reconsidering European regional policies. *Economic Policy*, 16, 207–53.

Borrás, S. (2003). *The Innovation Policy of the EU.* Cheltenham, UK and Northampton, MA, USA: Edward Elgar Publishing.

Commission of the European Communities. (1988). *Communication from the Commission, "First report on the state of science and technology in Europe"* [COM (88) 647].

Commission of the European Communities. (1989). *Communication from the Commission, "A framework for Community RTD actions in the 90's"* [SEC (89) 675 final].

Commission of the European Communities. (1994). *The European report on science and technology indicators 1994* (ERSTI). Brussels: European Commission.

Cooke, P., and Morgan, K. (1994). The creative milieu: A regional perspective on innovation. In M. Dodgson and R. Rothwell (eds), *The Handbook of Industrial Innovation* (pp. 25–32). Aldershot, UK and Brookfield, VT, USA: Edward Elgar Publishing.

Cornett, A.P., and Sørensen, N.K. (2008). International vs. intra-national convergence in Europe: An assessment of causes and evidence. *Investigaciones Regionales*, 13, 35–53.

Corpakis, D. (2016). *Fostering synergies between Horizon 2020 and Cohesion policy.* 6th Meeting of Horizon 2020 National Contact Points for Legal and

Financial Matters, Brussels, 16 March. At https://www.kpk.gov.pl/wp-content/uploads/2016/07/synergie-2016-03-17.pdf (accessed on 19 November 2019).

Dasgupta, P., and Stoneman, P. (1987). *Economic Policy and Technological Performance*. Cambridge: Cambridge University Press.

De Brujin, P., and Lagendijk, A. (2005). Regional Innovation Systems in the Lisbon Strategy. *European Planning Studies*, 13(8), 1153–72.

De Carli, M. (2017). *SEWP and Seal of Excellence: Fostering synergies*. Workshop, Aligning implementation of RIS3 and H2020 Funding across research priorities.

Edquist, C. (2004). Systems of innovation: Perspectives and challenges. In J. Fagerberg, D. Mowery, R. Nelson, J. Fagerberg, D. Mowery and R. Nelson (eds), *Oxford Handbook of Innovation* (pp. 181–208). Oxford: Oxford University Press.

EUR-Lex. (2019). Access to the European Union Law. At https://eur-lex.europa.eu/homepage.html?locale=en (accessed on 19 November 2019).

European Commission. (1993). *Communication from the Commission to the Council and the European Parliament, "Cohesion and RTD Policy: Synergies between research and technological development policy and economic and social cohesion policy"* [COM (1993) 203 final].

European Commission. (1995). *Green paper on innovation*. Brussels: European Commission.

European Commission. (1996). *First Action Plan for Innovation in Europe*. Brussels: European Commission.

European Commission. (1997). *Guide to Regional Innovation Strategies*. Luxembourg: European Commission.

European Commission. (2008). *Communication from the Commission to the European Parliament, the Council, the European Economic and Social Committee and the Committee of the Regions, "Towards Joint Programming in Research: Working together to tackle common challenges more effectively"* [COM (2008) 468 final].

European Commission. (2010). *Communication from the Commission to the European Parliament, the Council, the European Economic and Social Committee and the Committee of the Regions, "Regional Policy contributing to smart growth in Europe 2020"* [COM (2010) 553 final].

European Commission. (2013). *Innovation Union: A pocket guide on a Europe 2020 initiative*. Luxembourg: Publications Office of the European Union.

European Commission. (2014a). *Investment for jobs and growth: Promoting development and good governance in EU regions and cities. Sixth report on economic, social and territorial cohesion*. Luxembourg: Publications Office of the European Union.

European Commission. (2014b). *Mobilising regions for growth and jobs: Regions of Knowledge and Research Potential*. Luxembourg: Publications Office of the European Union.

European Commission. (2016). *The EU explained: Research and innovation*. Luxembourg: Publications Office of the European Union.

European Commission. (2017a). *LAB – FAB – APP Investing in the European future we want*. Report of the independent High Level Group on maximising the impact of EU Research & Innovation Programmes (Lamy Report). Brussels: European Commission.

European Commission. (2017b). *Synergies between Framework Programmes for Research and Innovation and European Structural and Investment Funds contributing to the Interim Evaluation of Horizon 2020*. Luxembourg: Publications Office of the European Union.

European Commission. (2018a). *Communication from the Commission to the European Parliament, the Council, the European Economic and Social Committee and the Committee of the Regions "Horizon 2020 interim evaluation: maximising the impact of EU research and innovation"* [COM (2018) 2 final].

European Commission. (2018b). *Communication from the Commission to the European Parliament, the European Council, the Council, the European Economic and Social Committee and the Committee of the Regions, "A renewed European Agenda for Research and Innovation: Europe's chance to shape its future"*. The European Commission's contribution to the Informal EU Leaders' meeting on innovation in Sofia, 16 May [COM (2018) 306 final].

Fagerberg, J. (2017). Innovation policy: Rationales, lessons and challenges. *Journal of Economic Surveys*, 31(2), 497–512.

Fernández, I., Castro, E., and Zabala, M. (2007). Estrategias regionales de innovación: el caso de regiones europeas periféricas. In X. Vence (ed.), *Crecimiento y políticas de innovación. Nuevas tendencias y experiencias comparadas* (pp. 157–89). Madrid: Pirámide.

Fernández, I., Mas-Verdu, F., and Tortosa, E. (2010). Regional innovation policies: The persistence of the linear model in Spain. *The Service Industries Journal*, 30(5), 749–62.

Foray, D. (2009). *The New Economics of Technology Policy*. Cheltenham, UK and Northampton, MA, USA: Edward Elgar Publishing.

Foray, D. (2014). *Smart Specialisation: Opportunities and Challenges for Regional Innovation Policy*. New York, NY: Routledge.

Foray, D., Morgan, K., and Radosevic, S. (2018a). *From rivalry to synergy: R&I policy and cohesion policy*. Policy Paper (Regional and Urban Policy), European Commission.

Foray, D., Morgan, K., and Radosevic, S. (2018b). *The role of smart specialization in the EU research and innovation policy landscape*. DG Regio Working Paper, European Union.

Gertler, M. (2001). Best practice? Geography, learning and the institutional limits to strong convergence. *Journal of Economic Geography*, 1(1), 5–26.

Guzzetti, L. (1995). *A Brief History of European Union Research Policy*. Brussels: European Commission.

Hudson, R. (2007). Regions and regional uneven development forever? Some reflective comments upon theory and practice. *Regional Studies*, 41(9), 1149–60.

Kaiser, R., and Prange, H. (2004). Managing diversity in a system of multi-level governance: The open method of co-ordination in innovation policy. *Journal of European Public Policy*, 11, 249–66.

Kok, W. (2004). *The High Level Group on Lisbon Strategy: Facing the challenge*. Luxembourg: European Communities.

Landabaso, M. (2000). Las nuevas políticas regionales de promoción de la innovación en la Unión Europea. *Economía Industrial*, 335–6, 51–66.

Landabaso, M., and Reid, A. (1999). Developing regional innovation strategies: The European Commission as animateur. In K. Morgan and C. Nauwelaers (eds), *Regional Innovation Strategies: The Challenge for Less Favoured Regions* (pp. 18–38). London: The Stationery Office.

Lundvall, B.Å. (ed.) (1992). *National Systems of Innovation: Towards a Theory of Innovation and Interactive Learning*. London: Pinter.

Lundvall, B., and Borrás, S. (2005). Science, technology and innovation policy. In

J. Fagerberg, D. Mowery, R. Nelson, J. Fagerberg, D. Mowery and R. Nelson (eds), *Innovation Handbook* (pp. 599–631). Oxford: Oxford University Press.

Maskell, P., and Malmberg, A. (1999). Localised learning and industrial competitiveness. *Cambridge Journal of Economics*, 23, 167–85.

Mazzucato, M. (2018). *Mission-oriented Research and Innovation in the European Union: A Problem-solving Approach to Fuel Innovation-led Growth.* Brussels: European Commission.

McCann, P. (2015). *The Regional and Urban Policy of the European Union: Cohesion, Results-orientation and Smart Specialisation.* Cheltenham, UK and Northampton, MA, USA: Edward Elgar Publishing.

Morgan, K., and Nauwelaers, C. (eds) (2003). *Regional Innovation Strategies: The Challenge for Less-favoured Regions.* London: Routledge.

OECD (2011). *Regions and Innovation Policy*, OECD Reviews of Regional Innovation. Paris: OECD.

Pontikakis, D., Doussineau, M., Harrap, N., and Boden, M. (2018). *Mobilising European Structural and Investment Funds and Horizon 2020 in support of innovation in less developed regions.* Seville: Joint Research Centre (JRC) Technical Reports, European Commission.

Reid, A. (2007). Innovation and regional development: Do European structural funds make a difference? *European Planning Studies*, 15(7), 961–83.

Reillon, V. (2015). *Overview of EU funds for research and innovation*, EPRS Briefings, 22 September. Brussels: EPRS (European Parliamentary Research Service).

Reillon, V. (2016). *EU innovation policy. Part I: Building up the EU innovation policy mix.* Brussels: EPRS (European Parliamentary Research Service).

Reillon, V. (2017). *EU framework programmes for research and innovation: Evolution and key data from FP1 to Horizon 2020 in view of FP9.* Brussels: EPRS (European Parliamentary Research Service).

Rodil, Ó. (2007). Innovación y competitividad en la Unión Europea: las nuevas políticas europeas en el período 2007–2013. In X. Vence (ed.), *Crecimiento y políticas de innovación. Nuevas tendencias y experiencias comparadas* (pp. 101–24). Madrid: Pirámide.

Rodil, Ó., Vence, X., and Sánchez, M.C. (2014). Disparidades en la Eurozona: el debate de la convergencia regional a la luz de las asimetrías en la estructura productiva. *Ekonomiaz: Revista Vasca de Economía*, 86, 274–305.

Rodríguez-Pose, A., and Novak, K. (2013). Learning processes and economic returns in European Cohesion policy. *Investigaciones Regionales*, 25, 7–26.

Rossi, F. (2005). *Innovation policy in the European Union: Instruments and objectives*, Munich Personal Research Archive Paper 2009. At https://mpra.ub.uni-muenchen.de/2009/ (accessed on 19 November 2019).

Rothwell, R. (1983). The difficulties of national innovation policies. In S. Macdonald, T. Mandeville and D. Lamberton (eds), *The Trouble with Technology* (pp. 202–15). London: Frances Pinter.

Rutten, R. (2016). Beyond proximities: The socio-spatial dynamics of knowledge creation. *Progress in Human Geography*, 41(2), 159–77.

SOCINTEC. (2005). *Ex-post evaluation of the RIS, RTTs and RISI ERDF Innovative Actions for the period 1994–1999. Final Synthesis Report.* At https://ec.europa.eu/regional_policy/sources/docgener/evaluation/doc/innoact/finalreport_post_erdf_94_99_en.pdf (accessed on 19 November 2019).

Tödtling, F., and Trippl, M. (2005). One size fits all? Towards a differentiated regional innovation policy approach. *Research Policy*, 34(8), 1203–19.

Uyarra, E., Koschatzky, K., and Héraud, J.A. (2007). *Understanding the multi-level, multi-actor governance of regions for developing new policy designs.* Position paper of the ERA-Spaces/ERISP projects prepared for the PRIME Annual Conference, Pisa, 29 January to 1 February. Manchester: PREST, University of Manchester.

Vanguard Initiative. (2014–2017). *Vanguard Initiative Annual Report.* Vanguard Initiative. At https://www.s3vanguardinitiative.eu/documents (accessed on 14 August 2019).

Vence, X. (1998). *La política tecnológica comunitaria y la cohesión regional. Los retos de los sistemas de innovación periféricos.* Madrid: Civitas.

Vence, X. (2007). Crecimiento económico, cambio estructural y economía basada en el conocimiento. In X. Vence (ed.), *Crecimiento y políticas de innovación. Nuevas tendencias y experiencias comparadas* (pp. 19–58). Madrid: Pirámide.

Vence, X., and Rodil, O. (2003). La concentración regional de la política de I+D de la Unión Europea. *Revista de Estudios Regionales,* 65, 43–73.

Vence, X., Guntín, X., and Rodil, O. (2000). Determinants of the uneven regional participation of firms in European technology Programmes. *European Planning Studies,* 8(1), 29–41.

Zabala-Iturriagagoitia, J.M., Jiménez-Sáez, F., and Castro-Martínez, E. (2008). Evaluating European Regional Innovation Strategies. *European Planning Studies,* 16(8), 1145–60.

7. Regional Innovation Systems and regional disparities in the Euro area: insights for regional innovation policy

Óscar Rodil-Marzábal and Xavier Vence-Deza

1. INTRODUCTION

The European Union (EU) currently faces critical issues. The response to economic crisis has led in recent years to remarkable changes in the European economic and policy landscape. The uneven impact of financial crisis and the subsequent austerity strategy were followed by a new economic divide, with diverging outcomes and a failure of traditionally precarious discourse on European cohesion. The process of Brexit is the paramount example of these issues. The future of the EU requires, more than ever before, a strengthening of the aim of regional convergence in order to comply with the foundational principle of regional cohesion and to render more socially attractive the integration process. Within the EU framework, the Economic and Monetary Union (EMU) area constitutes a deeper integration process, which makes the analysis more meaningful. Dealing with regional disparities in the EMU area provides a way to assess whether deeper integration (e.g., monetary union, financial harmonization) has shown real capacity to promote territorial cohesion and moderate regional inequalities. The present chapter focuses more specifically on the role of innovative capacity in the relative growth performance of different EMU regions, in an attempt to identify the relevance of different components of the Regional Innovation System (RIS) in the relative evolution.

This chapter analyses the growth patterns of the EMU regions (data at NUTS-2 level), considering differences regarding innovation and its effects on economic growth. The analysed period is 2000–2017 and the sample includes the regions of the 12 member states that have shared the monetary union practically since its creation (EMU-12). To perform this empirical analysis, we make use of the Eurostat REGIO database (economy dimension) and the Regional Innovation Scoreboard (innovation dimension).

The remainder of this chapter is organized as follows. Section 2 gives an overview of the debate concerning regional disparities in Europe. The third section presents trends of regional growth disparities within the EMU area for the period 2000–2017. Section 4 introduces the theoretical framework, paying special attention to the role of innovation from a systemic perspective. Next, in section 5, we seek to explain regional disparities by reference to the role of innovation. Finally, section 6 sets out our conclusions.

2. FACTS AND TRENDS OF THE REGIONAL GROWTH IN EUROPE: AN OVERVIEW OF THE DEBATE ON REGIONAL DISPARITIES

Despite the relatively large number of studies on regional disparities in Europe, there is no consensus when assessing the real trends. Depending on methodology, the period and the sample, the literature shows various results. On the one hand, some papers find evidence of convergence between the European regions (Barro and Sala-i-Martin, 1991; Sala-i-Martin, 1994; López-Bazo, 2003; Villaverde, 2003). On the other hand, there is evidence of divergence and/or mixed outcomes (Dunford, 1993; Suárez-Villa and Cuadrado-Roura, 1993; Armstrong, 1995; Dewhurst and Mutis-Gaitan, 1995; Neven and Gouyette, 1995; Fagerberg and Verspagen, 1996; Cuadrado-Roura, 2001; Martin, 2001; Cuadrado-Roura et al., 2002; Vence and Rodil, 2003b; Basile et al., 2001; Vence, 2014). These results are consistent with Armstrong (2002), who observed, first, the greatest convergence in the 1950s and especially in the 1960s; second, a considerable divergence in the late 1970s and early 1980s; and third, a slow process of convergence in the 1990s, although the regional disparities increased in the early 1990s (due to recession).

A recent paper on the long-term disparity trends from 1900 to 2010 (Rosés and Wolf, 2018) shows clear evidence of two broad periods: a large period of diminishing disparities from 1900 to 1980 and a period of increasing disparities from 1980 onwards. The authors constructed a data set containing information on population, employment (and sector distribution) and gross domestic product (GDP) at purchasing power parity for 173 regions covering 16 European nation states at the level of NUTS-2 (as of 2014) between 1900 and 2010. The results are pretty clear: there is a general trend of disparity reduction over the twentieth century, from 1900 until 1980, with a special period of convergence after 1945, and a divergence trend from about 1980 onwards, reinforced by a geographical re-concentration of economic activity.

The evolution of disparities is the result of uneven economic growth both between countries and within countries. The historical fluctuation in regional disparities is hard to match with the neoclassical hypothesis of linear trend to convergence in the long term. The uneven impact of major crisis, cyclical fluctuations, sector specialization, diffusion of new technologies, innovation capabilities and adaptability to external shocks, integration process, neoliberal policies and global change are all potential explanatory factors for this changing path in regional disparities (see, e.g., Grjebine et al., 2019; Bachtler et al., 2019). In this chapter, we focus on the diverse features of RISs.

3.   RECENT TRENDS OF REGIONAL GROWTH IN THE EMU

The present chapter focuses on the last two decades, from the introduction of the euro to the present. The study is conducted for the NUTS-2 regions of the EMU area. As well known, the NUTS-2 classification largely corresponds to the concept of region and to most of the existing political–administrative subdivisions. In this sense, the 12 member states of EMU-12 are subdivided, at NUTS-2 level, into a total of 165 regions.

An overview of economic growth in the total EMU (EMU-19) since the turn of the millennium shows a clear downward trend (Figure 7.1). In fact, most of the years of highest growth (≥ 2 per cent of annual variation) are concentrated in the period 1998–2007, while only one year (2017) of the subsequent period (2008–2018) shows an annual variation of real GDP per capita above 2 per cent, and two other years (2009, 2012) even have negative growth rates. These results confirm that the EMU has not yet reached its pre-crisis growth rates.

This evolution depicts a European economic cycle shared by all the EMU (EMU-19) countries (Figure 7.1), but especially by the 12 countries (EMU-12) that have been involved in the process since practically its beginning. This group of 12 countries shows a tighter profile, although there are some outlying cases such as Ireland and Greece (Figure 7.2).

Concerning the evolution of regional disparities, we make use of two well-known statistical tests: β-convergence and σ-convergence (popularized by Barro and Sala-i-Martin, 1991, and Sala-i-Martin, 1994). The meaning of σ-convergence is very intuitive: lower levels of dispersion (σ) means lower disparities, and the reverse. In this sense, between the years 2000 and 2017 (Figure 7.3), the increase of the dispersion of levels of

Source: Own calculation based on Eurostat database.

Figure 7.1   Real growth of GDP per capita (euros) in the EMU, 1998–
              2018 (percentage change on previous year)

regional income (GDP per capita in logarithms) draws increasing regional
disparities across the 165 regions of EMU-12 and could be viewed as an
overall trend towards divergence. However, as we can observe, it includes
two clearly opposite trends with a turning point around the year 2009.

   This empirical finding leads to an interesting distinction between
two sub-periods that show a different evolution of regional disparities:
2000–2009 (σ-convergence) and 2009–2017 (σ-divergence). Considering
this difference, the β-convergence test contributes to add a complementary
perspective in the analysis. In this sense, this second technique of analysis
shows a relationship of positive sign between the starting point of income
(GDP per capita in 2000) and the growth rate of income between the
beginning and the end of the overall period (2000–2017); in other words,
there is evidence of a slow process of β-convergence (Figure 7.4). However,
the sign of this relationship becomes positive for β-divergence between
2009 and 2017 (Figure 7.5).

   This set of empirical evidence highlights the importance of both the
different geography of integration and development within the EMU,
as well as the deep impact of the financial crisis of 2008 and the uneven
regional resilience to such a shock as revealed through analysis of regional

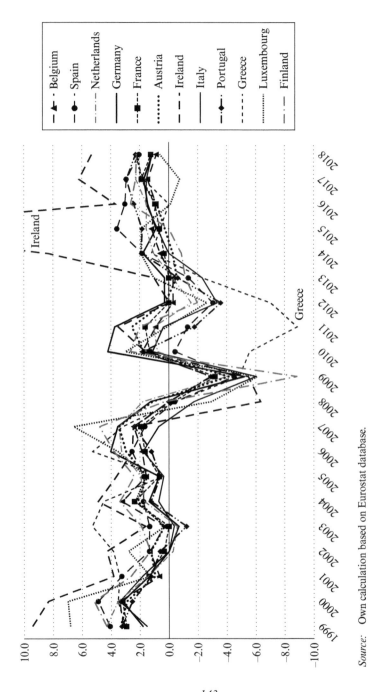

Source: Own calculation based on Eurostat database.

Figure 7.2   Real growth of GDP per capita (euros) in the EMU-12, 1998–2018 (percentage change on previous year)

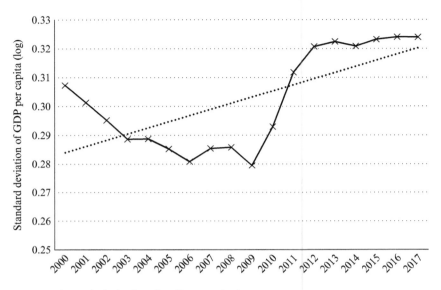

Source: Own calculation based on Eurostat database.

*Figure 7.3   σ-convergence test, EMU-12, NUTS-2 regions, 2000–2017
          (standard deviation of GDP per capita, in pps and logs)*

disparities. This differentiation allows for a more accurate analysis that
considers the existence of different speeds of integration within the EMU,
both in development and in the integration process, due to the particular moment of accession to the EU and the structural characteristics
(structural and productive specialization, diversity in financialization and
socioeconomic models, current account imbalances, European structural
funding, foreign direct investment relocation, etc.). In fact, two recent
contributions highlight the importance of sectoral and macroeconomic
aspects. First, Grjebine et al. (2019) show that not only sectoral reallocations are key drivers of productive divergence in Europe; the financial
dimension also plays a crucial role in the explanation of the lack of real
convergence in the EU (mainly through the combination of shocks from
financial sectors and the financial accelerator mechanism). The authors'
conclusions are in the same vein as those offered within other contributions on this topic (see, e.g., Vence et al., 2013, and Rodil et al., 2014).
Second, Crescenzi et al. (2016) discuss the pre-crisis macroeconomic conditions as explanatory factors for the resilience of regions and the post-2008
economic performance. They emphasize that current account surplus and
high public debt are relevant at the country level; at the regional level, they

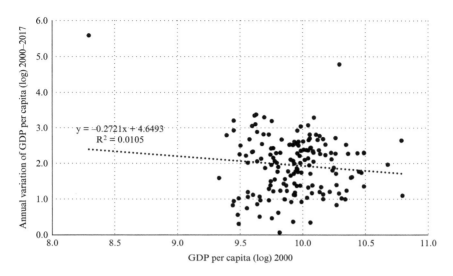

Source: Own calculation based on Eurostat database.

Figure 7.4 β-*convergence test, EMU-12, NUTS-2 regions, 2000–2017 (GDP per capita, in pps and logs)*

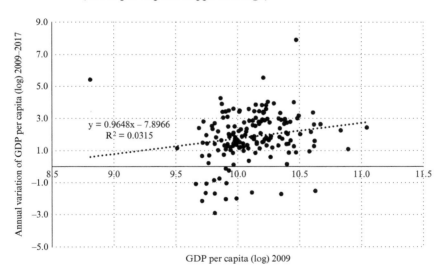

Source: Own calculation based on Eurostat database.

Figure 7.5 β-*convergence test, EMU-12, NUTS-2 regions, 2009–2017 (GDP per capita, in pps and logs)*

suggest that neither specialization patterns nor research and development (R&D) intensity comprises a reasonable explanatory factor for economic performance in the post-crisis period. Conversely, human capital and the capability of the regions to identify short-term innovative solutions to a changing external environment seem to be the main drivers of short-term resistance and economic growth: "this capacity does not necessarily derive from technology-driven processes supported by R&D investments but is more likely to be boosted by a skilled labour force that enhances rapid process and organizational innovation" (Crescenzi et al., 2016, p. 28). The next section discusses this topic as pertinent to the post-crisis period in the EMU-12.

4.   THE ROLE OF INNOVATION IN REGIONAL DISPARITIES FROM A SYSTEMIC PERSPECTIVE

To what extent is innovation crucial for growth and, consequently, does it matter for regional disparities? More specifically, what kind of innovative factor is more relevant? What feature of innovation? R&D? Non-R&D? Human resources?

The answers to these questions are crucial for understanding the role that innovation policy can play in reducing the disparities among the EMU regions.

There are two main reasons for focusing on the regions of EMU-12 when dealing with the interaction between innovation and growth. The first one is that these regions share a long integration process and thus they have the same currency and an increasingly homogeneous institutional framework, with strategic goals (external global competitiveness, economic stability) that may affect other specific objectives such as regional cohesion. The second reason for this empirical focus is that, despite the institutional homogeneity of the EMU, this territory is internally non-uniform. In fact, strong specificities and cumulative effects can affect its regions, leading to increasing disparities.

The underlying hypothesis is that innovative capabilities comprise a crucial driver in long-term economic growth. The Marx and Schumpeter approaches have emphasized the role of innovation as a major source of economic development (Nelson, 1996; Vence, 1995). Today, a vast array of contributions concerning evolution clearly supports these views (see, e.g., Freeman, 1987; Nelson, 1996; Fagerberg, 2018). Therefore, behind the regional differences in growth, it is very likely that there will also be differences in factors such as knowledge, technology and innovation performance (Vence, 1996; Metcalfe, 1996; Gaffard and Quéré, 1996;

Cooke et al., 2000; Cooke et al., 2011; Soete, 2011; Asheim et al., 2019). Moreover, both regional and local levels provide very interesting perspectives for analysis since these are levels where technological and innovation processes arise (OECD, 2007; Doloreux and Parto, 2004; Asheim et al., 2019).

Beyond the consideration of some individual factors and linear relationships, the role of innovation in the regional growth is built on a dynamic process of interactive and complex relationships between diverse actors. The concept of RIS tries to capture this complex and interactive process. An RIS can be defined as a structure at regional level composed of actors (organizations and institutions) and the relationships between them (Asheim et al., 2013; Asheim et al., 2019) that contributes to developing, diffusing and using innovations. Inspired by the concept of system of innovation (Freeman, 1987; Lundvall, 1992; Patel and Pavitt, 1994; Edquist, 2005), the RIS is based on the idea that innovations do not emerge in isolation but in an interactive learning process where localized learning processes are stimulated by geographical, social and cultural proximity (Cooke, 2001; Asheim et al., 2019). In this sense, many innovations usually take place in a context of a wide range of multilevel interactions but particularly intense at local–regional level, where some actors (e.g., firms) collaborate with others (e.g., organizations, consultancy, government research institutes or universities, etc.). In fact, these interactions among actors are the most relevant aspect for understanding the influence of the RIS on capital accumulation, technological progress and economic growth (Crescenzi and Rodríguez-Pose, 2009).

Considering that RIS is the core element underlying innovative behaviour of firms and a driver of economic development, study of the former becomes crucial for comprehending the evolution of regional disparities. The increasing availability of empirical data has allowed a flourishing literature focusing on RIS from different and complementary approaches (academic studies and policy reports) (see, e.g., Doloreux and Porto Gomez, 2017; Asheim et al., 2019). In short, from a descriptive point of view, this literature finds important and growing disparities in innovative capacities and performances among the European regions.

The literature on the RIS has been criticized for both the absence of accuracy and clarity in its statements and empirical findings (Edquist, 2005; Doloreux and Parto, 2004), and for not paying enough attention to failed cases (European Commission, 2014). In addition, the fact that the regional and national levels interact and are linked both with each other and with other territories – regions, countries or even at the supranational level (Tödtling and Trippl, 2005; Asheim and Gertler, 2006) – renders the RIS more complex and imprecise at the time of theorizing. Nevertheless, different growth patterns seem to persist in regions with similar innovation capacities (Kourtit et al., 2011; Asheim and Gertler, 2006; European Commission, 2014; Asheim et al., 2019). Diverse characteristics of regions concerning social capital, collaborative networks and knowledge sharing, share of industry in GDP and enterprise characteristics, are crucial for explaining regional differences within some key innovation indicators (e.g., business R&D expenditures, innovative enterprises, patent applications, etc.) (European Commission, 2017).

Finally, the role of certain EU policies (cohesion, R&D, etc.) is another important aspect in the multilevel framework of the RIS, as policies can affect the actors' performance and interactions between them. Several works have analysed the regional effects of some specific policies aimed at developing technological capabilities such as the R&D European Framework Programmes (Boldrin and Canova, 2001; Vence and Rodil, 2003a; Hudson, 2007; Reid, 2007; Esposti and Bussoletti, 2008). This policy tool was initially created to strengthen the EU competitiveness regarding the major global players (e.g., the USA and Japan), but it does not seem to have contributed to reducing pre-existing regional disparities, as the authors of the early approaches found. In this sense, there is a debate on the role played by European strategies devoted to the development of innovative capacities in regional disparities. Although these strategies can positively affect the EU competitiveness, they may not contribute to cohesion and reduction of regional disparities (Begg, 2008; Cornett and Sørensen, 2008; Rodríguez-Pose and Novak, 2013). A different assessment could be performed when dealing with common guidelines for regional innovation strategies such as Smart Specialisation Strategies developed in the 2014–2020 period (Foray, 2015; McCann and Ortega-Orgilés, 2015). Anyway, even in this case, the emphasis in reinforcing specialization as a common goal could be harmful for a long-term development strategy in very disruptive times (Cooke, 2012). In the end, one-size-fits-all policies are never the solution.

Data

To assess the performance of RIS, we make use of the statistical tool provided by the Regional Innovation Scoreboard. Following the same logic as the European Innovation Scoreboard (EIS),[1] although focusing on the role of small and medium-sized enterprises (SMEs), the Regional Innovation Scoreboard tries to cover the lack of innovation data at regional level using a systemic approach. The fact that there is a strong and positive association between regional innovation performance and regional competitiveness – the latter approached via the Regional Competitiveness Index (European

Commission) – seems to be a good indication of the systemic atmosphere that involves these processes.

The Regional Innovation Scoreboard 2017 uses data for 18 of the 27 indicators used in the EIS 2017, and it employs a composite indicator – the Regional Innovation Index (RII) – to summarize and measure the regional innovation performance. Compared with previous editions (e.g., 2016), the 2017 edition has increased the number of indicators, including regional indicators such as lifelong learning, international scientific co-publications, most-cited publications, public–private co-publications, trademark applications, and design applications. It is important to note that the Regional Innovation Scoreboard mainly adopts a linear approach in the study of the RIS and thus it focuses on its structure by distinguishing aspects such as inputs, throughputs and outputs (European Commission, 2017).

The Regional Innovation Scoreboard classifies regions into four innovation performance groups: Innovation Leaders (53 regions), Strong Innovators (60 regions), Moderate Innovators (85 regions) and Modest Innovators (22 regions). This classification receives a more detailed and precise sorting by differentiating an upper (+), middle and lowest (−) one-third within each group. Therefore, there are finally 12 sub-groups of regions within this fine-tune classification: from the least innovative regions (Modest Innovators −) to the most innovative ones (Innovation Leaders +). This sub-classification provides a more accurate view of the regional heterogeneity within EU, since many countries have most of their regions included in only one or two performance groups, but at the same time in four or more different sub-groups.

Compared with previous editions, the Regional Innovation Scoreboard 2017 shows a general improvement of innovation performance in most regions, mainly in regional Innovation Leaders and regional Strong Innovators and Moderate Innovators. However, a process of regional divergence in innovation performance is observed over time, with most performance reductions in geographically peripheral EU regions (European Commission, 2017).

5. THE ROLE OF INNOVATION IN REGIONAL ECONOMIC GROWTH: AN EMPIRICAL ASSESSMENT OF THE EMU CASE

According to the literature review, the evolution of regional disparities can be explained by factors such as the physical and human capital formation, the structural change towards high productivity activities, and a broad group of variables concerning innovation, among others. The

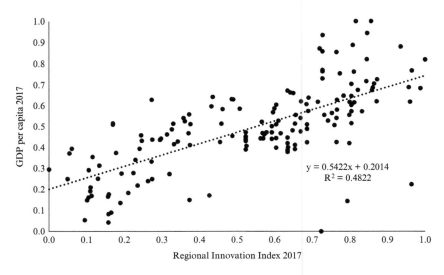

Source: Own calculation based on Eurostat database and Regional Innovation Scoreboard, 2017.

Figure 7.6   *Innovation performance (RII) versus income level (GDP per capita), EMU-12, NUTS-2 regions; rescaled positions (0–1), 2017*

RII summarizes the innovation performance of regions from a systemic perspective and it is highly associated with their income level (Figure 7.6).

The association between the innovation performance and the income level of regions can also be observed from a dynamic viewpoint, especially in the period from 2009 to 2017. This becomes clear when the distorting effect of the factors underlying the growth of the previous stage (credit and real estate bubbles) has stopped operating. In this sense, Figure 7.7 shows a positive relationship between the innovation performance, proxied by the simple average of RII for the years 2007, 2009 and 2011, and the regional growth of income per capita, proxied by the annual variation of GDP per capita in 2009–2017.

A deeper and more finely tuned analysis of the regional innovation performance requires considering separately the different indicators that serve to calculate the RII. These indicators allow us to approach different dimensions of the regional innovation performance, providing a picture of the systemic process of innovation. In this respect, Table 7.1 includes the Pearson correlation coefficients between several regional innovation indicators (simple average for the years 2007, 2009 and 2011) and the current level (2017) and growth (2009–2017) of regional income per capita.

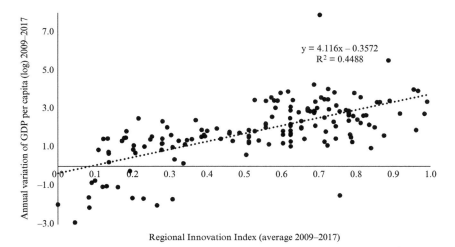

Source: Own calculation based on Eurostat database and Regional Innovation
Scoreboard, 2009–2017.

Figure 7.7   *Innovation performance (RII, average 2007–2011) versus*
                income growth (GDP per capita), EMU-12, NUTS-2 regions,
                2009–2017

As Table 7.1 shows, there is a positive statistical association between all the
regional innovation indicators (innovation performance) and the income
variables (economic performance), especially with regard to indicators that
stress the role of firms (business R&D expenditures; SMEs innovating in
house; patents; technological innovators; employment in medium-high/
high-tech activities, etc.) and also regarding interaction between agents
within the RIS. These findings are in line, first, with the role played by
firms as key actors in the process of knowledge creation and especially in
the implementation and economic valorization of innovations and, second,
with the role of linkages between agents (public–private collaboration,
firms collaborating with others) from a systemic approach.

Based on this preliminary evidence (statistical association), an econometric analysis is used to estimate the effect of the regional innovation performance on growth rates of income. This econometric approach enables a
deeper understanding of this relationship. Moreover, this analysis could be
useful for the assessment and design of regional innovation policy.

Beyond the obvious multicollinearity that exists when trying to combine
different innovation indicators, there are models that show the importance
of the articulation of the RIS measured by variables of collaboration
between agents. To address the methodological issue of multicollinearity,

Table 7.1 *Pearson correlation coefficients between the regional innovation indicators and the regional level and growth of income per capita, EMU-12, NUTS-2 regions*

Regional Innovation Indicator (simple average 2007, 2009, 2011)	GDP per capita 2017	Variation of GDP per capita 2009–2017
Population with tertiary education	0.436**	0.192*
Public R&D expenditures	0.286**	0.251*
Business R&D expenditures	0.585**	0.666**
Non-R&D innovation expenditures	0.300**	0.533**
SMEs innovating in house	0.533**	0.586**
Innovative SMEs collaborating with others	0.477**	0.417**
Public–private co-publications	0.641**	0.468**
European Patent Office patents	0.625**	0.641**
Technological (product or process) innovators	0.566**	0.575**
Non-technological (marketing or organizational) innovators	0.481**	0.591**
Employment in medium-high/high-tech manufacturing and knowledge-intensive services	0.617**	0.610**
Sales of new-to-market and new-to-firm products	0.445**	0.366**

Notes:
*   Correlation is significant at the 0.05 level (2-tailed).
**   Correlation is significant at the 0.01 level (2-tailed).

Source: Own calculation based on Eurostat database and Regional Innovation Scoreboard, 2009–2017.

the econometric analysis uses two types of estimates separately. The first set of models (Innovation growth models based on individual activity) includes variables relating to the innovative behaviour of firms, such as business effort in R&D, non-R&D innovation expenditures, share of employment in medium-high/high-tech sectors and share of SMEs innovating in house. The second set of models (Innovation growth models based on collaborative activity) includes variables relating to the quality of the linkages within the RIS such as the share of innovative SMEs collaborating with others and the share of public–private co-publications, together with other additional variables of the regional innovation performance.

This first set of econometric models (Innovation growth models based on individual activity) to be estimated can be summarized as follows:

$$GDP_i = \beta_0 + \beta_1\, BUSRD_i + \beta_2\, NONRD_i + \beta_3\, EMPHT_i + \beta_4\, SMEIH_i + \varepsilon_i$$

The second set of models (Innovation growth models based on collaborative activity) to be estimated can be summarized as follows:

$$GDP_i = \beta_0 + \beta_1 \, COPUB_i + \beta_2 \, SMECO_i + \beta_3 \, SALES_i + \beta_4 \, NONRD_i + \varepsilon_i$$

where GDP_i is the annual variation rate of GDP per capita from 2009 to 2017 (in percentage); the subscript *i* refers to the region ($i = 1, \ldots, n$); $BUSRD_i$ is the R&D expenditures in the business sector as percentage of GDP (average value of years 2007, 2009 and 2011, rescaled from 0 to 1); $NONRD_i$ is the non-R&D innovation expenditures in SMEs as percentage of turnover (average value of years 2007, 2009 and 2011, rescaled from 0 to 1); $EMPHT_i$ is the employment in medium-high/high-tech manufacturing and knowledge-intensive services as percentage of total workforce (average value of years 2007, 2009 and 2011, rescaled from 0 to 1); $SMEIH_i$ is the share of SMEs innovating in house as percentage of SMEs (average value of years 2007, 2009 and 2011, rescaled from 0 to 1); $COPUB_i$ is the number of public–private co-publications per million population (average value of years 2007, 2009 and 2011, rescaled from 0 to 1); $SMECO_i$ is the share of innovative SMEs collaborating with others as percentage of SMEs (average value of years 2007, 2009 and 2011, rescaled from 0 to 1); and $SALES_i$ refers to sales of new-to-market and new-to-firm innovations in SMEs as percentage of turnover (average value of years 2007, 2009 and 2011, rescaled from 0 to 1).

These multiple linear regression models were estimated by ordinary least squares (OLS) with standard errors robust for heteroscedasticity. Table 7.2 includes the summary statistics of variables included in estimation and Table 7.3 shows the results of estimation distinguishing between models based on individual activity and collaborative-activity-based models.

The estimation results provide useful findings, which enable verifying several hypotheses related to the relationship between the innovation performance and the economic growth of regions. First, it is important to note that all the variables included in the models show significant effects on income growth and the signs of the estimated coefficients are as expected. Moreover, this is true both for variables related to the business activity and for variables related to the linkages and collaborative activity (Table 7.3).

A variable with a high explanatory capacity is the R&D expenditures in the business sector as percentage of GDP (BUSRD), which shows a positive and significant effect on the income growth. This result reflects the crucial role that the most R&D-intensive firms play in the regional innovation performance and the economic valorization of it.

The variable of non-R&D innovation expenditures (NONRD) also shows a positive and significant effect on regional growth. This finding is

Table 7.2   Summary statistics of variables included in estimation[a]

Variables	Description / Regional Innovation Scoreboard indicator	Mean	S.D.	Min	Max
Dependent variable					
GDPpc 2009–17	Annual variation of GDP per capita 2009–2017 (log)	1.86	1.51	−2.91	7.90
Independent variables					
BUSRD	R&D expenditure business sector	0.511	0.243	0.00	1.00
NONRD	Non-R&D innovation expenditures	0.438	0.175	0.00	1.00
EMPHT	Employment medium-high/high-tech manufacturing and knowledge-intensive services	0.489	0.235	0.00	1.00
SMEIH	SMEs innovating in house	0.513	0.266	0.00	1.00
COPUB	Public–private co-publications	0.503	0.251	0.00	1.00
SMECO	Innovative SMEs collaborating with others	0.401	0.229	0.00	1.00
SALES	Sales of new-to-market and new-to-firm innovations	0.538	0.211	0.00	1.00

Note: [a]   Total of 165 observations, missing values were skipped.

Source: Own calculation based on Eurostat database and Regional Innovation Scoreboard, 2009–2017. The software used is Gretl, version 2019a.

in line with the fact that innovation involves much more than R&D activities, and that economic growth of regions also benefits to a significant extent on non-R&D activities. The share of innovative industries in the economy is also a key driver of regional growth; in fact, the employment share in medium-high/high-tech manufacturing and knowledge-intensive services (EMPHT) is another key determinant of the regional economic growth, as estimation of Models 3 and 4 shows. This result reveals that economic growth in the EMU is highly dependent on the capacity to develop on the new knowledge-based activities in sectors close to the technological frontier.

Another variable with positive and significant influence on growth rate is SMEIH, revealing the importance of SMEs with in-house innovation activities that have introduced any new or significantly improved products or production processes. This specific indicator puts the focus on SMEs because these firms face more obstacles to innovation than large ones and because there are differences among business structures across regions.

Finally, the estimation results for the innovation growth models based on collaborative activity particularly show positive and significant effects

Table 7.3   Results of the regression models (OLS)[a]

Innovation growth models based on individual activity

	1	2	3	4
BUSRD	4.146***	3.317***	2.390***	2.326***
	(0.43)[b]	(0.44)	(0.50)	(0.49)
NONRD	–	2.401***	2.224***	1.608***
		(0.47)	(0.44)	(0.59)
EMPHT	–	–	1.351***	1.115**
			(0.41)	(0.45)
SMEIH	–	–	–	0.707*
				(0.41)
Constant	−0.296	−0.951***	−1.057***	−1.006***
	(0.27)	(0.27)	(0.26)	(0.27)
Obs. num.	156	156	156	156
Adjusted R^2	0.44	0.49	0.50	0.51

Innovation growth models based on collaborative activity

	1	2	3	4
COPUB	3.098***	2.290***	1.220**	1.046*
	(0.47)	(0.52)	(0.59)	(0.56)
SMECO	–	1.129**	1.822***	1.201**
		(0.51)	(0.53)	(0.50)
SALES	–	–	2.437***	1.232**
			(0.59)	(0.55)
NONRD	–	–	–	2.898***
				(0.55)
Constant	0.215	0.193	−0.880**	−1.176***
	(0.30)	(0.29)	(0.38)	(0.38)
Obs. num.	156	156	156	156
Adjusted R^2	0.21	0.22	0.30	0.36

Notes:
[a] Dependent variable is GDP (annual variation of GDP per capita 2009–2017).
[b] Robust standard errors in parentheses.
  * $p<0.1$.
 ** $p<0.05$
*** $p<0.01$

Source: Own calculation based on Eurostat database and Regional Innovation Scoreboard, 2009–2017. The software used for estimation is Gretl, version 2019a.

on regional growth for the variables related to the collaborative activity and linkages (public–private co-publications and innovative SMEs collaborating with others). These results provide interesting and useful insights for the regional innovation policy, which should promote linkages between public and private agents according to a systemic approach of the relationship between innovation and economic growth.

6.   CONCLUSIONS

The EU has been characterized by stages of increasing growth disparities across regions both during the past decades and, particularly, since the irruption of the Great Recession. Although factors explaining these differences are diverse, and sometimes specific, innovation is widely recognized in the literature as a key determinant in these processes. This is especially clear when innovation is viewed as a complex and interactive process involving a variety of agents contributing to technology and non-technology changes. In this sense, the concept of RIS is a powerful tool for a better understanding of the existing linkages between innovation and growth. Moreover, this relationship acquires a higher level of specificity in a regional context rather than at country-level perspective. Beyond the traditional case studies on the matter or qualitative policy-oriented approaches, the empirical analysis can benefit from the availability of the new database Regional Innovation Scoreboard on RISs. In this regard, the data on innovation performance at regional level for the period 2009–2017 provided by the Regional Innovation Scoreboard allows a new empirical approach to the role of the RIS features on regional growth and regional disparities.

Focusing on the EMU-12 case, the analysis of regional disparities in economic growth from 2000 to 2017 shows two clearly differentiated stages: first, a period of convergence process between 2000 and 2008; and second, an increase of regional disparities in economic growth from 2009 onwards. It is important to note that the decrease in income growth disparities during the first stage (2000–2008) was accompanied by distorting factors such as credit expansion and a speculative price bubble linked to the pre-crisis accumulation model, particularly in regions from the South of Europe. However, in the subsequent period (from 2009 onwards), the mitigation of the above-mentioned distorting factors contributes to better capturing the influence of long-term growth factors, with innovation being crucial.

The results of the empirical study show a positive association between innovation performance and economic growth of regions of EMU-12, being statistically significant for most regional innovation indicators, both at specific and aggregate levels (RII). Moreover, the econometric approach finds in an accurate sense that income growth of regions positively depends on business-related factors such as business R&D expenditure, non-R&D innovation expenditure and employment share in medium-high/high-tech industries.

From a general perspective, these findings confirm not only that innovation matters for economic growth but also that innovation performance should be considered in a framework of systemic complexity in which business innovation plays a key role.

The results also give rise to some policy recommendations. The objective of boosting European economic growth is highly dependent on the improvement of RIS capabilities and the reinforcing complementarities between all RIS components. Moreover, the objective of a more cohesive European Union requires the reinforcement of the RIS of all European regions. More specifically, the policies to develop pro-growth RIS should be region specific and prioritize business capabilities in R&D and non-R&D (e.g., organization, marketing and innovative business models) innovation activities. Also of relevance are the positive and significant effects on regional growth of the variables related to the collaborative activity and linkages (public–private co-publications and innovative SMEs collaborating with others). These results suggest that regional innovation policy must prioritize the promotion of linkages between a large variety of private agents and between public and private agents according to a systemic approach.

ACKNOWLEDGEMENTS

The authors are grateful for the financial support received to carry out this research, from the Xunta de Galicia through the Galician Competitive Research Group grant ICEDE (ref. ED-431C 2018/23) and from the Spanish Government (AEI) through "La estrategia europea de transición a la economía circular: un análisis jurídico prospectivo y cambios en las cadenas globales de valor" project (ref. ECO2017-87142-C2-1-R). These programmes are co-funded by the European Regional Development Fund of the EU.

NOTE

1. The Regional Innovation Scoreboard replicates the European Innovation Scoreboard methodology used at national level to measure performance of RIS (European Commission, 2017).

REFERENCES

Armstrong, H.W. (1995). An Appraisal of the Evidence from Cross-Sectional Analysis of the Regional Growth Process within the European Union. In Armstrong, H.W., and Vickerman, R.W. (eds), *Convergence and Divergence among European Regions* (40–65), Pion Limited, London.

Armstrong, H.W. (2002). European Union Regional Policy: Reconciling the Convergence. In Cuadrado-Roura, J.R., and Parellada, M. (eds), *Regional Convergence in the European Union: Facts, Prospects and Policies* (231–72), Springer-Verlag, Berlin and New York, NY.

Asheim, B., and Gertler, M.S. (2006). The Geography of Innovation: Regional Innovation Systems. In Fagerberg, Jan, Mowery, David C., and Nelson, Richard R. (eds), *The Oxford Handbook of Innovation* (291–317), Oxford University Press, Oxford.

Asheim, B., Bugge, M., Coenen, L., and Herstad, S. (2013). *What Does Evolutionary Economic Geography Bring to the Table? Reconceptualising Regional Innovation Systems.* CIRCLE Working Paper no. 2013/05, Circle, Lund University.

Asheim, B., Isaksen, A., and Trippl, M. (2019). *Advanced Introduction to Regional Innovation Systems.* Edward Elgar Publishing, Cheltenham, UK and Northampton, MA, USA.

Bachtler, J., Oliveira, J., Wostner, P., and Zuber, P. (2019). *Towards Cohesion Policy 4.0*, Taylor & Francis, London.

Barro, R.J., and Sala-i-Martin, X. (1991). Convergence across states and regions, *Brooking Papers on Economic Activity*, 1, 107–82.

Basile, R., Nardis, S. de, and Girardi, A. (2001). *Regional Inequalities and Cohesion Policies in the European Union*, ISAE Working Paper No. 23. At http://dx.doi.org/10.2139/ssrn.936319 (accessed on 15 November 2019).

Begg, I. (2008). Structural policy and economic convergence, *CESifo Forum*, 9(1), 3–9.

Boldrin, L., and Canova, F. (2001). Inequality and convergence in Europe's regions: Reconsidering European regional policies, *Economic Policy*, 16, 207–53.

Cooke, P. (2001). Regional Innovation Systems, clusters and the knowledge economy, *Industrial and Corporate Change*, 10(4), 945–74.

Cooke, P. (2012). *Complex Adaptive Innovation Systems*, Routledge, Oxford.

Cooke, P., Boekholt, P., and Tödtling, F. (2000). *The Governance of Innovation in Europe: Regional Perspectives on Global Competitiveness*, Pinter Publishers, London.

Cooke, P., Asheim, B.T., Boschma, R., Martin, R., Schwartz, D., and Tödtling, F. (2011). Introduction to the Handbook of Regional Innovation and Growth. In Cooke, P., Asheim, B.T., Boschma, R., Martin, R., Schwartz, D., and Tödtling, F. (eds), *Handbook of Regional Innovation and Growth* (1–26), Edward Elgar Publishing, Cheltenham, UK and Northampton, MA, USA.

Cornett, A.P., and Sørensen, N.K. (2008). International vs. intra-national convergence in Europe: An assessment of causes and evidence, *Investigaciones Regionales*, 13, 35–56.

Crescenzi, R., and Rodríguez-Pose, A. (2009). Systems of Innovation and Regional Growth in the EU: Endogenous vs. External Innovative Activities and Socio-Economic Conditions. In Fratessi, U., and Senn, L. (eds), *Growth and Innovation of Competitive Regions* (167–91), Springer-Verlag, Berlin.

Crescenzi, R., Luca, D., and Milio, S. (2016). The geography of the economic crisis in Europe: National macroeconomic conditions, regional structural factors and short-term economic performance, *Cambridge Journal of Regions, Economy and Society*, 9, 13–32.

Cuadrado-Roura, J.R. (2001). Regional convergence in the European Union: From hypothesis to the actual trends, *Annals of Regional Science*, 35, 333–56.

Cuadrado-Roura, J.R., Mancha-Navarro, T., and Garrido-Yserte, R. (2002). Regional Dynamics in the European Union: Winners and Losers. In Cuadrado-Roura, J.R., and Parellada, M. (eds), *Regional Convergence in the European Union* (23–52), Springer, Berlin and New York, NY.

Dewhurst, J.H.L., and Mutis-Gaitan, H. (1995). Varying Speeds of Regional GDP Per Capita Convergence in the European Union, 1981–91. In Armstrong, H.W., and Vickerman, R.W. (eds), *Convergence and Divergence among European Regions* (22–39), Pion Limited, London.

Doloreux, D., and Parto, S. (2004). *Regional Innovation Systems: A Critical Review*, MERIT Working Paper.

Doloreux, D., and Porto Gomez, I. (2017). A review of (almost) 20 years of regional innovation system research, *European Planning Studies*, 25(3), 371–87.

Dunford, M. (1993). Regional disparities in the European Community: Evidence from the REGIO databank, *Regional Studies*, 27(28), 727–43.

Edquist, C. (2005). Systems of Innovation: Perspectives and Challenges. In Fagerberg, J., Mowery, D., and Nelson, R.R. (eds), *The Oxford Handbook of Innovation* (209–39), Oxford University Press, Oxford.

Esposti, R., and Bussoletti, S. (2008). Impact of Objective 1 funds on regional growth convergence in the European Union: A panel-data approach, *Regional Studies*, 42(2), 159–73.

European Commission (2014). *Regional Innovation Scoreboard 2014*, European Union, Brussels.

European Commission (2017). *Regional Innovation Scoreboard 2017*, European Union, Brussels.

Fagerberg, J. (2018). *Innovation, Economic Development and Policy: Selected Essays*, Edward Elgar Publishing, Cheltenham, UK and Northampton, MA, USA.

Fagerberg, J., and Verspagen, B. (1996). Heading for divergence? Regional growth in Europe reconsidered, *Journal of Common Market Studies*, 34(3), 431–48.

Foray, D. (2015). *Smart Specialisation*, Routledge, Oxford.

Freeman, C. (1987). *Technology Policy and Economic Performance: Lessons from Japan*, Pinter Publishers, London.

Gaffard, J.L., and Quéré, M. (1996). The Diversity of European Regions and the Conditions for a Sustainable Economic Growth. In Vence, X., and Metcalfe, J.S. (eds), *Wealth from Diversity: Innovation, Structural Change and Finance for Regional Development in Europe* (135–45), Kluwer AC, Dordrecht.

Grjebine, Th., Héricourt, J., and Triper, F. (2019). *Sectoral Reallocations, Real State Shocks and Productivity Divergence in Europe: A Tale of Three Countries*, CEPR Policy Brief n. 27.

Hudson, R. (2007). Regions and regional uneven development forever? Some reflective comments upon theory and practice, *Regional Studies*, 41(9), 1149–60.

Kourtit, K., Nijkamp, P., and Stough, R. (eds) (2011). *Drivers of Innovation, Entrepreneurship and Regional Dynamics*, Springer-Verlag, Berlin.

López-Bazo, E. (2003). Growth and Convergence across Economies: The Experience of the European Regions. In Fingleton, B., Eraydin, A., and Paci, R.

(eds), *Regional Economic Growth, SMEs and the Wider Europe* (49–74), Ashgate, Aldershot.

Lundvall, B.-Å. (ed.) (1992). *National Innovation Systems: Towards a Theory of Innovation and Interactive Learning*, Pinter Publishers, London.

Martin, R. (2001). EMU versus the regions? Regional convergence and divergence in Euroland, *Journal of Economic Geography*, 1, 51–80.

McCann, P., and Ortega-Orgilés, R. (2015). Smart Specialisation, regional growth and applications to EU Cohesion Policy, *Regional Studies*, 49(8), 1291–1302.

Metcalfe, J.S. (1996). Economic Dynamics and Regional Diversity: Some Evolutionary Ideas. In Vence, X., and Metcalfe, J.S. (eds), *Wealth from Diversity: Innovation, Structural Change and Finance for Regional Development in Europe* (19–38), Kluwer AC, Dordrecht.

Nelson, R.R. (1996). *The Sources of Economic Growth*, Harvard University Press, Cambridge, MA.

Neven, D., and Gouyette, C. (1995). Regional convergence in the European Community, *Journal of Common Market Studies*, 33(1), 47–65.

OECD (2007). *Globalisation and Regional Patterns of Innovation in EU-25 Regions: A Typology and Policy Recommendations Economies*, OECD, Paris.

Patel, P., and Pavitt, K. (1994). National Innovation Systems: Why they are important, and how they might be measured and compared, *Economics of Innovation and New Technology*, 3, 77–95.

Reid, A. (2007). Innovation and regional development: Do European structural funds make a difference?, *European Planning Studies*, 15(7), 961–83.

Rodil, O., Vence, X., and Sánchez, M.C. (2014). Disparidades en la Eurozona: el debate de la convergencia regional a la luz de las asimetrías en la estructura productiva, *Ekonomiaz*, 86, 274–305.

Rodríguez-Pose, A., and Novak, K. (2013). Learning processes and economic returns in European Cohesion policy. *Investigaciones Regionales*, 25, 7–26.

Rosés, J.R., and Wolf, N. (2018). *Regional Economic Development in Europe, 1900–2010: A Description of the Patterns*, CEPR, DP12749.

Sala-i-Martin, X. (1994). La riqueza de las regiones: evidencia y teoría sobre crecimiento regional y convergencia, *Moneda y Crédito*, 198, 13–80.

Soete, L. (2011). Regions and Innovation Policies: The Way Forward. In *Regions and Innovation Policy*, OECD Reviews of Regional Innovation, OECD Publishing.

Suárez-Villa, L., and Cuadrado-Roura, J.R. (1993). Regional economic integration and the evolution of disparities, *Papers in Regional Science*, 72(4), 369–87.

Tödtling, F., and Trippl, M. (2005). One size fits all? Towards a differentiated regional innovation policy approach, *Research Policy*, 34(8), 1203–19.

Vence, X. (1995). *Economía de la innovación y del cambio tecnológico*, Siglo XXI Ediciones, Madrid.

Vence, X. (1996). Innovation, Regional Development and Technology Policy. In Vence, X., and Metcalfe, J.S. (eds), *Wealth from Diversity: Innovation, Structural Change and Finance for Regional Development in Europe* (135–43), Kluwer AC, Dordrecht.

Vence, X. (2014). *Crisis y fracaso de la Unión Europea neoliberal*, Ediciones Eneida, Madrid.

Vence, X., and Rodil, O. (2003a). La concentración regional de la política de I+D de la Unión Europea, *Revista de Estudios Regionales*, 65, 43–73.

Vence, X., and Rodil, O. (2003b). La evolución de las disparidades regionales en la UE: ¿convergencia, divergencia o ambas? In González, F., and Sequeiros, J.G.

(eds), *Orden económico mundial: globalización y desarrollo* (785–803), Netbiblo, A Coruña.

Vence, X., Turnes, A., and Nogueira, A. (2013). *An Alternative Economic Governance for the European Union*, Centre Maurits Coppieters, Brussels.

Villaverde, J. (2003). Regional convergence, polarisation and mobility in the European Union, 1980–1996, *European Integration*, 25, 73–86.

8. The effects of projects funded by the EU Framework Programmes on regional innovation and scientific performance

**Pedro Varela-Vázquez and
Manuel González-López**

1. INTRODUCTION

The research and development (R&D) Framework Programmes (FPs) stand out as the main competitive instrument aimed at encouraging research and technological development within the European Research Area (Guzzetti, 1995; Vence, 1998; Reillon, 2017). In contrast to the research and innovation (R&I) European Structural and Investment Funds (ESIFs), allocation criteria are based on excellence in science and industrial leadership (Reillon, 2017; Pontikakis et al., 2018). This leads to a heavy concentration of projects in few hubs across the European Union (EU), as discussed in the literature (Vence, 1998; Özbolat and Harrap, 2018; Varela-Vázquez et al., 2019). Likewise, several authors analyse the impact of the international collaboration under FPs at firm level (Barajas and Huergo, 2010; Barajas et al., 2012). However, the effects of this programming and financial tool are almost unresearched at regional level (Izsak and Radošević, 2017; Dávid, 2016), especially regarding the effect on innovation and scientific capabilities. Given the relevance of the effects, it is advisable to analyse their global impact upon regional innovation and scientific performance.

The main aim of this study is to shed light on the effects of the FPs on regional innovation and scientific performance. In particular, this study analyses the impact of the coordination and participation numbers in projects under the 6th and 7th FPs according to four variables that may summarise innovation and scientific capabilities at regional level. The comprehensive database of projects was built by the authors from the Community Research and Development Information Service (CORDIS) dataset, as well as regionalised at Nomenclature of Territorial Units for Statistics (NUTS) 2 level. In addition, NUTS 2 regions are classified into three groups according to their economic development level in terms of gross domestic product (GDP) per capita. This classification facilitates analysis of regional singularities. Concerning the estimation of the impact on regional innovation and scientific performance, the analytical methodology is based on the ordinary least square (OLS) and Tobit techniques.

The chapter is structured in three sections. The first section deals with the main characteristics and current dynamics of the FPs. The following section introduces the analytical framework and data used in this study, as well as describing the main results. The last section discusses the main policy implications of both the results of this chapter and the allocation criteria of the FPs.

2. MAIN FEATURES AND RECENT DYNAMICS OF THE R&D FPs

Since their launch in 1984, R&D FPs have constituted the main programming and financial tool for fostering research and technological development within the European Research Area (Guzzetti, 1995; Vence, 1998; Reillon, 2017). In addition, their relevance is growing due to the sharp increase in their budget since the 7th FP (2007–2013), reaching 77 billion euros in the current multiannual programme (Reillon, 2017). Also worth noting is the increasing focus on firms and, especially, on small and medium-sized enterprises (SMEs) as a way to enhance industrial leadership (Rodil, 2007; Barajas and Huergo, 2010). In any case, universities account for the bulk of the funding from the 7th FP, reaching 44% of the total. SMEs are the third most popular group of agents, with 13% of the total funds (Dávid, 2016).

This study is focused on the 6th (2002–2006) and the 7th (2007–2013) FPs, because these represent the last two completed FPs with full data in the CORDIS dataset regarding project allocation. The ongoing 8th FP, also known as Horizon 2020 (H2020), address excellent science, industrial leadership and societal challenges as the three main issues (Pontikakis et al., 2018). This programme is not only structured by thematic areas, but also by challenges. In this regard, the main challenges are social ones, such as health, clean energy and transport.

One important issue is the allocation criteria in the EU FPs. In this regard, FPs may be classified as a place-blinded policy instrument (Reillon, 2017). Given their priorities regarding excellent science and industrial leadership, the geographical dimension and regional cohesion take second place. Despite recent efforts to introduce regional cohesion criteria mainly through leveraging synergies between these programmes (Corpakis, 2016; De Carli, 2017; Reillon, 2017), this is still a pending issue. As indicated by Reillon (2017), there is a conflict between excellence and cohesion criteria, as the application of the excellence criterion tends to concentrate funds in the pre-existing hubs. In fact, several authors emphasise that developed regions are usually the main beneficiaries in the distribution of funds and projects (Vence, 1998; Özbolat and Harrap, 2018; Varela-Vázquez et al., 2019).

As shown in Figure 8.1 and Figure 8.2, the allocation of coordination and participation in projects per million of inhabitants under the 6th and 7th FPs is highly concentrated on few hubs across the EU. This pattern is more pronounced with the coordination of projects. It should be noted that the number of regions in each category appears in brackets in the legend. In this regard, most of the regions with a relatively high number of coordinated projects are developed areas, such as Bavaria (DE21), Ile-de-France (FR10), Brussels (BE10), Wien (AT13), Copenhagen (DK01),

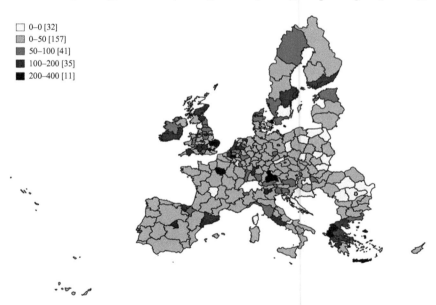

Note: Hereinafter, the number of regions is in brackets.

Source: Varela-Vázquez et al. (2019).

Figure 8.1   Number of coordinated projects under the 6th and 7th FPs per million inhabitants

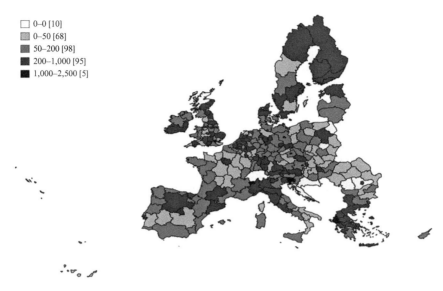

□ 0–0 [10]
▨ 0–50 [68]
▩ 50–200 [98]
■ 200–1,000 [95]
■ 1,000–2,500 [5]

Source: Varela-Vázquez et al. (2019).

*Figure 8.2   Number of participations in projects under the 6th and 7th FPs
per million inhabitants*

Great London (UKI) and Vlaams-Brabant (BE24) (Varela-Vázquez et al., 2019). Concerning participation in projects, projects are also concentrated on developed and middle-income regions.

These features regarding allocation criteria show remarkable effects on the geographical distribution of projects across the EU. The next sections of this study are aimed at analysing the effects, in terms of innovation and scientific performance, of the attractiveness of projects under the 6th and 7th FPs on the regional level. This analysis facilitates the discussion of the main policy implications of such spatial distribution on European regions, with a special focus on the different kinds of regions concerning GDP per capita.

3.   THE IMPACT OF R&D FPs ON REGIONAL INNOVATION CAPABILITIES AND SCIENTIFIC OUTPUT

This section describes methodological issues, as well as the main results regarding the effects of the 6th and 7th FPs on innovation capabilities and scientific output across Europe. Firstly, discussion of the analytical framework highlights the main statistical attributes of the variables used in this study. Secondly, key empirical evidences are drawn from the different proposed regression models.

3.1   Analytical Framework and Data

This study proposes an array of parallel regression models in order to assess the role played by the 6th and 7th FPs in the promotion of innovation and scientific output at regional level. The full sample includes 200 observations, which correspond to, mainly, the NUTS 2 regions and 28 NUTS 1 regions, due to the lack of available disaggregated data. In addition, regions are classified into three groups according to their economic development level in terms of GDP per capita. The analysis with the full sample and the sub-samples related to the GDP per capita enables examination of different geographical patterns within groups and between them.

As shown in Table 8.1, there are four different dependent variables that try to capture innovation and scientific output. In this regard, SMEs with product or process innovation (SME ppinov_14) and those with marketing or organisational innovation (SME mo_14) are related to innovation output. Data from these variables are gathered from the Regional Innovation Scoreboard (RIS) 2017 database (European Commission, 2019). According to the corresponding methodological report, data from these two variables refer to 2014. The proportion of innovative firms is a widely used indicator that sheds light on the innovative performance of the private sector (European Commission, 2017). Likewise, public–private co-publications (PPCP_15) and international scientific co-publications (ISCPUB_16) constitute two additional dependent variables that try to capture scientific output. Data from these two dependent variables are also collected from the RIS 2017. Thus, scientific publications are key elements in the regional performance and these variables also show the relevance of international collaboration, as well as between public and private agents (European Commission, 2017). Apart from these dependent variables, the authors would have included patent data at NUTS 2 level, but the lack of updated information prevented this use. The last available patent data refers to 2012, one year before the end of the 7th FP.

Concerning regressors, the number of projects coordinated under the 6th and 7th FPs per million inhabitants (C6_7FP) and the participation in projects per million inhabitants (P6_7FP) constitute the central part of this research. Given the uneven geographical distribution (Varela-Vázquez

Table 8.1 *Variable definition and summary statistics*

Variables	Definition	Obs.	Mean	Std. Dev.	Min.	Max.
Dependent variables						
PPCP_15	Public–private co-publications	200	0.25	0.15	0	0.79
SMEppinov_14	SMEs with product or process innovation	200	0.43	0.18	0	0.86
SMEmo_14	SMEs with marketing or organisational innovations	200	0.37	0.18	0	0.73
ISCPUB_16	International scientific co-publications	200	0.37	0.18	0.02	0.95
Independent variables						
C6_7FP	Number of coordination of projects under the 6th and 7th FPs per million inhabitants	200	50.59	66.19	0	395
P6_7FP	Number of participations in projects under the 6th and 7th FPs per million inhabitants	200	588.44	4,999.08	0	70.82
DumCap	Dummy for capital regions	200	0.10	0.31	0	1
Regiontype_14	Ordinal variable for regional economic development	200	2.09	0.85	1	3
R&D_14	Intramural R&D in PPS per inhabitant	198	419.93	436.05	6.5	2,816.20
R&D_15	Intramural R&D in PPS per inhabitant	200	450.39	454.44	8.4	3,177.90
TE_14	Percentage of people from 25 to 64 with tertiary education	194	27.12	8.99	11.4	53.7
TE_15	Percentage of people from 25 to 64 with tertiary education	194	27.85	9.00	11.6	55.1

Source: Own elaboration.

et al., 2019), this chapter is aimed at highlighting the role of the EU FPs in the promotion of innovation performance and scientific outcomes. Data were gathered from the CORDIS dataset (CORDIS, European Commission, 2018) and structured as proposed by Varela-Vázquez et al. (2019). Furthermore, this study includes a dummy variable to control for the agglomeration economies that stem from capital cities (DumCap). The regression includes a categorical variable (Regiontype_14) that facilitates analysis of the effects of regional economic development levels on innovation and scientific performance. In this way, those regions with a GDP per capita in 2014 below 75% of the EU average score 1, those between 75% and 100% score 2 and, finally, regions above the EU average score 3. Both DumCap and Regiontype_14 would have a positive expected impact upon innovation capabilities and scientific outcomes.

Finally, the inclusion of the intramural R&D expenditure in Purchasing Power Standards (PPS) per inhabitant and the percentage of people with tertiary education enables controlling for the regional efforts regarding basic, applied and experimental research, as well as for the quality of the stock of the human capital. It should be noted that the values of these variables refer to two years: 2014 and 2015. This is because there are two dependent variables referring to 2014 (SMEppinov_14 and SMEmo_14), one to the year 2015 (PPCP_15) and another to the year 2016 (ISCPUB_16). However, it is advisable to avoid 2016 data, due to the several missing values. Hence, there are two R&D expenditure variables (R&D_14 and R&D_15) and two concerning tertiary education (TE_14 and TE_15). Data from all of these are gathered from Eurostat. Both R&D and tertiary education would have an expected positive effect on regional innovative and scientific performance.

Given these dependent variables and regressors, this study is aimed at testing the following four hypotheses:

H1:   *EU FPs have a statistically significant effect on regional innovation capabilities and scientific outcomes.*

H2:   *EU FPs have a statistically significant effect on less developed regions (LDRs) (Regiontype_14=1) regarding innovation and scientific performance.*

H3:   *EU FPs have a statistically significant impact upon developed regions (DRs) (Regiontype_14=3) concerning innovation and scientific performance.*

H4: *EU FPs have a statistically significant effect on middle-income regions (MIRs) (Regiontype_14=2) with regard to innovation and scientific performance.*

A wide array of regression models is carried out in order to test the above hypotheses. All of them are based on either OLS models or Tobit models. Given that the range of the four dependent variables is constrained between 0 and 1, Tobit regression models may show more consistent results than OLS (Verbeek, 2013). In this regard, the authors have carried out the required test to fulfil the assumptions of each model, such as normality of residuals, collinearity or heteroscedasticity.

Equation 1 shows the generic OLS and tobit regression model specification:

$$y_i = \beta_0 + \beta_1 DumCap + \beta_2\ Regiontype\_14 + \beta_3 C6\_7FP(P6\_7FP) + \beta_4 R\&D\_14(15) + \beta_5 TE\_14(15) + \varepsilon_i \qquad (1)$$

where "i" is the region index, y_i might be any of the four aforementioned dependent variables, β_0 is the intercept and ε_i is the random error term. Moreover, parentheses show different options between regressors (C6_7FP or P6_7FP) or years (2014 or 2015).

Table 8.2 describes the correlations among all the variables in the full sample. In this regard, correlations are relevant and statistically significant between several dependent variables and regressors. Hence, it is advisable to analyse in further depth whether these correlations signify casual relations among variables by means of a multivariate regression model. Likewise, in Tables 8.3, 8.4, 8.5 and 8.6, some descriptive statistics and correlations of the sub-samples are shown.

3.2   Main Results

The multivariate regression models are estimated through OLS or the Tobit methodology with robust standard errors in order to avoid heteroscedastic residuals. It should be noted that the following tables only include the models that fit the basic assumptions of the OLS and the Tobit models. As more than one variable is used to measure the regional performance concerning innovation and scientific outputs, the results from both models are suitable for testing the hypotheses. Firstly, the results from the full sample are analysed. After that, the main outcomes from the sub-samples (LDRs, DRs and MIRs) are highlighted.

As can be seen in Table 8.7, coordination of projects under the 6th and 7th FPs shows a positive and statistically significant effect on the number

Table 8.2 *Variable correlations*

	C6_7FP	P6_7FP	DumCap	Regiontype14	R&D_14	R&D_15	TE_14	TE_15	PPCP_15	SMEppinov_14	SMEmo14	ISCPUB16
C6_7FP	1	0.093	0.355**	0.288**	0.352**	0.361**	0.445**	0.443**	0.528**	0.355**	0.356**	0.595**
P6_7FP	0.093	1	0.006	0.097	0.024	0.018	0.181*	0.180*	0.083	0.038	0.087	0.111
DumCap	0.355**	0.006	1	0.309**	0.228**	0.269**	0.480**	0.477**	0.318**	0.068	0.042	0.381**
Regiontype_14	0.288**	0.097	0.309**	1	0.621**	0.630**	0.518**	0.510**	0.713**	0.575**	0.555**	0.646**
R&D_14	0.352**	0.024	0.228**	0.621**	1	0.965**	0.433**	0.430**	0.708**	0.505**	0.534**	0.610**
R&D_15	0.361**	0.018	0.269**	0.630**	0.965**	1	0.484**	0.481**	0.742**	0.521**	0.528**	0.647**
TE_14	0.445**	0.181*	0.480**	0.518**	0.433**	0.484**	1	0.995**	0.647**	0.282**	0.269**	0.646**
TE_15	0.443**	0.180*	0.477**	0.510**	0.430**	0.481**	0.995**	1	0.648**	0.284**	0.267**	0.648**
PPCP_15	0.528**	0.083	0.318**	0.713**	0.708**	0.742**	0.647**	0.648**	1	0.588**	0.549**	0.918**
SMEppinov_14	0.355**	0.038	0.068	0.575**	0.505**	0.521**	0.282**	0.284**	0.588**	1	0.840**	0.510**
SMEmo_14	0.356**	0.087	0.042	0.555**	0.534**	0.528**	0.269**	0.267**	0.549**	0.840**	1	0.490**
ISCPUB_16	0.595**	0.111	0.381**	0.646**	0.610**	0.647**	0.646**	0.648**	0.918**	0.510**	0.490**	1

Notes:
* Correlation is significant at the level of 0.05.
** Correlation is significant at the level of 0.01.

Source: Own elaboration.

170

Table 8.3 *Summary statistics regarding regional economic development*

C6_7FP

	Obs.	Mean	Std. Dev.	Min.	Max.
LDR	64	34	78	0	358
MIR	54	29	16	2	114
DR	82	77	66	0	395

P6_7FP

	Obs.	Mean	Std. Dev.	Min.	Max.
LDR	64	129	222	0	1,037
MIR	54	148	148	17	1,026
DR	82	1,237	7,786	17	70,816

R&D_14

	Obs.	Mean	Std. Dev.	Min.	Max.
LDR	64	107.2	68.8	6.5	345.5
MIR	54	320.6	203.8	7.4	940.4
DR	82	737.2	504.6	18.0	2,816.2

R&D_15

	Obs.	Mean	Std. Dev.	Min.	Max.
LDR	64	114.5	65.3	8.4	294.4
MIR	54	348.4	202.3	36.5	964.8
DR	82	779.8	520.9	191.5	3,177.9

TE_14

	Obs.	Mean	Std. Dev.	Min.	Max.
LDR	64	20.1	4.9	11.4	27.8
MIR	54	29.7	6.6	16.5	40.8
DR	82	31.1	9.4	15.2	53.7

TE_15

	Obs.	Mean	Std. Dev.	Min.	Max.
LDR	64	20.9	4.8	11.6	29.1
MIR	54	30.5	6.9	17.0	41.8
DR	82	31.8	9.5	15.5	55.1

ISCPUB_16

	Obs.	Mean	Std. Dev.	Min.	Max.
LDR	64	0.22	0.10	0.02	0.52
MIR	54	0.36	0.11	0.05	0.62
DR	82	0.49	0.17	0.13	0.95

PPCP_15

	Obs.	Mean	Std. Dev.	Min.	Max.
LDR	64	0.11	0.06	0.00	0.25
MIR	54	0.23	0.10	0.03	0.47
DR	82	0.36	0.14	0.06	0.79

SMEppinov_14

	Obs.	Mean	Std. Dev.	Min.	Max.
LDR	64	0.29	0.16	0.00	0.68
MIR	54	0.45	0.14	0.15	0.70
DR	82	0.53	0.14	0.09	0.86

SMEmo_14

	Obs.	Mean	Std. Dev.	Min.	Max.
LDR	64	0.23	0.16	0.00	0.60
MIR	54	0.39	0.14	0.09	0.61
DR	82	0.46	0.14	0.07	0.73

Source: Own elaboration.

Table 8.4 Variable correlations in LDRs[a]

	C6_7FP	P6_7FP	R&D_14	R&D_15	TE_14	TE_15	PPCP_15	SMEppinov_14	SMEmo_14	ISCPUB_16
C6_7FP	1	0.984**	0.133	0.151	0.246	0.233	0.332**	0.429**	0.537**	0.433**
P6_7FP	0.984**	1	0.191	0.207	0.253*	0.242	0.378**	0.491**	0.586**	0.472**
R&D_14	0.133	0.191	1	0.963**	0.214	0.234	0.640**	0.455**	0.358**	0.575**
R&D_15	0.151	0.207	0.963**	1	0.240	0.264*	0.675**	0.409**	0.333**	0.604**
TE_14	0.246	0.253*	0.214	0.240	1	0.979**	0.202	0.026	-0.021	0.181
TE_15	0.233	0.242	0.234	0.264*	0.979**	1	0.208	0.017	-0.020	0.198
PPCP_15	0.332**	0.378**	0.640**	0.675**	0.202	0.208	1	0.344**	0.389**	0.813**
SMEppinov_14	0.429**	0.491**	0.455**	0.409**	0.026	0.017	0.344**	1	0.879**	0.461**
SMEmo_14	0.537**	0.586**	0.358**	0.333**	-0.021	-0.020	0.389**	0.879**	1	0.540**
ISCPUB_16	0.433**	0.472**	0.575**	0.604**	0.181	0.198	0.813**	0.461**	0.540**	1

Notes:

[a] DumCap is not shown in the table, because it is constant in LDRs.

* Correlation is significant at the level of 0.05.

** Correlation is significant at the level of 0.01.

Source: Own elaboration.

Table 8.5 *Variable correlations in MIRs*

	C6_7FP	P6_7FP	DumCap	R&D_14	R&D_15	TE_14	TE_15	PPCP_15	SMEppinov_14	SMEmo_14	ISCPUB_16
C6_7FP	1	0.564**	0.313*	0.373**	0.426**	0.588**	0.592**	0.612**	0.175	0.452**	0.675**
P6_7FP	0.564**	1	0.716**	0.330*	0.407**	0.351*	0.359*	0.423**	0.070	0.092	0.543**
DumCap	0.313*	0.716**	1	0.055	0.045	0.147	0.157	0.045	-0.120	-0.109	0.132
R&D_14	0.373**	0.330*	0.055	1	0.832**	0.103	0.084	0.380**	0.208	0.440**	0.371**
R&D_15	0.426**	0.407**	0.045	0.832**	1	0.271	0.250	0.571**	0.347*	0.441**	0.520**
TE_14	0.588**	0.351*	0.147	0.103	0.271	1	0.991**	0.446**	-0.011	0.144	0.453**
TE_15	0.592**	0.359*	0.157	0.084	0.250	0.991**	1	0.437**	0.002	0.153	0.444**
PPCP_15	0.612**	0.423**	0.045	0.380**	0.571**	0.446**	0.437**	1	0.400**	0.526**	0.832**
SMEppinov_14	0.175	0.070	-0.120	0.208	0.347*	-0.011	0.002	0.400**	1	0.676**	0.120
SMEmo_14	0.452**	0.092	-0.109	0.440**	0.441**	0.144	0.153	0.526**	0.676**	1	0.360**
ISCPUB_16	0.675**	0.543**	0.132	0.371**	0.520**	0.453**	0.444**	0.832**	0.120	0.360**	1

Source: Own elaboration.

173

Table 8.6 Variable correlations in DRs

	C6_7FP	P6_7FP	DumCap	R&D_14	R&D_15	TE_14	TE_15	PPCP15	SMEppinov14	SMEmo14	ISCPUB16
C6_7FP	1	0.060	0.412**	0.266*	0.288**	0.539**	0.541**	0.622**	0.148	0.015	0.699**
P6_7FP	0.060	1	-0.037	-0.061	-0.069	0.201	0.200	0.015	-0.042	0.060	0.069
DumCap	0.412**	-0.037	1	0.029	0.098	0.532**	0.525**	0.179	-0.200	-0.231*	0.311**
R&D_14	0.266*	-0.061	0.029	1	0.954**	0.226*	0.231*	0.512**	0.331**	0.392**	0.353**
R&D_15	0.288**	-0.069	0.098	0.954**	1	0.300**	0.304**	0.555**	0.336**	0.362**	0.415**
TE_14	0.539**	0.201	0.532**	0.226*	0.300**	1	0.997**	0.544**	-0.106	-0.166	0.572**
TE_15	0.541**	0.200	0.525**	0.231*	0.304**	0.997**	1	0.557**	-0.088	-0.162	0.583**
PPCP_15	0.622**	0.015	0.179	0.512**	0.555**	0.544**	0.557**	1	0.317**	0.154	0.880**
SMEppinov_14	0.148	-0.042	-0.200	0.331**	0.336**	-0.106	-0.088	0.317**	1	0.697**	0.155
SMEmo_14	0.015	0.060	-0.231*	0.392**	0.362**	-0.166	-0.162	0.154	0.697**	1	-0.007
ISCPUB_16	0.699**	0.069	0.311**	0.353**	0.415**	0.572**	0.583**	0.880**	0.155	-0.007	1

Source: Own elaboration.

Table 8.7   *Regression results with the full sample*

	OLS (robust se)[a]			Tobit (robust se)	
	M1 (SMEppinov_14)	M2 (ISCPUB16)	M3 (SMEppinov_14)	M4 (ISCPUB_16)	M5 (ISCPUB_16)
Constant	0.209025***	0.0144654	0.196005***	0.0144654	0.000797611
	(0.042846)	(0.029076)	(0.0459728)	(0.0286228)	(0.0317236)
DumCap	−0.0991938**	−0.000660591	−0.0739866*	−0.000660591	0.0334242
	(0.0429009)	(0.0274719)	(0.0443074)	(0.0270438)	(0.0287437)
Regiontype_14	0.0995068***	0.0594739***	0.0971449***	0.0594739***	0.0566267***
	(0.0141386)	(0.0132692)	(0.0148983)	(0.0130624)	(0.0151444)
C6_7FP	0.00068094***	0.00087476***		0.00087476***	
	(0.000151982)	(0.000178077)		(0.000175302)	
P6_7FP			−0.000000376		0.000000686
			(0.000000590)		(0.000000565)
R&D_14	0.000080753**		0.000102717***		
	(0.0000333635)		(0.000035751)		
R&D_15		0.000093394***		0.000093394***	0.000120077***
		(0.000034396)		(0.000175302)	(0.000040072)

Table 8.7 (continued)

| | OLS (robust se)[a] | | | Tobit (robust se) | |
	M1 (SMEppinov_14)	M2 (ISCPUB16)	M3 (SMEppinov_14)	M4 (ISCPUB_16)	M5 (ISCPUB_16)
TE_14	−0.00158496 (0.00148871)		−0.00065606 (0.0015413)		
TE_15		0.00516428*** (0.000990488)		0.00516428*** (0.00097505)	0.0068922*** (0.00112602)
N	192	194	192	194	194
Adjusted R²	0.413893	0.676189	0.365369		
Chi²				419.9089***	373.2995***
LogL	109.4886	165.5258	101.8527	165.5258	144.5906
Sigma				0.103089 (0.00603202)	0.114836 (0.00729375)

Notes:
[a] Standard errors in parentheses.
  * p<10%.
 ** p<5%.
*** p<1%.

Source: Own elaboration.

of SMEs with product or process innovations and the international scientific co-publications. However, the same does not apply to the participation in projects. Likewise, the level of regional economic development is also relevant for explaining innovation and scientific performance across Europe. In this way, the higher the GDP per capita, the higher the innovation and scientific performance. By contrast, regions that host their country's capital do not benefit from the agglomeration effects. In fact, empirical evidences underline that in the model one (M1) DumCap depicts a negative and statistically significant impact upon SMEppinov_14. As expected, R&D expenditure has a positive and statistically significant effect on innovation and scientific performance. In the case of the percentage of people with tertiary education, the positive and statistically significant effect can be viewed only regarding international scientific co-publications. Goodness-of-fit ranges between 0.365 and 0.676.

Concerning LDRs, Table 8.8 shows the results from the multivariate regressions using OLS and Tobit methodologies. DumCap and Regiontype_14 do not appear in these models, because all the regions in these sub-samples score the value 0 and 1 in these variables, respectively. It seems that C6_7FP depicts a positive and statistically significant effect on innovation and scientific performance (SMEppinov_14, PPCP_15 and ISCPUB_16). Exactly the same applies to P6_7FP, but with lower coefficients. Similarly to the full sample, R&D expenditures show a positive and statistically significant effect on all the dependent variables analysed. On the contrary, TE_14 and TE_15 are not statistically significant.

According to the results displayed in Table 8.9, C6_7FP shows a positive and statistically significant effect on SMEppinov_14, PPCP_15 and ISCPUB_16, but not on SMEmo_14. Furthermore, these coefficients are lower than in LDRs regarding SMEppinov_14 and higher in the other two. This may mean a higher importance of the coordination of projects in LDRs than in the DRs concerning fostering innovation, and the inverse relation to research outcomes. Likewise, the role played by P6_7FP is less relevant in comparison with LDRs. In this regard, this regressor is not statistically significant, except for SMEmo_14 under OLS, but with a tiny coefficient.

R&D expenditures show the expected positive and statistically significant effect on all the dependent variables, except for ISCPUB_16. In contrast, DumCap only shows a counter-intuitive negative and statistically significant effect on PPCP_15. Finally, the percentage of people with tertiary education tends to depict a positive and statistically significant effect on scientific outcomes (PPCP_15 and ISCPUB_16). It should be taken into account that tertiary education does not play a relevant role in LDRs.

Finally, MIRs show several singularities related to the impact of the EU FPs on innovation and scientific performance (Table 8.10). C6_7FP

Table 8.8 *Regression results with LDRs sample*

	OLS (robust se)[a]						Tobit (robust se)		
	M6 (SMEppinov_14)	M7 (PPCP_15)	M8 (ISCPUB_16)	M9 (SMEppinov_14)	M10 (PPCP_15)	M11 (ISCPUB_16)	M12 (PPCP_15)	M13 (SMEppinov_14)	M14 (PPCP_15)
Constant	0.262930*** (0.0755781)	0.0370842* (0.0216183)	0.115354*** (0.0408125)	0.261943*** (0.0745211)	0.0365670* (0.0215978)	0.113602*** (0.0404710)	0.0378104* (0.0211333)	0.25668*** (0.0736686)	0.0373069* (0.0211162)
C6_7FP	0.0008704*** (0.000267305)	0.0001847*** (0.00006484)	0.0004754** (0.000178761)				0.0001867*** (0.0000630)		
P6_7FP				0.0003376*** (0.000092011)	0.00006821*** (0.00002449)	0.0404710** (0.0000654)		0.0003383*** (0.0000895)	0.0000691*** (0.0000239)
R&D_14	0.0010377*** (0.000230580)			0.0009636*** (0.0002296)				0.0009793*** (0.0002280)	
R&D_15		0.0005905*** (0.0000905)	0.0008865*** (0.0001696)		0.0005760*** (0.0000922)	0.0008510*** (0.0001753)	0.0005938*** (0.0000883)		0.0005791*** (0.0000899)
TE_14	-0.0055965* (0.00309359)			-0.0058498* (0.0030116)				-0.00572073* (0.00293793)	
TE_15		-0.0002220 (0.001151)	-0.0006982 (0.0017636)		-0.0002394 (0.0011498)	-0.0007115 (0.0017547)	-0.0002909 (0.00114497)		-0.0003100 (0.0011445)
N	64	64	64	64	64	64	64	64	64
Adjusted R²	0.339586	0.485649	0.459767	0.374618	0.491049	0.466530			
Chi²							89.33271***	47.25367***	87.72079***
LogL	40.36059	112.6739	76.06837	42.10475	113.0116	76.47148	108.7045	39.39169	109.0530
Sigma							0.0421793 (0.00416124)	0.12698 (0.011258)	0.0419552 (0.00404209)

Note:
a Standard errors in parentheses.
  * $p < 10\%$.
  ** $p < 5\%$.
  *** $p < 1\%$.

Source: Own elaboration.

Table 8.9 *Regression results with DRs sample*

| | OLS (robust se)[a] | | | | | | | |
	M15 (SMEppinov_14)	M16 (SMEmo_14)	M17 (PPCP_15)	M18 (ISCPUB_16)	M19 (SMEppinov_14)	M20 (SMEmo_14)	M21 (PPCP_15)	M22 (ISCPUB_16)
Constant	0.539154***	0.465492***	0.0807961**	0.183272***	0.522348***	0.471323***	0.0442343	0.136938**
	(0.0481359)	(0.0474532)	(0.0398432)	(0.0465625)	(0.0501678)	(0.0473073)	(0.0439910)	(0.056854)
DumCap	-0.0673116	-0.0556133	-0.0685286**	-0.0287417	-0.0510833	-0.0390983	-0.0457177	0.011546
	(0.0529580)	(0.0446459)	(0.0278072)	(0.0355790)	(0.0544508)	(0.0439985)	(0.0345058)	(0.039619)
C6_7FP	0.0005350**	0.0002201	0.000915***	0.001371***				
	(0.0002341)	(0.0002237)	(0.0002426)	(0.0003381)				
P6_7FP					0.0000001	0.000002***	0.000001*	-0.0000002
					(0.0000007)	(0.000000)	(0.000000)	(0.0000007)
R&D_14	0.0000858**	0.0001185***			0.0000978***	0.000128***		
	(0.0000377)	(0.0000283)			(0.0000402)	(0.000032)		
R&D_15			0.000096***	0.000062*			0.00011***	0.000087**
			(0.00003245)	(0.00003281)			(0.00004)	(0.000040)
TE_14	-0.0030141	-0.0032477			-0.0015329	-0.003332*		
	(0.0019259)	(0.0019539)			(0.0021575)	(0.001855)		
TE_15			0.004840***	0.005140***			0.007737***	0.009022***
			(0.00154256)	(0.0016744)			(0.001866)	(0.002039)
N	80	80	82	82	80	80	82	82
Adjusted R²	0.164174	0.195186	0.585754	0.562817	0.117101	0.204396	0.461668	0.371949
LogL	54.97663	53.26260	82.58528	63.56507	52.78503	53.72297	71.84269	48.71204

179

Table 8.9 (continued)

	Tobit (robust se)					
	M23 (SMEppinov_14)	M24 (PPCP_15)	M25 (ISCPUB_16)	M26 (SMEppinov_14)	M27 (PPCP_15)	M28 (ISCPUB_16)
Constant	0.539154***	0.0807961**	0.183272***	0.522348***	0.0442343	0.136938**
	(0.0466074)	(0.0386094)	(0.0451206)	(0.0485748)	(0.0426287)	(0.055094)
DumCap	-0.0673116	-0.0685286**	-0.0287417	-0.0510833	-0.0457177	0.011546
	(0.0512764)	(0.0269461)	(0.0344772)	(0.0527217)	(0.0334372)	(0.038392)
C6_7FP	0.0005350**	0.000915***	0.001371***			
	(0.0002267)	(0.0002351)	(0.0003276)			
P6_7FP				-0.00000008	0.0000011*	0.00000022
				(0.0000007)	(0.0000004)	(0.00000071)
R&D_14	0.0000858**			0.000097**		
	(0.0000365)			(0.000039)		
R&D_15		0.0000960***	0.000062*		0.000111***	0.000087**
		(0.0000314)	(0.000032)		(0.000039)	(0.000039)
TE_14	-0.0030141			-0.001533		
	(0.0018648)			(0.002089)		
TE_15		0.0048397***	0.005140***		0.007737***	0.009022***
		(0.001494)	(0.0016225)		(0.001809)	(0.001976)
N	80	82	82	80	82	82
Chi²	12.77182***	87.28455***	87.91271***	28.08196***	66.31340***	71.96161***
LogL	54.97663	82.58528	63.56507	52.78503	71.84269	48.71204
Sigma	0.121706	0.088383	0.111456	0.125086	0.100754	0.133589
	(0.00885595)	(0.00706906)	(0.00928817)	(0.00989817)	(0.00947756)	(0.0121599)

Notes:

180

Table 8.10   Regression results with MIRs sample

| | OLS (robust se)[a] | | | | | | | |
	M29 (SMEppinov_14)	M30 (SMEmo_14)	M31 (PPCP_15)	M32 (ISCPUB_16)	M33 (SMEppinov_14)	M34 (SMEmo_14)	M35 (PPCP_15)	M36 (ISCPUB_16)
Constant	0.497965*** (0.09497)	0.367391*** (0.085972)	0.076707 (0.056266)	0.195691*** (0.071654)	0.440677*** (0.083137)	0.224641*** (0.079763)	0.025026 (0.054113)	0.133830* (0.068735)
DumCap	-0.114854* (0.064801)	-0.155785*** (0.033945)	-0.051132* (0.028324)	-0.028025 (0.059999)	-0.195773 (0.119630)	-0.113127 (0.109849)	-0.125294** (0.049307)	-0.180157*** (0.061268)
C6_7FP	0.001771* (0.001029)	0.003149*** (0.000820)	0.001711*** (0.000503)	0.002340*** (0.000670)				
P6_7FP					0.000287 (0.000188)	0.000066 (0.000145)	0.000268** (0.000121)	0.0004863*** (0.000142)
R&D_14	0.000070 (0.000094)	0.000168** (0.000081)		0.000157* (0.000080)	0.000085 (0.000097)	0.000290*** (0.000070)		
R&D_15			0.000167*** (0.000058)				0.000167** (0.000076)	0.000126573 (0.000080)
TE_14	-0.004048 (0.003590)	-0.004051 (0.002969)		0.001340 (0.002313)	-0.001816 (0.002928)	0.00224632 (0.00286726)		
TE_15			0.001500 (0.002031)				0.003669* (0.001822)	0.003859* (0.001971)
N	48	48	48	48	48	48	48	48
Adjusted R²	0.025098	0.344651	0.474144	0.473266	0.003213	0.158403	0.417495	0.456180
LogL	27.68660	38.28384	60.27749	51.83434	27.15379	32.28063	57.82203	51.06816

Table 8.10 (continued)

| | Tobit (robust se) | | |
	M37 (PPCP_15)	M38 (PPCP_15)	M39 (ISCPUB_16)
Constant	0.076707	0.025026	0.133830**
	(0.053255)	(0.051217)	(0.065057)
DumCap	-0.051132*	-0.125294***	-0.180157***
	(0.026808)	(0.046668)	(0.057989)
C6_7FP	0.001711***		
	(0.000476)		
P6_7FP		0.000268**	0.000486***
		(0.000115)	(0.000135)
R&D_14			
R&D_15	0.000167***	0.000167**	0.000127*
	(0.000055)	(0.000072)	(0.000076)
TE_14			
TE_15	0.001500	0.003669**	0.003859**
	(0.001923)	(0.0017265)	(0.001865)
N	48	48	48
Chi²	84.85741***	63.86805***	55.20500***
LogL	60.27749	57.82203	51.06816
Sigma	0.0689262	0.0725438	0.0835042
	(0.0076047)	(0.00711955)	(0.00812322)

Notes:
a Standard errors in parenthesis.
* p<10%.
** p<5%.
*** p<1%.

Source: Own elaboration.

182

has a positive and statistically significant effect on innovation outcomes measured by SMEmo_14, but not on SMEppinov_14. In addition, it shows a positive and statistically significant effect on scientific publications (PPCP_15 and ISCPUB_16). In this regard, the coefficients are higher than in LDRs and DRs. Thus, ensuring the attractiveness of these kinds of projects might be a good way to upgrade regional innovation and scientific performance. Concerning P6_7FP, its effects are limited to scientific publications. As can be seen in Table 8.10, the participation in projects under the 6th and 7th FPs has a positive and statistically significant impact upon public–private co-publications and international scientific publications.

MIRs that host their country's capital do not seem to take advantage of the agglomeration economies (urban economies). Thus, DumCap alternates negative and statistically significant effects on innovation and scientific outcomes with statistically insignificant outcomes. These results are in line with the descriptions in the other sub-samples. R&D expenditures depict an expected positive and statistically significant effect on innovation (SMEmo14) and scientific publications (PPCP_15). Lastly, the percentage of people with tertiary education only seems to have a positive and statistically significant impact upon publications (PPCP_15 and ISCPUB_16) under Tobit models (M38 and M39).

4. DISCUSSION AND POLICY IMPLICATIONS

The uneven geographical distribution of the EU FPs seems to trigger further effects on the regional innovation and scientific performance. Since innovation and scientific capabilities are the foundations of long-term growth, these patterns may be key. In this regard, empirical evidences highlight a generally positive and statistically significant impact of the coordination and participation in projects upon regional performance. Likewise, there are slight differences regionally, in terms of impact, when the same analysis is carried out in sub-samples with different economic development levels. Policy implications may arise from this feature and it would also invite policy design and implementation in the European Research Area.

Given the results shown above, the concentration of the coordination and participation in projects would lead to maintaining geographical differences, in terms of innovation and scientific performance. Hence, if the project allocation rationality will be ongoing, interregional disparities may be larger. In other words, the current rationality consolidates the existing European innovation hubs. As indicated by the main results, it is important to keep in mind that the level of regional economic development is already a relevant explanatory variable for the innovation and scientific performance. Concerning the sustainability of this trend, Rodríguez-Pose (2018) asserts that structurally uneven regional economic growth may be self-defeating in order to guarantee well-being, social peace or equality. In fact, empirical evidences are not at all unanimous regarding the capacity of the regional leaders to sustain the general economic growth and welfare through the spillovers towards lagging regions (Tomaney et al., 2010; McCann, 2016).

Concerning the differences among sub-samples, LDRs benefit more from the coordination of projects than DRs regarding innovation performance. By contrast, the opposite applies to scientific publications. Likewise, participation in projects plays a more relevant role in LDRs than in DRs. For these reasons, if the European policy goal were to foster innovation in peripheral regions, it is advisable to encourage the attractiveness capacity there and/or modify the allocation rationality. The same applies to the participation in projects. As indicated by Rodríguez-Pose (2018) regarding general policy design in Europe, place-based policies may be more suitable for overcoming this problem. Policies that do not take into account space dimension, such as in this case with the EU FPs, are actually reinforcing pre-existing hubs. In fact, Reillon (2017) recommends a greater relevance of place-based criteria in the EU innovation policy in order to enhance regional cohesion aims. The change towards more place-sensitive criteria in the allocation of projects would to some extent replace scientific excellence criteria.

Further attention is increasingly paid to those regions inside the middle-income trap (Rodríguez-Pose, 2018). In this regard, this study sheds some light on one of many ways to upgrade them. In MIRs, the effects of the coordination of projects are more significant than in the other two groups. It seems that playing the role of coordinators facilitates the improvement of innovation and scientific performance. Likewise, this could be used as a catching-up instrument to close the gap with European hubs. In fact, Iammarino et al. (2019) recommend the promotion of internationalisation for innovation projects in MIRs as a way to increase regional competitiveness. In any case, coordination of projects is more effective in fostering innovation in LDRs and MIRs than in DRs. Perhaps the reason behind this result is that DRs already have strong innovative capabilities.

Last but not least, it should be noted that the current allocation criteria, based on scientific excellence, may be contradictory with the criteria of the ESIFs for research and innovation. Despite the recent search for complementarities in the context of the Europe 2020 Strategy, lagging R&I regions show relatively low capabilities for attracting H2020 projects but a higher dependence on ESIFs (Pontikakis et al., 2018). The same pattern is noted by Varela-Vázquez et al. (2019) regarding regional economic development and the attractiveness of projects and funding. So, in terms of regional cohesion goals, it is advisable to consider whether the result of such combination is a zero-sum game. Further efforts of redesigning should be necessary in order to create synergies and virtuous cycles, and to enhance regional cohesion.

5. CONCLUSIONS

The EU R&D FPs are the main instrument aimed at fostering research and technology development in the European Research Area. As their allocation criteria are mainly based on scientific excellence and industrial leadership, projects are heavily concentrated on few hubs across Europe. Thus, it is advisable to analyse the effects of the coordination of and participation in projects under the FPs on the regional innovation and scientific performance. This information is useful for its implications regarding future policy design, as well as for the consequences of such geographical concentration of projects on regional cohesion.

The main results highlight a generally positive and statistically significant impact of the coordination of projects under the 6th and 7th FPs upon regional innovation and scientific performance. Nevertheless, the same does not apply to the participation in projects. In any case, the analysis of the sub-samples of regions facilitates detection of some singularities regarding GDP per capita levels. In this way, coordination and participation in projects seem to show a positive and statistically significant effect on the selected dependent variables, but participation in projects indicates lower coefficients. Likewise, coordination of projects shows a higher effect on regional innovation in LDRs than in DRs. However, the opposite applies to scientific publications. In addition, the role played by the participation in projects is less relevant in DRs than in LDRs. Finally, the higher positive and statistically significant coefficients of the coordination of projects corresponds to MIRs.

There is an array of policy implication that stems from these results. Firstly, the concentration of projects in few hubs leads to the increase of geographical differences in innovation and scientific performance and, therefore, in long-term economic growth. This trend may be only partially mitigated through the R&I ESIFs. Secondly, the attractiveness of coordination of projects is more effective in LDRs regarding innovation than in DRs. However, the opposite occurs when we analyse scientific publication. Thirdly, coordination of projects is also more effective in MIRs regarding both innovation and scientific performance than in the other two groups.

Fourthly, it seems that participation in projects shows the higher general impact in LDRs. To sum up, the results of the current allocation design hardly meet regional cohesion challenges.

Concerning limitations and future extensions, it should be noted that the dependent variables used in this study might be complemented by patent data, as patents are one of the main important outcomes of innovation. However, data from this variable cannot be obtained, because the last year available is 2012, one year before the 7th FP was completed. Future studies should be able to overcome this inconvenience. Finally, future extensions to this work should shed light on the effects in the long term of the combination of the EU FPs and R&I ESIFs at the regional level.

REFERENCES

Barajas, A., and Huergo, E. (2010). International R&D cooperation within the EU Framework Programme: Empirical evidence for Spanish firms. *Economics of Innovation and New Technology, 19*(1), 87–111.

Barajas, A., Huergo, E., and Moreno, L. (2012). Measuring the economic impact of research joint ventures supported by the EU Framework Programmes. *Journal of Technology Transfer, 37*, 917–42.

CORDIS. European Commission. (2018). *EU research projects under FP6 and FP7*. Retrieved from https://cordis.europa.eu/projects/home_en.html (on 21 June 2018).

Corpakis, D. (2016). *Fostering synergies between Horizon 2020 and Cohesion Policy*. 6th Meeting of Horizon 2020 National Contact Points for Legal and Financial Matters, Brussels, 16 March. Retrieved from https://www.kpk.gov.pl/wp-content/uploads/2016/07/synergie-2016-03-17.pdf (on 19 November 2019).

Dávid, Á. (2016). The participation of Austria and Hungary in the Framework Programmes for research and technological development of the European Union: A comparative analysis. *Romanian Journal of European Affairs, 16*(4), 48–67.

De Carli, M. (2017). *SEWP and Seal of Excellence: Fostering synergies*. Workshop, Aligning implementation of RIS3 and H2020 funding across research priorities.

European Commission. (2017). *Regional Innovation Scoreboard 2017*. Brussels: European Commission.

European Commission. (2019). *Regional Innovation Scoreboard 2017: Database*. Retrieved from https://ec.europa.eu/docsroom/documents/31644 (on 15 February 2019).

Guzzetti, L. (1995). *A brief history of European Union research policy*. Luxembourg: Office for the Official Publication of the European Communities.

Iammarino, S., Rodríguez-Pose, A., and Storper, M. (2019). Regional inequality in Europe: Evidences, theory and policy implications. *Journal of Economic Geography, 19*, 273–98.

Izsak, K., and Radošević, S. (2017). EU research and innovation policies as factors of convergence or divergence after the crisis. *Science and Public Policy, 44*(2), 274–83.

McCann, P. (2016). *The UK Regional–National Economic Problem: Geography, Globalisation and Governance*. London: Routledge.

Özbolat, N., and Harrap, N. (2018). *Addressing the innovation gap: Lessons for the Stairway to Excellence (S2E) project*. Seville: European Commission. ÇEUR (29287 EN), doi (10.2760/99850)m JRC 1118888.

Pontikakis, D., Doussineau, M., Harrap, N., and Boden, M. (2018). *Mobilising European Structural and Investment Funds and Horizon 2020 in support of innovation in less developed regions*. Seville: Joint Research Centre (JRC) Technical Reports, European Commision.

Reillon, V. (2017). *EU framework programmes for research and innovation: Evolution and key data from FP1 to Horizon 2020 in view of FP9*. Brussels: European Parliament. Retrieved from http://www.europarl.europa.eu/RegData/etudes/IDAN/2017/608697/EPRS_IDA(2017)608697_EN.pdf (on 17 September 2018).

Rodil, Ó. (2007). Innovación y competitividad en la Unión Europea: Las nuevas políticas europeas en el período 2007–2013. In X. Vence, *Crecimiento y políticas de innovación: Nuevas tendencias y experiencias comparadas* (pp. 101–24). Madrid: Pirámide.

Rodríguez-Pose, A. (2018). The revenge of the places that don't matter. *Cambridge Journal of Regions, Economy and Society, 11*, 189–209.

Tomaney, J., Pike, A., and Rodríguez-Pose, A. (2010). Local and regional development in time of crisis. *Environment and Planning A, 42*, 771–9.

Varela-Vázquez, P., González-López, M., and Sánchez-Carreira, M. (2019). The uneven regional distribution of projects funded by the EU Framework Programmes. *Journal of Entrepreneurship, Management and Innovation, 15*(3), 45–72.

Vence, X. (1998). *La política tecnológica comunitaria y la cohesión regional: Los retos de los sistemas de innovación periféricos*. Madrid: Civitas.

Verbeek, M. (2013). *A Guide to Modern Econometrics* (4th edn). Chichester: Wiley.

9. Evolution and change of the Galician innovation system and policies

Manuel González-López

1. INTRODUCTION

This chapter presents a case study of the innovation system and policies of Galicia, a European region in Northwest Spain. As this is a peripheral region both in geographical and in economic terms, analysis of the Galician case aims at extracting lessons about the innovation and policy dynamics of non-core territories. Galicia, which owns relevant legal and political competences on industrial and innovation policies, has progressively built an institutional set-up to support innovation and so to articulate its innovation system. Nevertheless, as we will observe in the following paragraphs, many structural weaknesses persist, explaining the relatively poor innovation performance of the region in comparison with the EU average. The late 2000s economic crisis, which hit particularly hard in southern European economies, accounts also for the difficulties involved in improving the innovation performance. All in all, the Galician economic structure has not experienced significant changes and a conservative pattern has dominated over the last two decades.

2. REGIONAL INNOVATION SYSTEMS AND REGIONAL INNOVATION POLICIES

The innovation system approach views innovation as a collective process in which regional innovation emerges from localized and institutionally supported networks. Such a "regionalization" of the phenomenon of innovation also explains the trend towards regionalization of science and technology (S&T) policy and governance (Cooke et al. 1997; Asheim and Isaksen 1997; Asheim and Gertler 2005). Firms, together with universities and regional governments, are key actors alongside the regional networks for creating, disseminating and using knowledge for economic purposes, and so they shape the evolution of the regional economies.

Regional innovation systems can be viewed from both a top-down and a bottom-up perspective (Howells 1999). From a bottom-up perspective, the concept of regional innovation system links to the economic geography literature, in which proximity and networking are determinant factors for knowledge production and diffusion and for the creation of spill-over effects. Such localized clusters follow a trajectory and moreover are narrowly shaped by social, cultural and institutional factors. In this case, the term "region" derives mainly from a geographical proximity dimension, as sometimes such clusters can be localized in the border spaces of two different countries. However, from a top-down perspective, regional innovation systems are conceived similarly to national innovation systems, so their delimitation depends on the regional governance structure (formal institutional specificities), as well as on productive issues referring to industrial specialization and core/periphery differences. The definition of "region" from this perspective refers largely to a historical or administrative space, i.e. formal institutions like governments and legal frameworks are relevant. This latter view is the one that we will apply to this study, as it fits better with the case of a region well defined from a historical, cultural and political point of view, such as Galicia.

Regarding innovation policies, there is a solid contribution from the Evolutionary School and the Innovation Systems approach on the rationality and type of policies needed for innovation. Evolutionary advocates have focused on the need to address systemic failures based on the understanding that learning processes needed for innovation are the result of multiple interactions in systems involving different agents and institutions (Metcalfe and Georghiou 1997). Such interactions, for instance between universities and industries, are not always fluid and sometimes they do not even exist, and for this reason policy intervention is required.

Nevertheless, as noted by Uyarra (2010), although the innovation literature has discussed in depth the role and rationality of innovation policies, it has generally disregarded the policy-making process itself. This author points out that Evolutionary scholars are usually biased towards normative analysis (what policy-makers ought to do), disregarding the positive analysis (i.e. what policy-makers actually do).

Most recently and linked to the literature about regional systems of innovation, there has been a growing interest in regional innovation policies (González-López et al., 2019). In this regard, the Smart Specialisation (SS) paradigm has been particularly successful both in academic and political terms, as it was adopted and is being applied by the European Union (EU) Cohesion Policy in European regions. The Smart Specialisation Strategy (S3) approach is linked to a topic of growing interest, related to how regional economies change and upgrade, and what is the role of the innovation systems and policies in such transformations (Asheim et al. 2019). Thus, the S3 approach focuses on the need to provoke regional structural change and path transformation (Foray 2014).

Moreover, the Evolutionary perspective identifies policy learning processes as a major source for policy change and evolution (Metcalfe and Georghiou 1997; Witt, 2003; etc.). Policy learning has actually become an area for study in its own right, based on the ideas of the interactive learning approach developed by Bengt-Åke Lundvall (1992) and other authors. Lundvall and Borrás (1998) established the basis of the understanding of innovation policies from this perspective. The authors refer to a new policy paradigm for innovation systems in which the policy-making process also consists of learning and adapting constantly to the new demands and conditions of the economy. Like some of the Evolutionary authors named above, Lundvall and Borrás consider that new practices of innovation policy evolve following an evolutionary logic rather than being created by deliberate design.

Lundvall and Borrás (1998) identify four mechanisms through which policy learning can be encouraged. First, there is policy evaluation for reformulation of innovation strategies. This is one of the commonest mechanisms for policy reformulation and it refers to the assessment of specific projects, programmes or whole policies. Second, the authors identify technology assessment and forecasting. Unlike evaluation, these processes are usually conducted externally and they have largely been used to pinpoint priorities and strategies in the medium and long term. Enhancing the social and political participation in the definition of technological alternatives, is the third mechanism. This usually takes the form of representative committees, in which different stakeholders independent from government structures are represented. Apart from the traditional policy discussion in parliaments, there seems to be an increasing trend towards a more real social participation. Lastly, there is learning from others. This refers to the need to look carefully at the design and implementation of policies in other countries (or regions). Moreover, Sanz-Menéndez and Borrás (2001), in a study about the evolution of EU technology policy, argue that ideas and policy frames provided by expert communities have had a powerful influence in S&T EU policy reformulation. In a similar vein, Mytelka and Smith (2002) point out that policy learning cannot be separated from the development of the field of innovation research itself. Finally, when dealing with the regional case, González-López (2019) identifies a learning channel flowing from a multi-level governance scheme, i.e. learning arises from the continuous interactions between the different administrative layers with competences on innovation policy.

In sum, despite the abundant academic contribution on innovation policies, more studies discussing regional innovation policy cases are needed, in order to extract relevant lessons for academic and policy-making purposes. By analysing the Galician case, we will try to shed some light on how regional economies transform and how this transformation affects and is affected by changes in its innovation system and the innovation policies implemented by the regional government.

3. THE GALICIAN SYSTEM OF INNOVATION

3.1 Changes in the Industrial Specialization

The Galician economy could be included within the group of late industrialized and peripheral European regions as it remained dominated by primary sectors until the 1970s and manufacturing boomed only during the second half of the last century. Nowadays the peripheral character of European regions shows a rather different profile from the one it had before. Now it is shown by a stronger presence of low-tech manufacturing industries and traditional or non-knowledge-intensive services (Vence-Deza and González-López 2008). This is also the picture of the Galician industrial structure in comparison with that of the EU-28 and, to a lesser extent, with that of Spain.

In comparison with the EU-28, the Galician economy specializes in primary activities and services related to retail, transport and accommodation, as well as those pertaining to activities concerning households, arts and entertainment. Other services, particularly those knowledge-intensive ones, are not relatively present within the Galicia economy, although their incidence did increase during the last decade. The weight of manufacturing and construction is at this moment similar to the EU average. Manufacturing has slightly reduced its weight in comparison with incidence within the EU, whilst construction activities have suffered a sharp reduction after the housing bubble burst in 2008, when construction registered abnormally high figures. A similar picture emerges when comparing the Galician economic structure with the Spanish one, with the only exception being the Galician higher specialization in manufacturing activities. Services activities, both low and high knowledge intensive, are in general more present in the Spanish economy (Figures 9.1 and 9.2).

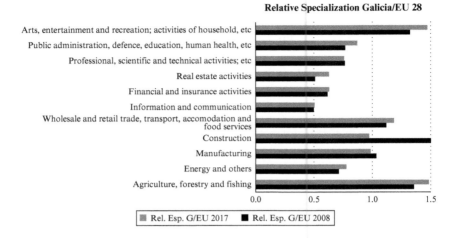

Source: Own elaboration based on data from the Galician Statistics Institute and Eurostat data.

Figures 9.1 and 9.2   Relative specialization, Galicia compared with EU 28 and Spain

The structure of the Galician manufacturing sector can also be analysed by using external trade data. The main exporting industries are the manufacture of wearing apparel, followed by the manufacture of motor vehicles and the manufacture of food products (Figures 9.3 and 9.4). These three activities form the core of the Galician manufacturing industry, each of them with its particularities. The wearing apparel industry stems from the emergence of a group of successful fashion firms during the 1980s, with the notable role of INDITEX (Industria de Diseño Textil, the matrix of Zara and other popular retail branches). Famous for the introduction of "just-in-time" practices in the fashion industry, this company is increasingly inserted within and even leads a global value chain in which the manufacturing itself does not take place in the region but in other parts of the world. This could explain why, at the same time as the industry exports beat a record in 2018, overcoming the car industry for the first time, its direct employment has suffered a sharp decline since the 2000s. In any case, we must not disregard the importance of INDITEX in the Galician economy, as many other activities (consultancy, logistics, metal industry, etc.) have indirectly benefited from the fashion group's expansion. Moreover, the car industry maintains its leading position thanks to the cluster located in Vigo, which was originally reliant on the foreign investment made by the French company Citroën (nowadays PSA Group) in 1957. Nowadays the cluster is formed by a group of supplier companies, many of them not dependent on the PSA Group but inserted in global value chains on their own. Finally, the food industry has historically been a major pillar of the regional economic structure, related to both the fish industry and the milk/ meat industry. Food production has experienced significant growth even during the recent crisis period, which has reinforced Galicia's traditional specialization in the industry.

In general terms, the evolution of the industrial structure of the Galician economy during the last two decades is characterized as follows.

1. Regarding manufacturing, there has been a reinforcement of the traditional specialization patterns as well as a drop in employment since the economic crisis, with the major exception of the food industry. There is no empirical evidence of the emergence of any new relevant specialization. Apart from the food industry, only some branches of manufacturing have registered a positive behaviour, for example computer, electronic and optical products, or machinery and equipment, but these still have a marginal relative weight.
2. Concerning service activities, the Galician economy has experienced a general growth in common with many other economies, but the main feature here is the relatively lower weight of knowledge-intensive services, typical of peripheral economies. As pointed out by González-López (2016) this feature is a major shortcoming of the Galician economy as it weakens the Galician innovation system and results in the draining of highly skilled people from the region.

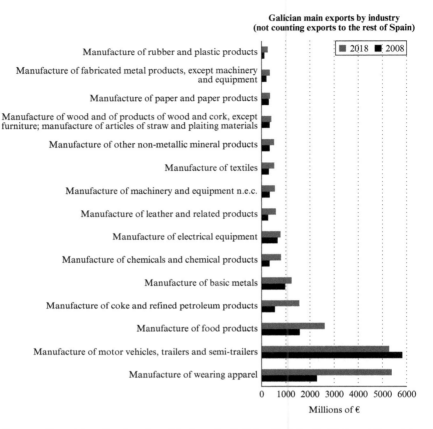

Source: Own elaboration based on data from the Galician Statistics Institute and Eurostat Data.

Figure 9.3   Galician main exports by industry in manufacturing industries

3.2   R&D and Innovation Performance

Galicia shows a moderately low innovation profile in the European context. During the 1990s and the first decade of the current century, research and development (R&D) expenditure on gross domestic product (GDP) continuously increased its share of GDP, reaching 1% in 2008, when the crisis broke out. Since that year, there has been a slight decrease in this indicator and at the time of writing it is lower than half of the EU-27 average. Differences from the EU are even larger when dealing with

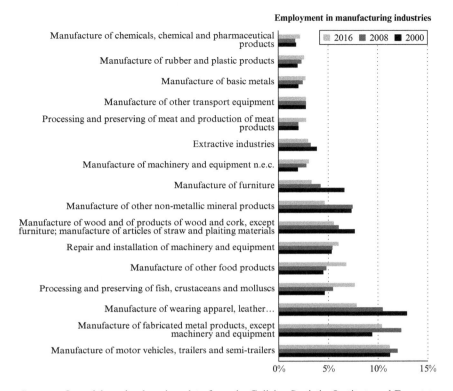

Source: Own elaboration based on data from the Galician Statistics Institute and Eurostat Data.

Figure 9.4 Galician main exports by employment in manufacturing industries

business R&D expenditure, which is approximately half of the total R&D expenditure. Patent activity is even lower than the previous indicators, as the average patent application to the European Patent Office (EPO) per million inhabitants was around 12 per year between 2006 and 2010, ten times lower than the EU average. Finally, the numbers of firms reporting innovation activities has suffered a significant decline since the crisis and only recently has this trend ceased (Figures 9.5 and 9.6).

3.3 Institutional Set-up Supporting Regional Innovation

Most references to Galician innovation policies mention studies of the Galician system of innovation. Yet none of these studies actually discusses

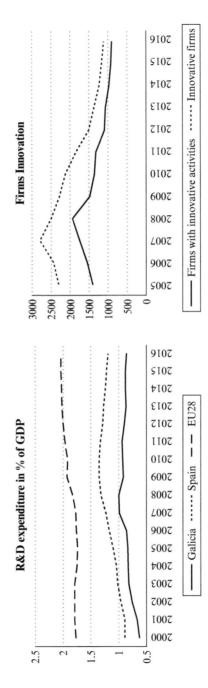

Source: Own elaboration based on Eurostat and Galician Statistics Institute data.

Figures 9.5 and 9.6   R&D expenditure in % of GDP and firms innovation

the policy-making process itself, just normative considerations about the role played by innovation policies on the innovation system performance. Only the paper by González-López (2019) explores in depth the innovation policies implemented in Galicia during the last two decades. This section will largely draw on the previous paper.

3.3.1   The legal framework and institutional organization

According to the Spanish Constitution and the Galician Statute of Autonomy, the Galician government (Xunta de Galicia) owns competencies in promoting industry as well as research activities. Such competencies experienced a major milestone with the passing of the Galician law for promoting research and technological development in 1993. This law presented an integrated view of research and innovation activities and gave legal coverage to the successive Galician Plans for R&D promotion, with the first plan launched in 1999. The next relevant legal change came with the law for promoting research and innovation in Galicia, passed in 2013, which substituted the 1993 law. The 2013 law explicitly regulates the Galician innovation system and the Galician Innovation Agency, which has been in charge of coordinating and executing the innovation policy and the Galician Plans of Research and Innovation since 2015 (see Table 9.1).

The 1st R&D plan was a 3-year plan and ran from 1999 to 2001. There was a significant delay in the approval of the first plan, and this is the reason why it was shorter than the following ones and had a certain transitory character. The plan was managed by the General Secretary's Office for R&D, which had been created by the new government in 1997 in order to integrate most resources and instruments related to innovation; until then, resources and instruments had been dispersed among several ministries. The office started from zero in terms of its very poor human and material resources, which were gradually increased. It was dependent on assistance from the Ministry of Presidency, which, from the institutional viewpoint, ensured its cross-sectional character and reinforced the coordination with all government departments and ministries. The office was created at the beginning of a new legislature but with the same political party and the same prime minister in charge, i.e. the emergence of the Galician innovation policy did not come about due to a political change. According to Mellizo-Soto et al. (2002) the new organization of the Galician innovation policy imitated the Spanish approach, which had been more business oriented due to the advent of the conservative government in the 1996 Spanish elections.

There were no important changes in the policy until 2003, when the General Secretary's Office for R&D became the Directorate-General

Table 9.1   Legal and institutional framework of the Galician innovation policy

R&D Plan	Legal reference	Responsible body
PGIDT 1999–2001	Galician law for promoting research and technological development (1993)	General Secretary's Office for R&D (Ministry of Presidency)
PGIDIT 2002–2005	Galician law for promoting research and technological development (1993)	DG of R&D (Ministry of Innovation, Industry and Trade) DG of Technology and Sectorial Development (Ministry of Innovation, Industry and Trade)
PGIDIT 2006–2010	Galician law for promoting research and technological development (1993)	DG of RD&I (Ministry of Innovation and Industry) DG of Universities S&T promotion (Ministry of Education and Universities)
PGIDIT 2011–2015	Galician law for promoting research and technological development (1993)	DG of RD&I (Ministry of Economy and Industry) substituted by the Galician Innovation Agency in 2015 (Ministry of Economy and Industry) DG of Universities (Ministry of Education and Universities)
RIS3 2014–2020	Galician law for promoting research and innovation (2013)	Galician Innovation Agency in 2015 (Ministry of Innovation, Employment and Industry)

Source: Own elaboration.

(DG) of R&D, dependent on the Ministry of Innovation, Industry and Trade. The reason for this was again the imitation of the Spanish organization design, which had changed in 2000. That meant the loss of the cross-departmental character of the innovation policy and, although the new DG continued to be in charge of coordinating the new R&D Plan (2002–2005), according to González-López (2019) such change was the prelude for a later sharper fragmentation of the innovation policy. In fact, in 2005, coinciding with the formation of a new government, a first (although minor) fragmentation of the R&D policy occurred and the DG of Universities took over some competences previously managed by the DG of R&D. However, the most relevant change took place in 2009, with the return of the conservative party to power. The new cabinet split the R&D resources (and so the R&D policy) between the DG of R&D and innovation (depending on the Ministry of Economy and Industry) and the DG of Universities (depending on the Ministry of Education and Universities). This division between the innovation policy concerning universities and the one concerning both the business sector and the rest of the innovation system agents continued with the creation of the Galician Innovation Agency in 2015. The reasons for this split are mainly the ideological orientation of the new government, which conceived the innovation process mainly as a matter for firms. Nevertheless, this approach is not consistent with the integrated view of innovation, in which research institutions and companies are seen as parts of the whole innovation system.

With regard to the creation of the Galician Innovation Agency (legally approved in 2012 but effectively running since 2015), the objective was basically to create a more flexible and less bureaucratic instrument for coordinating and implementing innovation policies. The political consensus was quite high in this regard, and most of the persons interviewed agreed that the relationship with firms and other stakeholders demanded more flexible structures.

Finally, from the planning viewpoint there is some continuity between 1999 and 2015, when four subsequent R&D plans were approved. This continuity ended in 2015, as no further plans have been elaborated or approved (at least at the time of writing). The persons interviewed opined that this was due to the elaboration of the regional S3 (approved in 2014), which somehow substituted the previous plans although they were methodologically and conceptually different. In fact, the 2013 law refers specifically to R&D Plans as the "fundamental instrument" for planning and coordinating innovation policies in Galicia. Therefore, not having a proper R&D plan appears as an inconsistency with the 2013 law.

3.3.2 Policy learning in Galician innovation policies

Table 9.2 lists the mechanisms of policy learning in Galician innovation policies. As expected, the accumulation of internal experiences and learning-by-doing processes has been identified as a major input for change and learning in Galician regional innovation policies. Apart from the first period when this policy actually started from zero, different types of learning processes have shaped the trajectory towards the consolidation of this policy. As we saw in the two previous sections, both minor and major changes affecting the policy organization, design procedures or instruments, can be related to learning from internal experiences. An example of major policy change is the creation of the Galician Innovation Agency, which was largely due to the need to avoid excessive bureaucratic costs whilst being more flexible and effective. Another change at least partially due to learning through experience is the move towards more

Table 9.2 Policy learning mechanisms

Plan	Experiences accumulation, learning by doing	Evaluation and/or monitoring	Technology assessment and forecasting	Social and political participation	Other regions or countries	Multi-level governance channels	Theoretical rationales
PGIDT 1999–2001	Poor (emergence of the policy)	No	No	Very low (during the plan design) and standard parliament discussion before approval	No	Very important; Spanish innovation policy model	Systematic approach of innovation (abandoning linear model)
PGIDIT 2002–2005	Relevant (initiating the consolidation of the policy)	No	Yes; external reports on R&D priorities were hired (before plan design and during implementation)	Low; seminar with experts during the plan design and standard parliament discussion before approval	Yes; Basque model of technological centres; Catalan model for human resources (both models were poorly adapted)	Important; Spanish R&D plan lineament with EC FwP priorities	Regional Innovation Systems approach

PGIDIT 2006–2010	Relevant (consolidation of the policy)	Formally yes, not in practice	Yes; external reports on R&D priorities were hired (before plan design and during implementation)	Low; standard procedure of discussion at government and parliament	Yes; Basque model for talent attracting Catalan model, Nordic models	Important; lineament with EC FwP priorities	Regional Innovation Systems approach
PGIDIT 2011–2015	Relevant (e.g. change towards more selective instruments)	Formally yes, not in practice	Yes; an external report on R&D priorities was hired before plan design	Low; standard procedure of discussion at government and parliament	Yes; American model (prioritizing credits instead of non-refundable grants)	Important; Spanish innovation policy model	Regional Innovation Systems approach; open innovation theories
RIS3 2014–2020	Relevant (e.g. creation of the Galician Innovation Agency)	Formally yes, not in practice so far	Yes; following RIS³ lineaments, a diagnosis report on innovation potentialities was made before the strategy design	High; working groups with stakeholders, policy-makers, experts, etc.	Yes; Basque model (technological centres network), Catalonia (competitive research groups and talent attracting)	Very important; European Commission lineaments for RIS3	Smart Specialisation

Source: Own elaboration.

selective instruments (a lower number and with higher budgets), which also aimed at reducing bureaucratic costs and increasing their impact. Finally, the implementation of instruments such as the recent programmes of public procurement for innovation has also been the result of a learning-by-doing internal process. As indicated by one of the persons interviewed, "the adoption of these programmes has needed continuous interaction with internal financial and audit units because the general administration was not prepared to deal with such initiatives; in a sense we have been quite innovative in this regard".

Moreover, formal learning channels like evaluation and/or monitoring and technological assessment and forecasting have generally been little used in the Galician innovation policy. There is a very poor policy evaluation tradition in the Galician administration (in common with many other European administrations). Evaluation and monitoring mechanisms have been formally included since the 3rd R&D Plan, but they have not been implemented so far (including the S3 [Smart Specialization] strategy). Regarding technology assessment and forecasting, some reports on R&D and technological trends were hired to private consultants or universities, particularly to support the plans' design.

Learning through social and political participation for policy design and implementation has also been quite poor, with the only exception being the most recent period. Most plans were submitted only to a process of formal socialization and political discussion, and not to a systematized participative process. The most remarkable change happened during the design of the SmaSpe strategy, in which the procedure followed the European Commission (EC)'s requirements by creating working groups with stakeholders, policy-makers and experts, particularly with a view to promoting the entrepreneurial discovery process. Besides this, there are plans for continuing such process of social participation during the implementation of the strategy.

Moreover, one of the most-used channels for policy learning comes from the interaction with the other two governance levels, the Spanish and the European. From the beginning, the Galician innovation policy was especially influenced by the Spanish policy and governance structure. Adaptation of organizational models and instruments has been a constant trend throughout the period analysed. Sometimes it is even difficult to distinguish between policy changes due to learning processes occurring through the interaction with the Spanish government or simply being imitated due to political or normative reasons. As we have previously indicated, the move from a General Secretary's office with a cross-sectional character (directly dependent on the Ministry of Presidency) towards a rather sectorial General Directorate (dependent on the Ministry of

Industry) is an example of change due to imitation. In any case, even if policy change is due to simple imitation of another government level, it also implies some kind of learning, notwithstanding the results of such learning process. Ultimately, as noted by Mytelka and Smith (2002), learning is usually a response to a problem that generates a search with uncertain outcomes.

Likewise, the EU level has also been significant as a source of learning and imitation for the Galician innovation policy, in particular during recent times. Again, the S3 strategy is a key milestone, as it was designed following the EC's guidelines. As pointed out by the person responsible for the innovation policy at that time, "the implementation of the strategy meant a great effort by officers and policy makers regarding learning about the rationality and procedures of the S3" (González-López 2019, p. 114). Furthermore, as indicated in previous sections, the adoption of the S3 implied that all the efforts of the innovation agency were put on its design and implementation. That meant the abandoning of the R&D Plans that were already a consolidated trend in the Galician innovation policy, something with an impact that should be assessed in the future.

Learning from other regions and countries has also been recognized as a relevant learning channel by the Galician policy-makers. Thus, most of the persons interviewed identified two regional models, the Basque and the Catalan, as mirrors to look at in different aspects and particularly when dealing with instruments. The Basque policy for technology centres and the Catalan policies for human resources are two significant examples. These two regions have demonstrated a strong industrial tradition, in addition to a pronounced ambition for deeper political autonomy in Spain. This has probably led in turn to increased ambition and experimentation with regard to their innovation policies. Other models, like the Nordic or the American ones, were identified by some of the interviewees as relevant to specific aspects of the innovation policy.

Finally, regarding the theoretical rationales, according to the persons interviewed the Galician innovation policy has been largely influenced by some of the most remarkable theoretical approaches on regional innovation to have emerged in the previous two decades. The 1st R&D Plan, indicating the emergence of a real innovation policy in Galicia, was an explicit attempt to incorporate a systemic view of innovation and to depart from the linear model. Moreover, the regional innovation systems approach has been much in evidence for the design of the Galician innovation policy particularly since the 2nd Plan (2002–2005). As indicated in the previous section, several instruments have aimed at enhancing the interaction of the different agents of the system (firms, universities, research centres, etc.). Other theoretical approaches have been in one way or another incorporated into the policy, for instance the open innovation theories (included in the rationality of the 4th R&D Plan). Finally, the SS theoretical approach has indirectly been very influential for policy learning during the last period, with the implementation of the Galician Research and Innovation Strategy for Smart Specialisation (RIS3).

4. CONCLUSIONS

This chapter has discussed the case of how the Galician economy, its innovation system and the innovation policies implemented by the region, have changed during the last two decades.

The Galician economy has not experienced deep changes during this time. There has been a reinforcing of the traditional specialization patterns based on the automobile and food industries and the most recent fashion retail sector, with the notable role of the INDITEX business group. There is no empirical evidence of the emergence of any new relevant specialization. With regard to service activities, the Galician economy has experienced a general growth like many other economies, but the main feature is the relatively lower incidence of knowledge-intensive services, typical of peripheral economies. This feature is a major shortcoming of the Galician economy as it weakens the Galician innovation system and results in the draining of highly skilled people from the region.

Concerning its innovation performance, Galicia shows a moderately low innovative profile in the European context. Most of its innovation indicators are below the EU and Spanish average; and the differences, particularly with the EU, have widened after the economic crisis.

Moreover, both innovation policies and the Galician innovation system have gradually consolidated since the end of the 1990s. We have seen how this process has largely been a case of policy learning. In particular, as shown by González-López (2019), the interaction with other government levels constitutes one of the most-used channels for policy learning. Sometimes learning is associated with simple imitation, for various reasons. In the Galician case, imitation of the Spanish innovation policy was a constant trend, particularly during the initial stages, but also when political changes happened at the Spanish level. At other times, learning through multi-level governance channels is needed because it is legally or politically mandatory to adapt to a new political rationality. The implementation of the S3 strategy also constitutes a clear (and maybe extreme) example of this kind of policy learning, as its adoption was mandatory in order to gain access to structural funds. Nevertheless, the need to adopt the S3 strategy has not only implied an important learning process in itself for the Galician policy-makers; it has also been key to enhancing policy learning through other mechanisms. It is a case of learning through social and political participation, as for the first time a systematized process of participation was used for designing and implementing the Galician innovation policy.

All in all, we can conclude that the articulation of a regional innovation system and the progressive consolidation of innovation policies have not served to induce significant changes in the Galician economy. It is an example of a region where a conservative pattern of continuity has dominated and many features typical of peripheral economies persist.

REFERENCES

Asheim, B.T., and M.S. Gertler (2005). The geography of innovation: regional innovation systems. In *The Oxford Handbook of Innovation*, edited by J. Fagerberg, D. Mowery and R. Nelson, 291–317. Oxford: Oxford University Press.

Asheim, B.T., and A. Isaksen (1997). Location, agglomeration and innovation: towards regional innovation systems in Norway? *European Planning Studies*, 5(3), 299–330.

Asheim, B.T., A. Isaksen and M. Trippl (2019). *Advanced Introduction to Regional Innovation Systems*. Cheltenham, UK and Northampton, MA, USA: Edward Elgar Publishing.

Cooke, P., M.G. Uranga and G. Etxebarria (1997). Regional innovation systems: institutional and organisational dimensions. *Research Policy*, 26(4–5), 475–91.

Foray, D. (2014). *Smart Specialisation: Opportunities and Challenges for Regional Innovation Policy*. New York, NY: Routledge.

González-López, M. (2016). A economía galega en perspectiva internacional: avances, feblezas e retos de futuro. *Tempo Exterior*, 33, 69–83.

González-López, M. (2019). Understanding policy learning in regional innovation policies: lessons from the Galician case. *Innovation: The European Journal of Social Science Research*, 32(1), 104–18, DOI: 10.1080/13511610.2018.1519780

González-López, M., B.T. Asheim and M.D.C. Sánchez-Carreira (2019). New insights on regional innovation policies. *Innovation: The European Journal of Social Science Research*, 32(1), 1–7, DOI: 10.1080/13511610.2018.1537121

Howells, J. (1999). Regional systems of innovation. In *Innovation Policy in a Global Economy*, edited by D. Archibugi, J. Howells and J. Michie, 67–93. Cambridge: Cambridge University Press.

Lundvall, B.-Å. (1992). *National Systems of Innovation: Towards a Theory of Innovation and Interactive Learning*. https://doi.org/10.1080/08109029308629360

Lundvall, B.-Å., and S. Borrás (1998). *The Globalising Learning Economy: Implications for Innovation Policy*. Brussels: European Commission.

Mellizo-Soto, M.F., L.S. Menéndez and L.C. Castro (2002). Diseño institucional y preferencias políticas: o cómo equilibrar los intereses académicos en la política de ciencia, tecnología e innovación gallega. *Documento de Trabajo*, 2(9). CSIC.

Metcalfe, J.S., and L. Georghiou (1997). *Equilibrium and evolutionary foundations of technology policy*. CRIC Discussion Paper No. 3, Centre for Research on Innovation and Competition, University of Manchester.

Mytelka, L.K., and K. Smith (2002). Policy learning and innovation theory: an interactive and co-evolving process. *Research Policy*, *31*(8–9), 1467–79.

Sanz-Menéndez, L., and S. Borrás (2001). Explaining changes and continuity in EU technology policy: the politics of ideas. In *The Dynamics of European Science and Technology Policies*, edited by Simon Dresner and Nigel Gilbert, 28–54. Aldershot: Ashgate Publishing.

Uyarra, E. (2010). What is evolutionary about "regional systems of innovation"? Implications for regional policy. *Journal of Evolutionary Economics*, *20*(1), 115–37. https://doi.org/10.1007/s00191-009-0135-y

Vence-Deza, X., and M. González-López (2008). Regional concentration of the knowledge-based economy in the EU: towards a renewed oligocentric model?, *European Planning Studies*, *16*(4), 557–78. DOI: 10.1080/09654310801983472

Witt, U. (2003). Economic policy making in evolutionary perspective. *Journal of Evolutionary Economics*. https://doi.org/10.1007/s00191-003-0148-x

10. The evolution of regional innovation policy in a peripheral area: the case of Apulia region

Ivano Dileo and Francesco Losurdo

1. INTRODUCTION

Over the last years, the topic of innovation has become one of the most important challenges in the regional policy debate as it impacts both directly and indirectly several aspects of a regional economic system. Evidence of these effects suggests the need to analyse in more depth the different application modes of such a policy, differentiating between core and peripheral regions. However, within peripheral regions differences are often highly marked (González-López et al., 2014). These differences mostly depend on various technological paths and trajectories, innovation models and strategies, as well as the legal and institutional framework that each region has experienced over time (Uyarra and Flanagan, 2010).

As pointed out by Tödtling and Trippl (2005) and Isaksen and Jakobsen (2017), the success of innovation systems in less developed and peripheral regions is triggered by diverse basic conditions and push factors (Pylak, 2015) and selection processes (Fitjar and Rodríguez-Pose, 2011).

This circumstance highlights the need for new place-based and territory-oriented approaches, particularly within peripheral and less developed regions where several elements are involved, such as structural factors, abilities and human capital. In the case of Apulia region, apart from geographical peripherality, relational peripherality also plays an important role through the requirement to apply a new regional innovation policy vision capable of meeting new needs and of resolving emerging issues within the global society.

This chapter comprises an attempt to analyse the evolution of regional innovation policy and characteristics of legal and institutional frameworks in Apulia region, as well as examining how long and in what way the related applied actions and instruments have been implemented over the last four EU planning periods. Overall the chapter seeks to understand how to overcome the old policy innovation approach towards the Research and Innovation Strategies for Smart Specialisation (RIS3) model.

The chapter is organized as follows. We begin by focusing on some aspects of the theoretical framework that has been adopted, which includes elements from the debate concerning theoretical elements in peripheral regions. Next, we explain our methodology, particularly with regard to the evolution of regional innovation policy in Apulia, focusing on the legal and institutional frameworks and instruments used within a "three-step process" (formalization, systematization, application). Within this discussion, the Smart Specialisation Strategy for Apulia region is considered. Finally, we present our conclusions on the criticality and strengths of the application of a regional innovation process in Apulia region.

2. THEORETICAL FRAMEWORK

2.1 From the Evolutionary Approach to Regional Innovation Systems

The evolutionary approach to technological change focuses on a long-run perspective in which a variety of technologies is considered. This model was formalized by Schumpeter (1918) to explain the evolution of firms, industries and economies and the creation of new knowledge for entrepreneurial growth (Nelson and Winter, 1982; Malerba and Orsenigo, 1995).

At first, Schumpeter did not emphasize policy support for entrepreneurial and knowledge development, rather highlighting the role of SMEs. Only at a later stage (Schumpeter, 1939) did he mostly focus on the role of larger firms and the need for higher investments in R&D for innovation.

Unlike neoclassical models (Samuelson, 1973), evolutionary economics supported state intervention in market failures and the non-linear path of the innovation process to increase technological capabilities (Edler and Fagerberg, 2017; Tödtling and Trippl, 2005). Accordingly, the evolutionary approach considers public policy as a key instrument for removing lock-in processes and reducing barriers that impede the adaption of technologies in learning mechanisms (Dosi, 1988). Scholars such as Metcalfe (1994, 1995, 2002) and Witt (2003) have observed linkages between the generation of new inventions and the selection process for long-run development. Subsequently, the evolutionary model has included the policy debate in a wider context, corroborating the existence of diverse selection processes and innovation policies supported by different government mechanisms and regulations (Borrás and Edler, 2014).

Since the 1980s, thanks to innovation systems models, the perspective has changed and the impact of public policy has started to be more dominant. The rationale behind this development is based on the interplay among different actors, institutions and technologies (Edquist, 1997), which generates synergies. Scholars including Lundvall (1992) first formalized the concept of the National Innovation System (NIS) and following this Cooke (1992, 2002, 2003) emphasized the differences between the NIS and the Regional Innovation System (RIS), indicating that an RIS aims at defining elements able to operate throughout the region, such as competences in regional financing, cooperation between actors, and networking processes among stakeholders and policy makers (Asheim and Coenen, 2005). Pekkarinen and Harmaakorpi (2006) have fostered the multi-actor innovation models as a crucial approach for reducing cultural barriers to innovation.

According to Tödtling and Trippl (2018), regions vary depending on their specific characteristics, as well as their capacity to attract and absorb innovation. Boschma (2005) has opined that regional innovation policy should address the reconstruction of old institutions by discovering new opportunities. In this wide framework, a mixed approach to policy making may be suitable, in accordance with the level of investment planned. It follows that a unique efficient policy does not exist, as it depends on economic structure, regional differences in innovation capabilities, and the related complexities that may impact the performance of an innovation and research and development (R&D) policy whose effects are lagging by ten or twenty years. Moreover, also in terms of the impact of innovation policies, the selection of policy instruments is significant too (Uyarra and Flanagan, 2010).

Particularly in peripheral areas, this approach is strongly hindered by lock-in processes, weaker absorption capacity of innovation and a modest RIS structure. Unlike Schumpeterian and neoclassical views, RIS rationale accounts for the importance of policy not only as a mere instrument able to respond to market failures but also as a reaction to the failure of capabilities, scarce capacity to absorb skills and poor relationships among regional actors (Weber and Truffer, 2017).

Both innovation-oriented regional policies and learning processes are crucial for the success of a region in an RIS. Benneworth et al. (2017) and Jiao et al. (2016) have observed the significant role of universities and research centres in stimulating a cultural environment based on innovation. In this regard, policy makers should pay more attention to institutional changes, as these mostly affect the level of interactions among actors and innovation performance in an RIS (Zhao et al., 2015).

Additionally, a new approach to capabilities in an RIS (Zhao et al., 2015) shows that institutions should require only a small group of performing industries and sectors to obtain higher productivity gains and innovation advantages. Recently, the concept of "differentiated knowledge bases" (Asheim et al., 2011) has revealed the need for a new and broader systemic approach in which greater integration among different knowledge bases emerges depending on the region's capacity to innovate.

2.2   Innovation Policy in Peripheral Regions

Regions are not homogenous entities, as they present a variety of different characteristics. According to Rosenfeld (2002), there are three types of regions: (1) old industrialized regions dominated by labour-intensive industries; (2) semi-industrialized regions, based on the presence of small and medium-sized enterprises (SMEs) and low-tech industries; (3) peripheral regions or less populated ones.

Although the concept of peripheral regions arises from the geographical location of a region, scholars provide various interpretations of the term (Crescenzi, 2005). For instance, Keeble et al. (1988) define peripheral regions as those regions with scarce access to the market, which in turn impedes the rise of their competitive advantage. Copus (2001) has observed that a region is increasingly peripheral when its creation of new knowledge and related infrastructures is lacking. Other scholars (Tödtling and Trippl, 2005) have pointed out that the lack of dynamic clusters increases the gap with more developed and central regions; in fact, differences between central and more peripheral regions are exacerbated by the fact that many functions are often located in core regions, due to the presence of broader relationships between firms and universities and stronger cooperation networks among stakeholders (Morgan and Nauwelaers, 1999). Peripheral regions are also constrained by the risk of political lock-in (Hassink, 2005), which slows the shift of innovation policy from old political practices towards new policy-making approaches (Lorenzen, 2001). Also, Oughton et al. (2002) have noted that the lagging regions are less able to use public funds for innovation-based activities because of their lack of learning capacity and competences (Morgan and Nauwelaers, 1999); the right use of financial resources may support institutions to create new instruments and methods (North and Smallbone, 2006; Karlsen et al., 2011; Melancon and Doloreux, 2011).

Peripherality can also mean lack of network with outside actors (Copus and Skuras, 2006). In this respect, regional institutions play a crucial role in setting up external linkages. For instance, addressing actions to improve relationships between university and regional government represents a strong factor for boosting innovation and building higher education infrastructure systems (e.g., Benneworth and Charles, 2005; Kempton, 2015; Pinto et al., 2015; Eder, 2019).

However, it is widely acknowledged that a well-targeted innovation policy is crucial for triggering a real performing innovation process in a long-run view; there cannot be a "one-size" innovation policy capable of fitting all solutions for different region cases (Niosi, 2011). To date, a range of concerns and critical issues have arisen from studies in this field (e.g., Liagouras, 2010; Karlsen et al., 2011; Brown, 2016).

3.   METHODOLOGY

This section discusses the methods, data and research design we have selected for our analysis. The case study aims at illustrating the characteristics of the industrial system in Apulia region, underlining peculiarities, new trends and criticalities regarding the structure of the regional economic system, through the use of data drawn from the Italian National Institute of Statistics and Eurostat. After that, we consider the RIS, mostly focusing on some innovation indicators used in the literature and using these to compare Apulia region with the European Union (EU) as a whole.

Finally, we discuss the evolution of the regional legal and institutional framework with a particular emphasis on the policy changes that occurred during four EU planning periods. We seek to show the main changes that have taken place since the emergence of the regional innovation policy to the present. In particular, we show the changes and improvements in the instruments and phases that have influenced the structure of the regional innovation policy organization.

3.1   The Regional Innovation System in Apulia Region

3.1.1   The regional production system
According to the Regional Innovation Scoreboard (2017), Apulia is a moderate innovation region. The contribution of regional value added to the national value was 4.3% in 2017 (Istat, 2018), whereas the regional gross domestic product (GDP) per capita is about 6.3% of the national average.

The gap between southern and northern regions is somewhat wide. In 2017, GDP per capita in the South was 24,500 and in the North it was 34,850. Moreover, during 2011–2016, the southern macroarea accounted for the highest GDP decrease (–0.6%) within all the macroareas.

The regional production system shows relatively high productivity in the agricultural sector, which generates a large part of the regional GDP. Other economic branches, such as agro-food production, chemicals and sofas, are mostly oriented towards non-local and international markets (Apulia Region, 2014). However, the Apulia regional productive system is also characterized by a services sector that is weak yet constantly increasing. Most of the firms located in the region are family-owned businesses that for the most part have fewer than twenty employees. Also, the R&D sector and high-tech economic activities show a specialization index slightly higher than 0.5.

Before the Maastricht Treaty, Italy was not yet characterized by regional innovation systems within peripheral regions. Since the treaty took effect, Innovation and Technology (I&T) activities have been shifted from old industrialized regions to peripheral ones following the decentralization process of the biggest public and private companies, in line with the path-dependence model. Over the last twenty years, the industrial structure of Apulia region has changed radically. Alongside highly capital-intensive large-scale industry – such as Ilva, which operates in the steel-making sector in Taranto, and Eni (petrochemicals) in Brindisi – a network of SMEs has gradually expanded. Consequently, highly specialized areas have emerged, such as food processing and vehicles in the province of Foggia; footwear, textiles, wood and furniture in the Barletta area north of Bari; engineering, wood and furniture, and computer software around the Bari area; wood and furniture in the Murge area to the west; textiles and clothing in Monopoli-Putignano to the south; and footwear and textiles in the Casarano area. The result of this emergence has been increasing performance both inside and outside the regional economic system.

Almost all these large companies have become sources of technological innovation in Apulia region, as they have also involved several small local firms in the production process and triggered a radical transformation in the education and knowledge infrastructure system. This process has been strongly supported by regional policy makers and today the design of the RIS is based on a path-dependent road-map.

3.1.2   The science and technology system

To analyse the innovative output of a region, a variety of indicators may be used. We make use of data collected from databases and official documents of Eurostat. Despite increasing attention to innovation by policy makers and improved dynamics in high-tech activities, Apulia region is still lacking substantial innovation performance (Table 10.1).

During the 1990s and the first decade of the current century, R&D expenditure continuously increased its share of the GDP, reaching 0.76% in 2012. Although it registered a slight increase, the share of intramural R&D expenditure in total regional GDP is still low. Indeed, R&D expenditure accounts for just 0.99% in 2015, in contrast to the EU28 average of 2.04%.

The contribution of high-tech sectors is generally modest and largely concentrated in northern Italy. In particular, the regional share of employment

Table 10.1   Some innovation indicators in Apulia region and in the EU28

	Apulia	EU 28
Population (2018)	4,048,242	508,273,732
GDP capita (pps) (2017)	18,700	29,800
Unemployment rates, % (2017)	18.90	7.60
Intramural R&D expenditure, % GDP (2015)	0.99	2.04
Persons with tertiary education and employed in science and technology (% of active population) (2018)	12.90	21.80
Patent applications to the EPO (per million inhabitants) (2011)	16.36	113.87
Employment in high-tech sectors (% of total employment) (2017)	1.40	4.00

Source: Own elaboration based on Eurostat.

in high-tech sectors in total employment level was somewhat low in Apulia in 2017 (1.4%), as was the percentage of persons with tertiary education and employed in science and technology in 2018 (12.9% vs. 21.8% EU28).

Applications to the European Patent Office (EPO) are even lower than the previous indicators; in fact, the average patent application to the EPO per million inhabitants was around 16.36 in 2011, i.e. almost seven times lower than the EU 28 average.

Despite its lagging development and structural imbalances in its innovation activities, Apulia region is able to leverage on some peculiarities such as the aerospace industry and substantial investments made in the area of nanotechnologies, also characterized by increasing technical competences.

Moreover, Apulia region is characterized by a good research infrastructure system. The region contains three public universities (Bari, Foggia and Salento), one polytechnic university and a private university (LUM, Libera Università Mediterranea). Apulia also boasts a structure in which the National Institute for Nuclear Physics (INFN) operates, as well as, for instance, the Center for Biomolecular Nanotechnologies, a research centre, and the Institute of Energy and Sustainable Development.

The University of Salento specializes in the fields of biotechnologies, applications, nanosciences and aerospace. Local aerospace companies operate in global value chains, strongly contributing to the growth of suppliers of components.

According to ARTI (Regional Agency for Technology and Innovation), in 2012 Apulia accounted for the highest amount of new spin-offs (17) and in 2015 Apulia was positioned first in southern Italy in terms of spin-off concentration. Finally, important private research centres such as Cetma, Alenia, Augusta, Planetek, Masmec, Bosch group, Mer Mec and Itel are located in the region. Among the technological districts, one of the most representative is the Mechatronics District, which was established in Apulia as a strategic tool for research and innovation (R&I) policy.

3.2   Regional Innovation Policy in Apulia Region

3.2.1   The evolution of legal and institutional frameworks

In Italy, regional governments play an important role in outlining innovation policy (Table 10.2). During the 1994–1999 EU planning period, Apulia region launched the POP (Progetto Operativo Plurifondo) 1994–1999, established by the regional act n.5/95. During this period, the regional innovation governance system started to be based on innovation leverage.

The reform of the Italian constitutional law in 2001 allowed for reorganizing regional institutions and shifting some administrative functions from the national level to the regional governments, under the rationale of the multi-level governance principle.

In the case of Apulia, the main authority in charge of innovation policy is the Apulia Region's Office for Economic Development, Jobs and Innovation. This body has full legislative and constitutional powers in developing innovation and control of regional policy in the R&I sector. Since its inception, Italian regions have progressively increased their legislative power in defining R&D and technological innovation strategies as well as the creation of their own regional agencies for innovation and research centres.

During the 2000–2006 planning period, Apulia designed the first organic Regional R&D Strategy (2001), and in 2003 established the Regional R&D Strategy Realization Plan. As a convergence region, the Apulia innovation system was supported by EU funds (such as ERDF [European Regional Development Fund] and ESF [European Social Fund]) and operation programmes such as the Regional Operational Programme (POR), according to general lines enacted by the National Operational Programme (PON) and the Interregional Operational Programme (POI).

POR 2000–2006 represented the reference document for regulating regional interventions aimed at developing innovation and the technological infrastructure system in Apulia region. The main coordination body was the State–Regions Conference alongside the Committee for the National Operational Programme for Research and Competitiveness, which defines the Framework Programme Agreement (APQ).

Nevertheless, the distribution of competences for supporting innovation was still vague; this means that in some cases the national government may promote similar initiatives in overlap to those promoted by regional governments, thus causing critical issues in terms of coordination of the actions between these two levels of government. This complexity is further exacerbated by a large number of bodies created during the last twenty years for supporting innovation and R&D development, such as technological parks, research centres and so on.

However, during previous years, regional government has made some important progress in innovation fields. At the time of writing, the innovation strategy is based on a bottom-up approach and elaborated through the support of ARTI, which was established in 2005 to facilitate matching between demand of innovation and implementation of policy actions (e.g., for the elaboration of the Regional Strategy for Research and Innovation), and for the first time to rationalize and support regional institutions to improve cooperation between public sectors and private firms.

The consultation mechanism includes the involvement of other regional organizations, such as the regional ILO (Industrial Liaison Office) network, the productive districts and the university system, in line with the priorities launched by the Regional Strategy for Innovation.

The regional government is also supported by other stakeholders, such as InnovaPuglia and Puglia Sviluppo, which were established in 2008. They represent intermediate bodies, with the aim to replace the role of the technological parks Technopolis and FinPuglia. InnovaPuglia supports regional administrative functions in terms of investment plans in technology and innovation initiatives for local production and implements the Digital Agenda for Europe; Puglia Sviluppo implements initiatives for supporting innovation in local productive systems with the assistance of the ERDF. During this phase, Apulia region has mostly concentrated on policy learning mechanisms, including the preparation of tools and implementation actions. The foundation for a knowledge-based society was laid thanks to a stronger focus on the role of human capital, higher education levels and integration into international networks of research cooperation.

During the 2007–2013 period, Italian regions started to systematize their policy approach (Caloffi et al., 2013), shifting the rationale to a more technology-based system. After the creation of productive districts in traditional sectors with the law n. 317/1991, in 2007 the Ministry of Education and Research (MIUR) introduced law n. 23, which launched technological districts, formed by high-tech local firms and spatially agglomerated. Within this frame, Apulia effectively organized the territory into technological districts in the fields of aerospace, food, cultural heritage, biotechnology and life science, energy and environment, logistics and production technology, mechanics and mechatronics, new materials and nanotechnology, and information and communication, and strengthened

Table 10.2 Main legal references for outputs and instruments in Apulia region (1994–1999; 2000–2006; 2007–2013)

R&I planning period	Legal reference	Most important output/s	Responsible body	Instruments
1994–1999	Regional act n. 5 (1995), "Norms for the realization of the POP 1994–1999"	POP 1994–1999	Regione Puglia, Area Politiche per lo Sviluppo, il Lavoro e l'Innovazione, Servizio Ricerca Industriale e Innovazione	– Financial subsidies for R&D and innovation – Promotion of technological innovation in SMEs
2000–2006	DM (Decreto Ministeriale) n. 593 (2000)	Regional R&D Strategy (2001) Regional R&D Plan (2003) POR 2000–2006 Scientific Research Framework Programme (2005)	Regione Puglia, Area Politiche per lo Sviluppo, il Lavoro e l'Innovazione, Servizio Ricerca Industriale e Innovazione	– Aids to industrial system, SMEs and handicrafts – Funds to empower risk capital of SMEs – Actions for human capital (grants, loans, internships) – Long-life education and training in Hard Sciences – Financial support to private research laboratories

| 2007–2013 | Regional law n. 23 (2007) Regional acts n. 146 (2008) and n. 2941 (2011) Regional acts n. 20 and 25 (2008) Regional act n. 507 (2010) | Technological Districts POR 2007–2013 Regional Strategy for R&I 2007–2013 | Regione Puglia, Area Politiche per lo Sviluppo, il Lavoro e l'Innovazione, Servizio Ricerca Industriale e Innovazione | – ILO Puglia (Industrial Liaison Offices), Research and Technology Organizations, nonprofit organizations, support infrastructures
– Public–private research laboratories networking (TTO, Technology Transfer Offices)
– Back to the Future (research grants)
– R&D investment support for SMEs
– Support to newly established innovative SMEs – start-up (risk capital, skilled workers employment)
– Support to SMEs networks for the diffusion of ICT (post-diploma and post-degree education; post-degree and research scholarships; support to researchers' mobility to companies; excellence training, Competence Centers)
– Future in Research (funds for academic fellowships) |

Source: Own elaboration based on Regional Innovation Monitor Plus (2016) and POR 2007–2013.

the cooperation strategy by involving universities, research institutions and other stakeholders in the consultation process. This represents the region's first attempt to formalize and apply public policy to advanced technological activities.

Thus, Apulia region created the Regional Strategic Document, the National Strategic Framework (QSN) and the Strategic Document for the Mezzogiorno (DSM), all targeted towards defining strategies for a joint use of EU and national funds, and adopted the PON on Research and Competitiveness for 2007–2013. Finally, the regional act n. 507 (2010) launched the Regional Strategy for R&I for the period 2007–2013.

This new technology-based approach was an attempt to marginalize the diffusion-based model (Muscio and Orsenigo, 2010), thus lowering the fragmentation of financial resources and increasing the concentration of funds to priority areas. Nevertheless, in the case of Apulia region, the increasing autonomy of the regional administrations did not yet match the autonomy in terms of fundraising and financing of policy initiatives as defined by the PON.

During the 2007–2013 period, more instruments were addressed concerning innovation and R&D. Indeed, targeted actions were increasingly devoted to improving human capital level and higher education systems, as well as to supporting high-tech innovative SMEs.

Although 2000–2006 was characterized by strong and direct support of technological innovation, during 2007–2013 many instruments were more focused on the relationships between R&D sector and innovative firms, including Information and Communications Technology (ICT).

3.2.2 SmartPuglia 2020: RIS3 main characteristics in Apulia region

The new strategy for innovation 2014–2020 emphasizes innovation and technology as cross-cutting factors for implementing a systematic and integrated long-term vision carried out jointly by the regional government, stakeholders and R&D structures within a very small set of priority sectors and actions based on higher competences (Table 10.3). The so-called SmartPuglia 2020 strategy was prepared between 2012 and 2013, but regional government formally approved it through the regional act n. 1732 (2014).

During the current phase, the POR is articulated in the attempt to overcome some structural barriers such as low productivity and low employment rates. Indeed, through the Digital Agenda Flagship initiative, Europe 2020 recognized the main role of the ICT sector. From this point forwards, Apulia region started to implement a more synergic policy model thanks to the interrelation between the Smart Specialisation Strategy and the Digital Agenda strategy in the attempt to identify a new policy approach for integrating cross-cutting policies on R&D, innovation, competitiveness and training with other vertical policies such as those for improving environment, transport and healthcare.

This new innovation model identifies five actors in a sort of "Quadruple Helix" model (Carayannis et al., 2012), an extension of the model based on the "Triple Helix" (Etzkowitz and Leydesdorff, 2000), in which government, industry, university, research centres and society cooperate to face societal challenges and improve research infrastructures in a more open vision. Low demand for innovation in the region makes this goal quite difficult to achieve, in the context of an industrial system mostly based on SMEs and a low absorption capacity of graduates.

However, thanks to new measures such as technology clusters, openlab and Future in Research (FIR), Apulia region acquired impressive financial resources. The so-called Openlabs Initiative enforced the pre-commercial procurement scheme of the past planning period in an attempt to foster regional actors for supporting innovation ICT actions as leverage for the "open innovation" process. FIR is a regional initiative aimed at supporting the employment of non-tenured researchers in the academic research area. The initiative was financed for the first time during the 2007–2013 period with the support of the Development and Cohesion Fund and once again in 2018, consistently with the overall regional innovation strategy goals (the REFIN initiative).

The Apulian ICT Living Labs is an "open ecosystem" project that was created for active participation of potential users in the research and experimentation process of innovative solutions, through the use of ICTs. Finally, Pass Laureati is a project consistent with the Europe 2020 Strategy, with the objectives of RIS3 and KETs (key enabling technologies), aimed at favouring and supporting higher education and attending university master's courses in Italy and abroad. These measures demonstrate that SmartPuglia 2020 is not a static plan but continuously on the move, dynamic, and considered the main tool for a long-term strategic and systemic view.[1]

4.   CONCLUSIONS

Apulia region lags behind the national and European economic systems in terms of innovation performance. Despite the recent financial crisis, regional institutions started a process aimed at enforcing both regional innovation governance and an innovation policy approach. Nevertheless, existing limits and the fairly large delay in R&D actions are still evident in the whole region. The ongoing reorganization does not seem to have realized long-term investments for human resources training and the

Table 10.3   Main instruments, goals and budget (R&I 2014–2020)

R&I period	Instruments/ measures	Goal	Budget (Million Euros)	Funds (direct and indirect)	Responsible
2014– 2020	Open labs	Support for innovation and ICT actions	9	FESR*/ FEASR**, Horizon	Regione Puglia, Area Politiche per lo Sviluppo, il Lavoro e l'Innovazione. Servizio Ricerca Industriale e Innovazione
	FIR	Funds for fellowships	26	FSE***, Horizon 2020	
	REFIN	Funds for fellowship	25	FSE, Horizon 2020	
	Action Pacts for cities	Regional network based on advanced digital services	11	FESR, Horizon 2020, Life	
	Living Labs	Developing new products and services for companies and families	24	FESR, Cosme, Life	
	Pass Laureati	Voucher for post-university training	10	FSE, Horizon 2020, ERASMUS+, Europa creativa, PSCI****	
	Regional Technology Clusters	Collaborative research targeted at businesses and research institutions that are part of a regional technological district.	30	FESR/ FEASR, Cosme, Life	

Notes:
   *   Fondo Europeo per lo Sviluppo Regionale (European Regional Development Fund [ERDF]).
  **   Fondo Europeo Agricolo per lo Sviluppo Rurale (European Agricultural Fund for Rural Development [EAFRD]).
 *** Fondo Sociale Europeo (European Social Fund [ESF]).
**** Programma per il Cambiamento Sociale e l'Innovazione (Programme for Social Change and Innovation).

Source: Elaboration based on Regional Innovation Monitor Plus (2016) and SmartPuglia 2020 (2015).

regional system shows a deep dependence on the supply of innovation by the university system.

    Thanks to the increasing support of ARTI and other regional agencies, the regional government has implemented an increasing consultation process involving regional stakeholders aimed at discussing the priorities of the POR 2014–2020. In fact, the current POR is more articulated, showing the new role of stakeholders and a wider university–industry cooperation process within the regional innovation system. The SmartPuglia 2020 Strategy has certainly provided new insights in this perspective to better address the cross-cutting approach of innovation and digital policies through new applied policy measures and instruments.

However, the capacity to convert the conceptual and methodological RIS3 framework into concrete projects is still uncertain. This is also true for both less developed and peripheral regions where the strategy requires the operationalization of concepts introduced only recently and where the risk of overlap with past models is difficult to avoid.

In Apulia region, involvement of local actors through Living Labs helped the process of identifying technological needs during the RIS3. The academic system has achieved important goals in terms of responding to the regional demand for human capital through increasing academic courses in the science fields.

While regional stakeholders are trying to foster university–industry interaction, it will be very hard for businesses to interact with academics on technology transfer initiatives if there is too much cognitive distance and they lack the human capital required for engaging in collaborations.

NOTE

1. Two important structural funds, European Structural and Investment Funds (ESIFs) and Horizon 2020 (H2020), have been established to meet the goals of the Regional Digital Agenda.

REFERENCES

Apulia Region (2014). Smart Specialization Strategy. *Smartpuglia 2020*, March 2014.
Asheim, B., and Coenen, N. (2005). Knowledge bases and regional innovation systems: Comparing Nordic clusters. *Research Policy*, 34(8), 1173–90.
Asheim, B., Boschma, R., and Cooke, P. (2011). Constructing regional advantage: Platform policies based on related variety and differentiated knowledge bases. *Regional Studies*, 45(7), 893–904.
Benneworth, P., and Charles, D. (2005). University spin-off policies and economic development in less successful regions: Learning from two decades of policy practice. *European Planning Studies*, 13(4), 538–57.
Benneworth, P., Pinheiro, R., and Karlsen, J. (2017). Strategic agency and institutional change: Investigating the role of universities in regional innovation systems (RISs). *Regional Studies*, 51(2), 235–48.

Borrás, S., and Edler, J. (2014). Introduction: On governance, systems and change, in S. Borrás and J. Edler (eds), *The Governance of Socio-Technical Systems: Explaining Change*, Eu-SPRI Forum on Science, Technology and Innovation Policy, Cheltenham, UK and Northampton, MA, USA: Edward Elgar Publishing, 23–48.

Boschma, R.A. (2005). Proximity and innovation: A critical assessment. *Regional Studies*, 39(1), 61–74.

Brown, R. (2016). Mission impossible? Entrepreneurial universities and peripheral regional innovation systems. *Industry and Innovation*, 23(2), 189–205.

Caloffi, A., Rossi, F., and Russo, M. (2013). Does participation in innovation networks improve firms' relational abilities? Evidence from a regional policy framework. DRUID, Copenhagen Business School, Department of Industrial Economics and Strategy/Aalborg University, Department of Business Studies: DRUID Working Papers 13-07.

Carayannis, E., Thorsten, B., and Campbell, D. (2012). The Quintuple Helix innovation model: Global warming as a challenge and driver for innovation. *Journal of Innovation and Entrepreneurship*, 1(2), 1–12.

Cooke, P. (1992). Regional innovation systems: Competitive regulation in the new Europe. *Geoforum*, 23(3), 365–82.

Cooke, P. (2002). Regional innovation systems: General findings and some new evidence from biotechnology clusters. *The Journal of Technology Transfer*, 27(1), 133–45.

Cooke, P. (2003). Strategies for regional innovation systems: Learning transfer and appplications, Policy Paper. United Nations Industrial Development Organization, Vienna.

Copus, A.K. (2001). From core-periphery to polycentric development: Concepts of spatial and aspatial peripherality. *European Planning Studies*, 9(4), 539–52.

Copus, A., and Skuras, D. (2006). Business networks and innovation in selected lagging areas of the European Union: A spatial perspective. *European Planning Studies*, 14(1), 79–93.

Crescenzi, R. (2005). Innovation and regional growth in the enlarged Europe: The role of local innovative capabilities, peripherality and education. *Growth and Change*, 36, 471–507.

Dosi, G. (1988). The nature of the innovative process, in G. Dosi, C. Freeman, R. Nelson, G. Silverberg and L. Soete (eds), *Technical Change and Economic Theory*, London: Pinter, 221–38.

Eder, J. (2019). Innovation in the periphery: A critical survey and research agenda. *International Regional Science Review*, 42(2), 119–46.

Edler, J., and Fagerberg, J. (2017). Innovation policy: What, why, and how. *Oxford Review of Economic Policy*, 33(1), 2–23.

Edquist, C. (1997). Systems of innovation approaches: Their emergence and characteristics, in C. Edquist (ed.), *Systems of Innovation: Technologies, Institutions and Organisations*, London: Pinter, 1–35.

Etzkowitz, H., and Leydesdorff, L. (2000). The dynamics of innovation: From National Systems and "Mode 2" to a Triple Helix of university–industry–government relations. *Research Policy*, 29, 109–23.

Eurostat [n.d.]. Regional Accounts, via https://ec.europa.eu/eurostat/web/national-accounts/regional-accounts (accessed on 26 November 2019).

Fitjar, R.D., and Rodríguez-Pose, A. (2011). Innovating in the periphery: Firms, values and innovation in southwest Norway. *European Planning Studies*, 19(4), 555–74. DOI: 10.1080/09654313.2011.548467.

González-López, M., Dileo, I., and Losurdo, F. (2014). University–industry collaboration in the European regional context: The cases of Galicia and Apulia region. *Journal of Entrepreneurship, Management and Innovation*, 10(3), 57–87.

Hassink, R. (2005). How to unlock regional economies from path dependency? From learning region to learning cluster. *European Planning Studies*, 13(4), 521–35.

Isaksen, A., and Jakobsen, S.E. (2017). New path development between innovation systems and individual actors. *European Planning Studies*, 25, 355–70.

Istat (2018). Conti Economici Territoriali, via https://www.istat.it/it/archivio/conti+ territoriali (accessed on 26 November 2019).

Jiao, H., Zhou, J., Gao, T., and Liu, X. (2016). The more interactions the better? The moderating effect of the interaction between local producers and users of knowledge on the relationship between R&D investment and regional innovation systems. *Technological Forecasting and Social Change*, 110, 13–20.

Karlsen, J., Isaksen, A., and Spilling, O. (2011). The challenge of constructing regional advantages in peripheral areas: The case of marine biotechnology in Tromsø, Norway. *Entrepreneurship and Regional Development*, 23, 235–57.

Keeble, D., Offord, J., and Walker, S. (1988). *Peripheral regions in a community of twelve member states*. Luxembourg: Commission of the European Communities.

Kempton, L. (2015). Delivering smart specialization in peripheral regions: The role of universities. *Regional Studies*, 2(1), 489–96.

Liagouras, G. (2010). What can we learn from the failures of technology and innovation policies in the European periphery? *European Urban and Regional Studies*, 17, 331–49.

Lorenzen, M. (2001). Localized learning and policy: Academic advice on enhancing regional competitiveness through learning. *European Planning Studies*, 9(2), 163–85.

Lundvall, B.Å. (1992). *National Systems of Innovation*. London: Anthem Press.

Malerba, F., and Orsenigo, L. (1995). Schumpeterian patterns of innovation. *Cambridge Journal of Economics*, 19(1), 47–65.

Melancon, Y., and Doloreux, D. (2011). Developing a knowledge infrastructure to foster regional innovation in the periphery: A study from Quebec's coastal region in Canada. *Regional Studies*, 46, 1–18.

Metcalfe, J.S. (1994). Evolutionary economics and technology policy. *The Economic Journal*, 104(425), 931–44.

Metcalfe, J.S. (1995). Technology systems and technology policy in an evolutionary framework. *Cambridge Journal of Economics*, 19, 25–46.

Metcalfe, J.S. (2002). Knowledge of growth and the growth of knowledge. *Journal of Evolutionary Economics*, 12, 3–15.

Morgan, K., and Nauwelaers, C. (1999). A regional perspective on innovation: From theory to strategy, in K. Morgan and C. Nauwelaers (eds), *Regional Innovation Strategies: The Challenge for Less-favoured Regions*, Norwich: Regional Studies Association, 1–18.

Muscio, A., and Orsenigo, L. (2010). Politiche nazionali e regionali di diffusione della conoscenza, in P. Bianchi and C. Pozzi (eds), *Le Politiche Industriali alla Prova del Futuro: Analisi per una Strategia Nazionale*, Bologna: Il Mulino, 155–84.

Nelson, R., and Winter, S.G. (1982). *An Evolutionary Theory of Economic Change*, Cambridge, MA: The Belknap Press of Harvard University Press.

Niosi, J. (2011). Building innovation systems: An introduction to the special section. *Industrial and Corporate Change*, 20(6), 1637–43.

North, D., and Smallbone, D. (2006). Developing entrepreneurship and enterprise in Europe's peripheral rural areas: Some issues facing policy-makers. *European Planning Studies*, 14, 41–60.

Oughton, C., Landbaso, M., and Morgan, K. (2002). The regional innovation paradox: Innovation policy and industrial policy. *Journal of Technology Transfer*, 27(1), 97–110.

Pekkarinen, S., and Harmaakorpi, V. (2006). Building regional innovation networks: The definition of an age business core process in a regional innovation system. *Regional Studies*, 40(4), 401–13.

Pinto, H., Fernandez-Esquinas, M., and Uyarra, E. (2015). Universities and knowledge intensive business services (KIBS) as sources of knowledge for innovative firms in peripheral regions. *Regional Studies*, 49(11), 1873–91.

POR (2007–2013). Regional Operation Programme, Apulia Region, via https://ec.europa.eu/regional_policy/en/atlas/programmes/2007-2013/italy/operational-programme-puglia (accessed on 26 November 2019).

Pylak, K. (2015). Changing innovation process models: A chance to break out of path dependency for less developed regions. *Regional Studies, Regional Science*, 2, 46–72.

Regional Innovation Monitor Plus (2016). Regional Innovation Report, Puglia, via https://ec.europa.eu/growth/tools-databases/regional-innovation-monitor/report/innovation/regional-innovation-report-2016-puglia (accessed on 22 November 2019).

Rosenfeld, S.A. (2002). Creating smart systems: A guide to cluster strategies in less favoured regions. European Union-Regional Innovation Strategies, via http://www.competitiveness.org/article/articleview/376/1/27/ (accessed on 11 April 2019).

Samuelson, P. (1973). *Economics* (9th edn). Tokyo: McGraw-Hill Kogakusha.

Schumpeter, J.A. (1918). *Die Krise des Steuerstaates*. Leipzig: Leuschner & Lubensky.

Schumpeter, J.A. (1939). *Business Cycles: A Theoretical, Historical, and Statistical Analysis of the Capitalist Process* (vol. 1). New York, NY: McGraw-Hill.

SmartPuglia 2020 (2015). Policy document, European Commission, via https://ec.europa.eu/growth/tools-databases/regional-innovation-monitor/policy-document/smartpuglia-2020 (accessed on 22 November 2019).

Tödtling, F., and Trippl, M. (2005). One size fits all? Towards a differentiated regional innovation policy approach. *Research Policy*, 34(8), 1203–19.

Tödtling, F., and Trippl, M. (2018). Regional innovation policies for new path development: Beyond neo-liberal and traditional systemic views. *European Planning Studies*, 26(9), 1779–95.

Uyarra, E., and Flanagan, K. (2010). From regional systems of innovation to regions as innovation policy spaces. *Environment and Planning C: Government and Policy*, 28(4), 681–95.

Weber, K.M., and Truffer, B. (2017). Moving innovation systems research to the next level: Towards an integrative agenda. *Oxford Review of Economic Policy*, 33(1), 101–21.

Witt, U. (2003). Economic policymaking in evolutionary perspective. *Journal of Evolutionary Economics*, 13, 77–94.

Zhao, S.L., Cacciolatti, L., Lee, S.H., and Song, W. (2015). Regional collaborations and indigenous innovation capabilities in China: A multivariate method for the analysis of regional innovation systems. *Technological Forecasting and Social Change*, 94(1), 202–20.

11. Regional innovation system and policy in Malopolska, Poland: an institutionalised learning

Marta Gancarczyk, Marta Najda-Janoszka and Jacek Gancarczyk

1. INTRODUCTION

This chapter adopts a positive perspective in policy research (Uyarra, 2010; González-López, 2019) to describe the processes of formulating, adjusting and implementing the innovation policies in Malopolska, after Poland's accession to the European Union (EU) in 2004. As a context for policy analysis, the region's innovation system has been synthesised to include its structure and major indicators compared with those in Poland and the EU.

The aim of this study is to present the evolution of the regional innovation system and policies in Malopolska, Poland as a learning process. Based on the theoretical background of innovation systems and policy learning, as well as new institutional economics, we focus our analysis on the dynamics of the Malopolska innovation system, the ways the policies form the regional specialisation and promote entrepreneurial discovery and innovation, and the types of learning that have stimulated evolution of the region's innovation policies.

Our findings point to the increasingly positive potential of the Malopolska innovation system (input characteristics) and its less positive but improving performance (output characteristics). In this context, we identify formalised learning that stems from regulations, institutional hierarchy and academic research as the major driver of policy evolution. When analysing the changing policy objectives, measures, and budgets, we note the positive outcomes of this learning. First, the industrial specialisation of Malopolska evolved from an unfocused approach involving a combination of the dominant knowledge base and industries of new opportunities, following the smart specialisation (SS) concept. Second, policy measures and budgets are increasingly targeted towards entrepreneurship support. Further positive evolution of the region's system and policies requires strengthening the interaction and synergies between the dominant and emerging areas of specialisation and enhancing the collaborative links among businesses as well as among businesses and academia.

This research provides a contribution to the knowledge on policy learning in terms of regional transformation towards new paths (Asheim, 2019; Isaksen et al., 2019; Hassink et al., 2019) and it also assists with understanding how regional specialisation evolves towards SS (Foray, 2014; McCann and Ortega-Argilés, 2015).

2. THEORETICAL FRAMEWORK

In the innovation system and policy framework, as in the new institutional economics, a distinction is made between institutions as rules of the game and organisations and agents as players that implement the rules (Edquist, 2011; Williamson, 1998). In this view, regional innovation policies can be treated as formal institutions that constrain societal actions towards a dominant direction (North, 1990, 2005; Vatn, 2007; Ostrom, 2005). It may be expected that this dominant direction would lead to a clear focus and regional specialisation. However, the constraining nature of institutions is also one of the explanations for path dependence that might lead to rigid specialisation and related lock-in (Martin and Sunley, 2006; Hassink, 2005; Martin, 2010). This calls for the enabling role of regional innovation policies to launch new directions and entrepreneurial opportunities, i.e. to overcome path dependence and lock-in and to make a regional specialisation smart (Foray, 2014, 2017; Uyarra, 2010). For transforming and growing regions, such as Malopolska, the direction and efficiency of new path development represents one of the key issues in innovation policies (Isaksen et al., 2019; Hassink et al., 2019).

The need for new path development is addressed by theoretical advancements in the area of regional innovation systems and policies, particularly by the concept of SS (Foray, 2014, 2017). SS promotes a specialised diversification based on region-specific capacities and region-specific entrepreneurial opportunities to enable sustainable growth (Foray, 2014, 2017; Rodrik, 2014; McCann and Ortega-Argilés, 2015; Foray et al., 2018). This requires a concurrent exploitation of the extant dominant base of industries and entrepreneurial exploration of opportunities in new, related industries (Grillitsch, 2018; Foray, 2014, 2017; McCann and Ortega-Argilés, 2015). As they are the source of breakthrough innovations and new industries, entrepreneurial processes are at the centre of the smart specialisation strategy (S3). However, entrepreneurial activities do not happen in a vacuum, but are specific to the context, including multiple actors, institutional arrangements and development path interactions (Hassink et al., 2019).

The context for S3s can primarily be captured and framed as the regional innovation system, its structure and its governance (Asheim, 2019; Asheim et al., 2019). The concept of innovation systems stresses the importance of industry, research and government agents interconnected by complex relationships and activities in order to generate innovations (Edquist, 2011). Lately, this agent- and activity-oriented view has been complemented by the emerging concept of entrepreneurial ecosystems (EEs) (Mason and Brown, 2014; Acs et al., 2017; Stam, 2015). The EE perspective marks a shift in industrial and innovation policies from general entrepreneurship support to support for productive or high-quality new ventures (Brown and Mason, 2017). Productive entrepreneurship, i.e. innovative and growing enterprises, forms a link between the inputs to innovation, such as human resources and research and development (R&D) expenditures, and the outcomes, in terms of innovations and new industries (Acs et al., 2017; Stam, 2015).

Conceptual developments in innovation systems and policies are both the outcomes and the drivers of policy learning, the topic that organises this study (Lundvall and Borrás, 1998; Malerba and Nelson, 2011; Edquist, 2011; Isaksen and Karlsen, 2011). Our chapter is guided by the positive approach to policy analysis, which focuses on recognising the real processes and outcomes of policy formulation and implementation (Uyarra, 2010; González-López, 2019). Such an approach is relevant for policy learning, since it reveals either consistency or mismatch between regional policies and priorities set at regional and EU levels, as well as between these policies and the theoretical background concerning regional development (Asheim, 2018). Moreover, it is a self-reflexive approach that seeks to recognise extant sources of learning. The mechanisms of policy learning at the regional level include: (1) policy evaluation through formal, ex-ante, on-going and ex-post reports; (2) technology assessment and forecasting based on the specialised scientific research; (3) social and political participation through multi-stakeholder and multi-layer policy design; and (4) learning from others, such as following the guidelines of the country and the EU government or benchmarking other regions (Lundvall and Borrás, 1998; González-López, 2019).

Based on the above theoretical considerations, we formulate four research questions that structure our analysis of the Malopolska innovation system and policies:

RQ1.   What dynamics are observed in the evolution of the Malopolska innovation system?

RQ2. How do the innovation policies in Malopolska develop the region's specialisation towards SS that would exploit extant region-specific capacities (dominant industries) and explore new entrepreneurial opportunities (new prospective industries)?

RQ3. How do the budgets and measures of the Malopolska innovation policies stimulate entrepreneurial activities towards R&D commercialisation and innovation development?

RQ4. What are the learning mechanisms that drive the evolution of the Malopolska innovation policies? What is the dominant type of learning that effects this evolution?

3. METHOD

We apply the case study method as the major approach to investigating the evolution of the Malopolska regional system and policies. Methods supporting the case study include analysis of secondary sources, such as policy documents, evaluation reports and public statistics, complemented by a direct and semi-structured interview with the key informant. The investigation examines the period after Poland's accession to the EU, since the accession launched systematic activities in and reflection on the systems and policies for innovation. The analysis of public statistics and structured content analysis of policy documents focused on the themes of our research questions (Ndofor et al., 2015). Specifically, the investigation concerned the dynamics of the innovation system, the way the region's specialisation emerged, and the allocation of policy measures and budgets. Finally, the types of learning mechanisms were identified as drivers of change within the region's specialisation and the allocation of policy measures and budgets. Two researchers screened the policy documents, comprising strategies, operational plans, technology and industrial forecasts, and evaluation reports for the period 2005–2020. We have coded and tabulated the characteristics related to the major themes for different phases of policy evolution separately, to see the differences in the approaches to objectives, measures and budgets. A third researcher was consulted to reconcile ambiguities in the findings. The interview with a key informant from the Malopolska regional government provided insights into the processes involved in designing policies. This interview was also an important source for understanding the policy setting within the institutional hierarchy of the EU Structural Funds' management and the Polish central government. Our interviewee can be treated as a key informant, being the only longer-term employee with managerial responsibilities related to regional innovation strategies.

4. THE REGIONAL INNOVATION SYSTEM OF MALOPOLSKA

4.1 The Structure of the Regional Innovation System

4.1.1 Firms and industrial specialisation

The regional government system in Poland comprises 16 territorial units holding the constituting and executive power within the unitary state. Malopolska is located in the southern part of Poland, which historically has been a less-developed and lower-income area, with massive outward international migration. The region holds the twelfth position among the 16 territorial government units by area. However, it demonstrates a high population density, being in fourth position in this regard with 3.33 million inhabitants, including the population of 763,000 within Krakow, its capital, in 2016.

Despite considerable economic growth following Poland's accession to the EU, the gross domestic product (GDP) in purchasing power standard (PPS) per inhabitant is still lower in the Malopolska region than both the EU and Polish average (Table 11.1).

In terms of industry structure, Malopolska is a transforming region, changing its industrial profile from heavy and mature industries towards knowledge-intensive and high-technology services and manufacturing. Its major manufacturing industries, such as metallurgy, heavy chemicals, mining, metal, tobacco and food, maintain a large share in the regional economy (Malopolska Regional Government Office, 2018). The largest contributors to industrial employment are shown in Table 11.2.[1]

Among the major industrial employers, knowledge-intensive services, i.e. legal and accounting activities, computer programming, consultancy and related activities, and activities of head offices featured the highest dynamics (Table 11.2). These activities form the Business Service Sector (BSS), comprising Business Process Outsourcing, Shared Services Centres,

Table 11.1   GDP in Malopolska and Poland as percentage of the EU-28 in PPS per inhabitant, 2004–2016

Unit / Year	2004	2005	2006	2007	2008	2009	2010	2011	2012	2013	2014	2015	2016
EU-28	100	100	100	100	100	100	100	100	100	100	100	100	100
Poland	50	50	51	53	55	60	62	65	67	67	67	68	68
Malopolska	44	45	46	47	50	53	55	58	59	59	60	62	62

Source: Eurostat (2018).

Table 11.2   The major industries of Malopolska (percentage share in the region's industrial employment)

NACE* Rev. 2	2009 %	2011 %	2013 %	2015 %
Specialised construction activities	9.0	8.5	8.3	8.3
Land transport and transport via pipelines	5.4	5.4	5.5	5.3
Manufacture of food products	4.2	3.9	4.0	4.1
Construction of buildings	4.9	4.7	3.9	4.0
Legal and accounting activities	2.1	2.3	3.2	4.0
Manufacture of fabricated metal products, except machinery and equipment	3.3	3.2	3.2	3.2
Wholesale and retail trade and repair of motor vehicles and motorcycles	2.9	3.0	3.1	3.0
Computer programming, consultancy and related activities	1.6	1.6	2.1	2.7
Food and beverage service activities	2.9	2.5	2.6	2.6
Civil engineering	2.5	2.7	2.4	2.3
Architectural and engineering activities; technical testing and analysis	2.0	2.2	2.0	2.1
Real estate activities	0.0	1.9	2.1	2.1
Manufacture of rubber and plastic products	1.8	1.6	1.6	1.6
Manufacture of basic metals	1.8	1.5	1.6	1.6
Accommodation	1.7	1.4	1.6	1.5
Manufacture of wood and of products of wood and cork, except furniture; manufacture of articles of straw and plaiting materials	1.5	1.4	1.4	1.5
Activities of head offices; management consultancy activities	0.8	0.9	1.0	1.4

Note: *   Statistical classification of economic activities in the European Community.

Source: Based on Malopolska Regional Government Office (2018).

information technology (IT) and R&D centres, and are predominantly occupied by foreign direct investors (ABSL, 2018). The BSS generates 64,000 jobs in Krakow, the largest employment among Polish cities in this sector. Krakow is also recognised as the largest BSS concentration in Central Europe and the sixth largest in the world (ABSL, 2018; OECD, 2019). Another distinctive characteristic of the Malopolska industrial specialisation is its growing position in the area of creative industries, including IT, particularly animation and software games, as well as design. Other dynamic industries include biotech, automotive, tourism and leisure (Malopolska Regional Government Office, 2018).

Malopolska has been recording an increasing employment in the service and manufacturing high-technology sectors, as measured by the percentage in total employment (from 2.4% in 2004 to 3.6% in 2016) (Eurostat, 2018). Over the same period, Poland remained stable and the EU even declining in this regard. The region significantly exceeds the country share of high-tech employment in total employment (3.6% relative to 2.9% for Poland in 2016). However, it remains slightly below the EU value of 4.0% (Eurostat, 2018).

Employment in knowledge-intensive services (KIS) follows the growing share of KIS in employment in the EU and in Poland (from 23% in 2004 to 31.7% in 2016). However, the lower shares both for Malopolska and Poland (30.9% in 2016) in relation to the EU (40% in 2016) were persistent over 2004–2016 (Eurostat, 2018).

4.1.2   The science and technology system

Malopolska is a leading Polish academic centre, with 29 higher education institutions (Statistics Poland, 2018a). Jagiellonian University, the oldest university in Poland and in Central Europe, ranks as Poland's top university, beside the University of Warsaw. Krakow Technical University and AGH University of Science and Technology are among the best Polish technical universities, recognised internationally as well. The number and quality of higher education and scientific institutions generates high potential in human resources. Krakow universities educate 170,000 students and 68% of the region's population aged 19–24 has been students, of which 7,000 are in the doctoral programmes. Moreover, in 2016, 49% of inhabitants aged 30–34 had accomplished tertiary education relative to the country share of 45.7% (Eurostat, 2018).

The region is also a recognised R&D location, with 436 R&D units (Statistics Poland, 2018a). It holds the second position in Poland by the number of R&D units, namely 14.2 units per 100,000 inhabitants. Among 19,000 R&D personnel and researchers, 10,000 people hold a doctorate or even higher degree, which contributes to the overall potential in the area of R&D personnel. In 2016, the share of R&D personnel and researchers in total employment (1.62%) significantly exceeded the Polish average of 1.08% – however, it was still lower than the EU mean (2.03% in 2015). Similarly, the percentage of researchers employed in the business enterprise sector was the second highest in Poland, but still below this share in the EU (Eurostat, 2018).

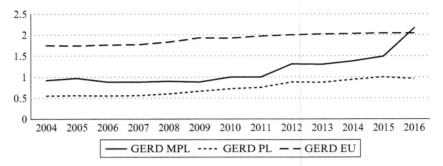

Source: Eurostat (2018).

Figure 11.1   GERD in Malopolska compared with Poland and the EU-28,
2004–2016

4.2   R&D and Innovation Indicators

Over the period 2004–2016, intramural R&D expenditure as a percentage
of the regional GDP (GERD) was considerably below the EU average,
except for 2016, when this share reached 2.16% and exceeded the EU reference value (2.04%). As regards the Polish context, it was predominantly
the second-largest GERD after the capital region of Mazowieckie in the
period considered (Figure 11.1).

However, the indicator of R&D per inhabitant in euro purchasing power
standards (RDPI) is more distinctive and informative in highlighting the
differences in R&D expenditures between Malopolska and the EU. Based
on this method, even though the region's GERD exceeds the average

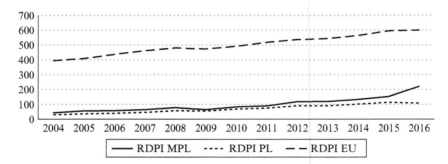

Source: Eurostat (2018).

Figure 11.2   RDPI in Malopolska compared with Poland and the EU-28,
2004–2016 at 2005 prices

GERD in the EU in 2016, it is still 2.7 times lower according to the RDPI (37% of the EU RDPI) (Figure 11.2).

Relative to other Polish regions, Malopolska consistently scores highly in business sector R&D expenditures as a percentage of the regional GDP (BERD), forming 44% of the regional GERD in 2015, and 77% in 2016 (Eurostat, 2018). However, the BERD of Malopolska represented from 21% (2004) to 50% (2015) of the EU BERD. The exception is the 2016 indicator, higher than the European one by 25%, but with uncertain perspective for continuity (Eurostat, 2018). The positive dynamics of the enterprise R&D investment are stimulated by the institutions promoting a collaboration between business and academia, such as technology and science parks and 20 cluster initiatives in the area of medical sciences, the printing industry, clean technologies and life sciences. That said, this knowledge transfer infrastructure brings a moderate academia–industry collaboration, with even fewer vital links between small and medium-sized enterprises (SMEs) and research institutions (STOS, 2017; Statistics Poland, 2018a).

The region features increasingly positive characteristics of innovative potential in terms of human resources, knowledge transfer institutions and R&D indicators. This potential corresponds with Malopolska's position as one of three top Polish regions in terms of innovation performance over 2004–2016. Nevertheless, Malopolska was only a moderate performer among European regions in 2004–2016 (European Commission, 2009, 2012, 2016, 2017). According to the Regional Innovation Scoreboard (European Commission, 2017), the normalised score for the region in 2009–2017 ranged from 54% to 58.7% of the EU score in 2011. The strengths of the innovation system compared with the EU countries include design applications, non-R&D innovation expenditures and the population with tertiary education. Relative weaknesses are marketing and organisational innovations, SMEs innovating in house, and sales of new-to-market and firm-level innovations (European Commission, 2017).

Overall, the region is stronger in terms of the potential and input char-acteristics than in its outputs of R&D investment and activities (STOS, 2017; PARP, 2013; Malopolska Regional Government Office, 2018). The expected output would be the commercialisation of R&D efforts into patent, design and trademark applications, as well as innovations through productive entrepreneurship. Patent and trademark applications are predominantly higher than the country average. However, as regards the number of patents per 1 million inhabitants, only four out of 28 EU countries recorded rates lower than Poland in 2012. At the same time, 11 countries had lower rates of trademarks in 2015. Over 2004–2015, Malopolska demonstrated relative strength in design applications per million inhabitants (47.08 in 2015), exceeding both the Polish score (43.67 in 2015) and, in 2017, the EU average performance as well (Eurostat, 2018; European Commission, 2017).

The entrepreneurial activity forms a basis for knowledge commercialisation; however, this activity was weaker in 2010–2016 than Poland's average of enterprises per 1,000 population, only in 2017 reaching the country mean value (Statistics Poland, 2018a). The quality of entrepreneurial activities, in turn, is reflected in the innovative performance and high-growth firms. According to the panel data 2005–2017, the percentage of innovative enterprises in Malopolska was predominantly stronger than the Polish average, particularly in 2015–2017. However, this share declined to 21.25% in 2017 from 39.05% in 2005, and both the observed percentage and dynamics of innovative firms are insufficient to upgrade the performance in relation to the EU (Table 11.3).

The efficiency from innovations, in terms of sales from new products, is decreasing or stable, and predominantly below the national performance in this regard. Additionally, a decreasing to stable share of net revenues from sales of new-to-market products in total sales raises concerns about the competitive value and sustainability of innovations introduced (see Table 11.4). These characteristics of output indicators evidence a modest R&D commercialisation through entrepreneurial activities. The innovation activities are concentrated in a narrow group of large enterprises that report the highest and increasing share of sales from innovations. Small and medium-sized businesses demonstrate much lower rates (Statistics Poland, 2019b).

A promising phenomenon comprises high-growth enterprises that accomplish at least 20% revenue growth over three years (Statistics Poland, 2017, 2018b). Although in 2011–2013 their share in all enterprises of Malopolska was in the eleventh and eighth positions among Polish regions, the results for 2013–2016 place the region as the third or second top location for high growers (Statistics Poland, 2017, 2018b). By nature, high-growth enterprises are a small but impactful group (Acs et al., 2017). Therefore, as long as their dynamics continues, they will provide prospects for the region's better performance in terms of productivity from innovations. These prospects can be evaluated as positive, being indicative of a vibrant start-up community in high-tech industries such as software games, animation, internet of things, satellites and cyber security, located in the Krakow academic and technology park incubators (OECD, 2019). These start-ups are potential scale-ups and high growers, commercialising the R&D investment.

Table 11.3   *Innovative industrial enterprises in Malopolska and Poland, 2005–2017*

Indic/ Year	2005	2006	2007	2008	2009	2010	2011	2012	2013	2014	2015	2016	2017
% innovative enterprises[a] MPL	39.05	22.09	38.80	22.81	19.25	16.29	19.50	17.37	18.05	15.55	20.43	21.25	20.74
% innovative enterprises PL	42.04	23.68	37.40	21.39	18.06	17.10	16.10	16.51	17.13	17.52	17.58	18.68	18.51
% sales from innovative products[b] MPL	10.89	10.89	10.59	13.87	10.37	10.63	7.60	6.48	6.49	7.71	9.45	9.91	9.71
% sales from innovative products PL	13.47	13.47	11.89	12.43	10.56	11.34	8.93	9.22	8.65	8.78	9.50	8.12	7.08
% sales new to market products[c] MPL	–	6.02	7.05	9.71	4.03	6.79	3.97	3.51	4.02	4.74	4.29	3.95	3.51
% sales new to market products PL	–	6.13	7.01	6.48	4.12	7.08	5.22	3.82	3.80	3.70	4.05	3.95	3.44

Notes:
[a]   Innovative enterprises as percentage of total industrial enterprises.
[b]   Net sales from innovative products as percentage total net sales of industrial enterprises.
[c]   Sales from new to market products as percentage total sales of industrial enterprises.

Source: Statistics Poland (2019a).

5.   REGIONAL INNOVATION POLICIES IN MALOPOLSKA IN THE YEARS 2005–2020

5.1   Institutional and Governance Framework

The first Regional Innovation Strategies (RISs) were developed in Poland during the years 2000–2005. Development of the innovation policy at the regional level began shortly after the introduction of the major territorial reform of the state in 1999. Thus, the work on the first RIS of Malopolska (2005–2013) (Malopolska Regional Government Office, 2005) was conducted in parallel with the initial programming of the socio-economic development of Malopolska, which was a region newly

Table 11.4   Budget structure of RIS Malopolska

Component	RIS 2005–2013	RIS 2020
Business	Mixed instruments within single tasks – support for enterprises with parallel support for business environment institutions	Instruments clearly targeted towards business activity
Budget Business & Science cooperation	**331,200,000 PLN (20.26%)** Instruments for stimulating cooperation, no direct grants	**4,717,000,000 PLN (39.81%)** Instruments for stimulating cooperation including direct grants for applied research and spin-off ventures
Budget Business environment institutions	**1,000,000 PLN (0.06%)** Elaborated portfolio of instruments for stimulating knowledge and technology transfer, developing systems for gathering and analysing data related to innovations	**168,000,000 PLN (1.46%)** Limited number of instruments for stimulating knowledge and technology transfer, funding for R&D equipment
Budget Administration	**1,203,000,000 PLN (73.60%)** Instruments for establishing institutional bodies for analysing knowledge and technology development	**5,247,600,000 PLN (45.51%)** Instruments for broadband network development, computerisation of public institutions and development of public digital content
Budget	**100,000,000 PLN (6.12%)**	**1,397,200,000 PLN (12.12%)**
TOTAL BUDGET	**1,635,200,000 PLN**	**11,529,800,000 PLN**

formed from several different provinces, as well as with the development of the national-level structural strategies. Development of the regional policy programming system in Poland took several years, as there were no general or indicative guidelines regarding programming of socio-economic development at the regional level (Szlachta, 2014). Given that the regions in Poland were newly established, the first regional development strategies exhibited more of an inventorial approach with aims to consolidate newly defined territory. Hence, RIS Malopolska 2005–2013 (Malopolska Regional Government Office, 2005) followed a similar logic, with action lines targeted broadly towards all areas of strategic development defined in the Regional Development Strategy (RDS) of Malopolska 2000–2006. However, the first RIS for Malopolska was developed for a period that largely exceeded the time frame set for the mid-term national strategies as well as RDS Malopolska. Such time inconsistency resulted from attempts to align the development programming in Poland with the programming of the EU, since the EU funds provided through operational programmes represented the main potential source of financing tasks defined in the RIS.

Challenged by the upcoming new financial scheme of the EU, Malopolska implemented the project "Strengthening the Regional Innovation Strategy: InnoRegio Malopolska" under the 6th Framework Program for Technical Research and Development already running in the year 2005. The project was run by the consortium of Polish and international partners (e.g. technology transfer centres, technology parks) and coordinated by the Regional Government Office of Malopolska with the help of a newly established Malopolska Innovation Council that represented business, research institutions and the local government. The council established initially as a steering committee for the project later became a consultative and advisory body in the management system of the RIS.

In the year 2008, the regional self-government accepted an updated version of the RIS (Malopolska Regional Government Office, 2008) to ensure alignment of the RIS with the new RDS of Malopolska (2007–2013) and with the new financial perspective of the EU (2007–2013). Introduced changes (the structure and scope of defined tasks and goals) corresponded with a greater appreciation of the regional dimension in the national-level policies. With the new financial perspective in place, the share of structural funds managed at the regional level rose from 25% to around 50%. Moreover, actions undertaken also involved organisational changes in the RIS management structure by creating the special Office for Monitoring and Management of the RIS. Development of organisational structures was accompanied by development of the monitoring system for RIS (2009–2012).

Preparatory work for the next RIS had already begun in 2011. The new approach involved multi-level advisory teams, a system of broad public consultations, and a bringing together for active participation various actors representing business, research and business environment institutions. Work on RIS Malopolska 2020 (Malopolska Regional Government Office, 2012) was conducted in quite demanding conditions, since the new long-term as well as mid-term national development strategies were also under construction. On the other side, unlike with the first RIS, the new perspective was built on a quite detailed indicative guide to research and innovation strategies for smart specialisation (RIS3). Thus, the distinct characteristic for the programming of the new RIS was a direct and on-going control and consultation practice between regional bodies and EU units. The public consultation process lasted until the end of 2015, and in 2016 the final version of RIS Malopolska 2020 was officially accepted by the Management Board of the Malopolska Region. By that time, all the national-level long-term and mid-term strategies had been accepted and all operational programmes (requiring allocation of EU funds) had been implemented.

5.2   Regional Specialisation Development

Attempts to identify the leading industries in Malopolska had already been made during the process of developing the first RIS, when Malopolska, as a recently established region, was struggling to build its development strategy. Thus, the RIS indicated a relatively strong inventorial perspective and excessive attention directed towards the general development of the region, instead of its innovativeness. Implementation of a horizontal approach led to identification of strategic development areas, which basically covered all major industries present in Malopolska. Such an unfocused approach accompanied by inconsistencies between strategic and operational levels (mismatch between priorities and action lines) weakened the enabling role of the regional innovation policies, in terms of both exploiting the extant dominant industries and exploring new prospective ones. Also not without significance was the low level of social participation in the strategy's development process. Although there were teams of experts representing various institutions for innovation supply, the regional authorities and business, participation in the meetings of the working panels was neither regular nor intensive.

Confronted with the priority lines of the new financial perspective of the EU (2007–2013), the regional authorities and business environment institutions recognised the need to look into longer-term development trajectories of science and technologies and their potential impacts on the economy, society and the natural environment. Several foresight projects were performed (e.g. Hausner, 2008; Skulimowski, 2013; KPT, 2010) that allowed for identification of ten technologies within the three most promising areas of specialisation for the Malopolska region, namely (1) safety and comfort of life; (2) medicine and health; (3) information and visualisation. Drawing on those expert analyses, a first draft version of the new RIS presented in 2012 (Malopolska Regional Government Office, 2012) included four initial proposals for the regional S3: (1) life science; (2) sustainable energy; (3) information and communication technologies; and (4) multimedia (see Figure 11.3). In the same year, the

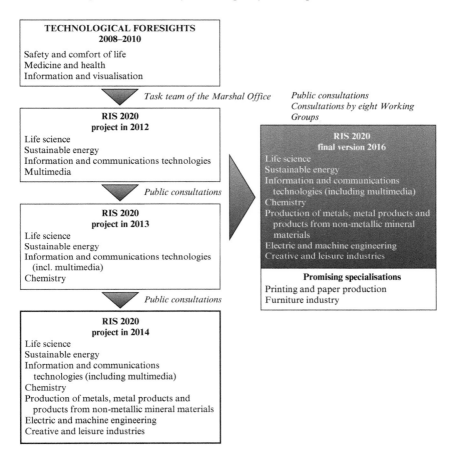

Figure 11.3   Development of smart specialisations in Malopolska region

project underwent a public consultation procedure with expert groups involving a combined representation of business, research institutions and the local government. A revised version of the new RIS (Malopolska Regional Government Office, 2012) with a modified list of four potential areas for S3 was accepted in 2013. Instead of classifying multimedia as a separate category, the list included chemistry, which represented an extant dominant industry in Malopolska. Public consultations provided a voice to business stakeholders, who began expressing concerns that the RIS might lead to discontinuation of support for areas outside the developed specialisation. Subsequently performed verification analysis of specialisation areas (Fundacja GAP, 2014) and social consultations resulted in further modification of the strategy. The engaged stakeholders generated a quite elaborate list of proposals for further extending the catalogue of regional specialisations. Proposals were thoroughly verified in terms of effectiveness and efficiency of resource use in the R&D sphere, and the relative advantage of Malopolska in comparison to other Polish regions, and as a result the document accepted in 2014 introduced three additional areas for S3 (Figure 11.3).

In 2015, eight working groups for SS were appointed, seven groups corresponding to the areas of S3 and one interdisciplinary group focused on searching for new, prospective areas. During an open recruitment period, 261 applications were received and half of them had been submitted by entrepreneurs. This confirmed a high interest in the programme and more importantly in deciding on S3 boundaries, since the working groups were responsible for developing detailed descriptions of specialisations. In order to manage strong tensions between business stakeholders pressing for an extension of the catalogue and experts suggesting a further narrowing of the RIS, in 2015 an additional verification of specialisations was performed. Provided recommendations included maintaining the status quo with the defined catalogue. Hence, in 2016 the Management Board of the Malopolska Region accepted the final version of RIS Malopolska 2020 with seven areas of S3 (Malopolska Regional Government Office, 2012). The document reflects a cohesive approach towards specialisation, as support lines have been directed towards implementation of projects compatible with areas of S3, yet with a limited stream of funds allocated to support projects from outside the areas identified as the current SS. The approach clearly complies with the direction described as exploitation of region-specific capacities. However, considering that the developed strategy exhibits a rather modest recognition of relations among defined areas of Regional Smart Specialisation (RSS), it raises concerns with regard to the parallel direction of exploration of new prospective industries. Moreover, the regional authorities seem to be aware of the fact that the catalogue of seven areas of RSS might be too broad, as argued by experts, yet they tend to maintain a cautious approach on the matter due to strong pressure from the business advocating for RSS extension.

5.3   Policy Instruments and Budgets

The lack of focus characteristic of the first RIS[2] can be referred not only to the areas of strategic development but also observed with regard to introduced policy measures. The documentation contained many inconsistent linkages between strategic objectives, planned tasks and defined instruments. Moreover, among the planned tasks were items that had little to do with innovation and in fact should not be included in RIS. According to the budget structure of the RIS 2005–2013 (Malopolska Regional Government Office, 2005), the main, dominant support was directed towards establishing and strengthening business environment institutions (Table 11.4). However, the indicated level of 73.6% of the total budget should be treated as underestimated, since instruments for supporting business environment institutions were also included as an integral part within tasks directed towards actual business activity (Tables 11.4 and 11.5). The distribution of EU funds for the innovation policy of Malopolska complied with the institution-oriented support of RIS, as only 34% of funds were directly targeted at business ventures.

The subsequent RIS Malopolska 2020 (Malopolska Regional Government Office, 2012) has exhibited a major improvement in terms of focused prioritisation and internal cohesiveness. The types of defined instruments as well as the overall budget structure have shown a substantially better alignment with the key weaknesses of the Malopolska innovation system, i.e. entrepreneurial activity and commercialisation of knowledge (see Tables 11.4 and 11.6). Instruments targeted towards business activity have accounted for almost 40% of the total budget of the RIS. Moreover, there has also been a greater recognition of the entrepreneurial potential of the cooperation between business and science (shown in a significant increase in budget share and introduction of grants for developing spin-offs). This shift in orientation has been of a comprehensive nature, including allocation of EU funds managed at the regional level. Almost 60% of those funds has been directed towards business ventures.

Regarding the design and configuration of the instruments supporting knowledge commercialisation and development of innovative and high-growth enterprises, the structure of the business component of RIS Malopolska 2005–2013 (Malopolska Regional Government Office, 2005) exhibits a questionable arrangement of defined instruments (Table 11.5). Within one task, instruments representing various types and areas of intervention were grouped together. Moreover, there was a very weak emphasis on the innovative dimension of supported activities. Direct funding was planned for only two selected industries, while a dominant form of support was represented by promotional actions.

RIS Malopolska 2020 (Malopolska Regional Government Office, 2012), however, has shown a completely different approach (Table 11.6). All instruments included in the business component have been clearly and coherently directed towards business ventures. The innovative dimension has been highlighted across defined forms of support. Further, there has been an extended spectrum of support instruments directed towards de-novo enterprises. Unlike in the previous strategy, support actions have

Table 11.5   Business component of RIS Malopolska 2005–2013

Instruments grouped according to tasks with assigned budget*	Budget of the task (PLN)	% of the total budget
• Promotion of available funding for innovative activity	30,000,000	9
• Establishing and funding for seed capital funds		
• Establishing and funding for venture capital funds		
○ *Establishing a regional fund for supporting research and implementation projects of academics and PhD students*		
• Supporting agricultural production and agro-food processing (incl. regional traditional products)	100,000,000	30.2
○ *Support for developing technology and industrial parks, clusters*		
○ *Establishing and developing the Industrial Design Center*		
• Funding and consulting for agro-tourism business	200,000,000	60.4
• Establishing and funding for incubators		
○ *Construction and development of exhibition and congress facilities*		
• Promotional campaign on EU financial support programmes	600,000	0.2
• Promotion of innovativeness through competitions (no funds)		
○ *Broad promotional campaign on innovations*		
• Supporting participation in trade fairs	600,000	0.2
○ *Promotional campaign on investment in Malopolska (incl. FDI)*		
○ *Promotion of Malopolska for foreign academics*		
Total support in the business component	331,200,000	100

Note: *   Text in italics indicates tasks not included in the business component yet directed towards supporting institutions.

been based on direct funding, grants, and vouchers. Promotion has also been included, albeit not as a dominant but as a complementary action line.

Observed differences between strategies across budget structures, types and areas of interventions have indicated a shift from a quite blurred support, directed mainly at establishing and strengthening business environment institutions, towards a focused approach with multiple action lines directed at an entrepreneurial and innovative business activity.

Table 11.6   Business component of RIS Malopolska 2020

Instruments grouped according to tasks with assigned budget	Budget of the task (PLN)	% of the total budget
● Funding for industry research projects and experimental projects	2,240,000,000	47.5
● Funding for R&D infrastructure development		
● Funding for contracting and implementing R&D projects		
● Funding for investment activity (purchasing/ modernising) in fixed assets, knowledge assets	1,700,000,000	36
● Funding for expert services related to innovative activity		
● Support for firms operating in clusters		
● Support for living labs		
● Funding for training and consulting for starting business		
● Financial support for starting business		
● Bridge support for starting business		
● Employment support for starting business		
● Innovation vouchers for SMEs	80,000,000	1.7
● Funding for venture capital and seed funds	570,000,000	12.1
● Funding for loan and guarantee funds		
● *Support for internationalisation of SMEs through promotion*	127,000,000	2.7
● *Support for innovation through promotion*		
Total support in the business component	4,717,000,000	100

5.4   Monitoring and Evaluation: The Learning Mechanisms of Policy Evolution

Due to the lack of legal regulations as well as overall practice in the area of policy evaluation in Poland (Olejniczak, 2010), capacity building for evaluation of the regional innovation policy in Malopolska was conducted in parallel with the policy implementation. The initial activity in the area, related to the ex-ante evaluation of the RIS, was practically imposed by the implementation of European cohesion policy in Poland (Haber, 2007). Interest in on-going and ex-post evaluations was observed as the implementation of the RIS progressed and formal requirements emerged. Four years after launching the first RIS, work began on construction of the appropriate monitoring system. The process was carried out in three main stages, starting in 2009 with design of the system, and then continuing in 2010 and 2012 with examination of set indicators (FundEko, 2012a). Along with measure-ment, subsequent stages included reviews of the original concept of the RIS monitoring system for further improvement works. However, although some on-going evaluations had been carried out already (e.g. CEM Instytut Badań Rynku i Opinii Publicznej, 2009; FundEko, 2012b), the results of those first reviews of the system were not distributed to a wider audience, leading to limiting the learning process. Despite that, a major evaluation of the monitoring system performed in 2015 indicated some enhanced knowledge and practice in the area (FundEko, 2015). The main premise for conducting that verification was preparation of a new monitoring system convergent with the new perspective of RIS. Thus, unlike with the first RIS, the methodology for monitoring and evaluating RIS Malopolska 2020 was agreed at the same time as a public intervention was planned. Moreover, a new planning perspective also introduced a more pronounced emphasis on the comparability of monitoring results across regions in Poland. To enhance the possibility of comparing the quality of the innovation progress in the country, a list of core indicators common to all regions was developed, yet each region was allowed to extend the list according to its needs. The list was developed as part of workshops organised by the World Bank on behalf of the Ministry of Infrastructure and Development.

The measurement methodology and the catalogue of indicators devel-oped during the years 2009–2012 were further used to perform ex-post evaluations of the first RIS. The two major evaluations were carried out in the years 2016 and 2017 (MSAP UEK, 2016; STOS, 2017), providing for the first time a comprehensive picture rather than a narrow thematic or instrumental focus exhibited in on-going evaluations. Moreover, addressing the requirements of the strategic evaluation process (Georghiou, 2007), the catalogue of used research methods was significantly extended to include desk research, surveys, telephone interviews, in-person interviews, case studies and expert panels. Nevertheless, due to quite vaguely defined objectives and internal inconsistencies within the RIS, there were some difficulties in attributing wider effects of analysed interventions.

The current RIS Malopolska 2020 has undergone several on-going thematic evaluations, performed according to the reformulated monitoring system. The strategy has been updated regularly (the most recent update occurred in 2018) yet introduced changes have concerned rather formal corrections and financial data updates than substantive issues. Further, to improve policy instruments for entrepreneurship and knowledge com-mercialisation, Malopolska has engaged in trans-national review of the RIS by joining, in 2016, the Interreg programme "InnoBridge – Bridging the innovation gap through converting R&D results into commercial success in a more effective and efficient way". That cooperation has enhanced the learning process by shifting from mere passive observation and distant comparison with other regions, as practised during the first RIS, towards active participation in regular international workshops involving peer reviews, exchange of good practices and assisted development of action plans.

6. CONCLUSIONS

This study has presented the evolution of the Malopolska regional innovation system and policies as a process of learning. Our analysis focused on four major themes reflected in the research questions. The first theme concerned the dynamics observed in the innovation system. In the period after Poland's accession to the EU, the Malopolska innovation system featured a transformation from dominant mature and heavy industries towards emerging prospective areas, such as BSS, ICT and biotech. In the period 2004–2016, one can observe the overall improved position of the Malopolska RIS, due to the input characteristics, i.e. potential in the area of R&D investment and infrastructure and highly qualified human resources (HR), among others. Nevertheless, the output characteristics, in terms of intellectual property and innovations, have been improving less than expected. There is a mismatch between regional innovation capacity and the level of R&D commercialisation to create value from R&D investment and infrastructure and to ensure employment opportunities for qualified HR professionals. FDI in the form of business process offshoring has been filling this gap. However, this raises concerns about the overreliance of the regional economy on inward FDI (OECD, 2019). A positive sign for the reverse trend is an increasingly productive entrepreneurship in terms of high-tech start-ups and high growers, as well as significant dynamics in high-tech and knowledge-intensive industries.

The second theme for research related to the way Malopolska's innovation policies have shaped the regional specialisation towards SS, with a rationale to create a new path and avoid lock-in (Hassink et al., 2019). We found this evolution in the area of developing the region's specialisation, from a broad approach emphasising a horizontal development of the region (2005–2013) to an active industrial policy in search of a new development path (2014–2020). The latter phase has additionally been featured in the transition from an expert approach focused on limited areas of new advanced technologies to a more context-oriented approach that combines the dominant industrial base and areas with prospects for new path creation (McCann and Ortega-Argilés, 2015).

The third research theme led us to explore how the budgets of Malopolska's innovation policies have stimulated entrepreneurial activities towards commercialising knowledge and innovation development. We acknowledge evolution in the area of policy measures to support knowledge commercialisation and innovation development. In the years 2005–2013, the policy was broadly dedicated to developing components of the regional innovation system (business environment institutions) rather than to support for innovative entrepreneurial activities. The transition to a more focused approach, addressing the entrepreneurial and innovative business activity, was in evidence in 2014–2020 (Brown and Mason, 2017).

The final research issue concerned the mechanisms of learning that were driving the evolution of the region's innovation policy in the area of industrial specialisation and the allocation of measures and budgets. We found strong mechanisms of learning enhanced by formal institutions, such as legal regulations and structured procedures within the hierarchy of policy making (Lundvall and Borrás, 1998). This institutionalised learning has been regulated by the law since 2000, and in 2004 it was delegated to regional authorities responsible for Structural Funds (Bober, 2007; Miedziński, 2008). Since 2004, regional management of the EU programmes has been involved in formalised and iterative policy evaluations at the design, on-going implementation and ex-post implementation stages. Besides major evaluation reports, the evaluation process has engaged much expert analysis and academic research. The major legal framework of public evaluations has stimulated other learning mechanisms that were complementary to the major evaluation reports, including technology assessments and forecasting produced by academic researchers. Another strong mechanism of institutional learning stems from the structured procedures and consultations within the hierarchy of policy making, especially from direct interactions and consultations with the management of EU programmes (Lundvall and Borrás, 1998). The latter mechanism was the primary transmission channel for new policy directions, consistent with advancements in the theory and practice of innovations systems and policy at the EU level. Moreover, the mechanism of learning from the EU Structural Fund's management (learning from others, peer learning) was also the stimulus for the stakeholder engagement in the process of setting up policy objectives, measures and budgets. Finally, the learning stems from other regions based on the benchmarking initiatives of Interreg.

This study offers two contributions to the innovation system and policy literature. First, it adds to the knowledge of policy learning in the context of regional transformation towards new paths (Isaksen et al., 2019; Hassink et al., 2019). Second, it enhances the understanding of how regional specialisation evolves towards SS, and particularly how the SS concept is implemented from the policy perspective (Foray, 2014, 2017; Rodrik, 2014; McCann and Ortega-Argilés, 2015; Foray et al., 2018). Our focus is the mechanisms and outcomes of policy learning. The current profile of the regional specialisation results both from evaluation reporting and foresight learning (the emphasis on exploration and new path pursuit) and from stakeholder participation (the emphasis on the exploitation of the extant base of industries) (Lundvall and Borrás, 1998). This combination resonates well with the idea of SS (Foray, 2014; McCann and Ortega-Argilés, 2015). Moreover, the most recent policy measures and budgets focus on the support for productive entrepreneurship (Brown and Mason, 2017). This shift in the policy responds to the learning from evaluation and expert reports that indicates insufficient innovative performance. It is also consistent with recent conceptual advancements promoting innovation systems as a complex context for the processes of entrepreneurial discovery (Stam, 2015; Hassink et al., 2019). Further positive evolution of the region's innovation system and policies is dependent on synergies between the dominant and emerging areas of specialisation, to ensure synergies from exploration and exploitation (McCann and Ortega-Argilés, 2015). Another prerequisite is strengthening knowledge transfer among businesses as well as businesses and academia to enhance productive entrepreneurship instead of crowding out private enterprise by publicly supported ventures (Acs et al., 2017).

NOTES

1. Apart from retail trade and wholesale trade, with a combined share of 25% in industrial employment in 2015.
2. Due to the lack of detailed financial data broken down by tasks and instruments for the strategy update undertaken in 2008, the document RIS Malopolska 2008–2013 was not included in the analysis.

REFERENCES

ABSL (2018). *Sektor nowoczesnych usług biznesowych w Polsce* (The sector of modern business services in Poland). Warsaw: ABSL.
Acs, Z.J., Stam, E., Audretsch, D.B., and O'Connor, A. (2017). The lineages of the entrepreneurial ecosystem approach. *Small Business Economics*, *49*(1), 1–10.
Asheim, B.T. (2018). Learning regions: a strategy for economic development in less developed regions? In Paasi, A., Harrison, J., and Jones, M. (eds), *Handbook on the Geographies of Regions and Territories*. Cheltenham, UK and Northampton, MA, USA: Edward Elgar Publishing, 130–40.
Asheim, B.T. (2019). Smart specialisation, innovation policy and regional innovation systems: what about new path development in less innovative regions? *Innovation: The European Journal of Social Science Research*, *32*(1), 8–25.

Asheim, B.T., Isaksen, A., and Trippl, M. (2019). *Advanced Introduction to Regional Innovation Systems*. Cheltenham, UK and Northampton, MA, USA: Edward Elgar Publishing.

Bober, J. (2007). Formalno-prawne podstawy Unii Europejskiej w zakresie ewaluacji (Formal and legal foundations of evaluation in the European Union). In Mazur, S. (ed.), *Ewaluacja Funduszy Strukturalnych: perspektywa regionalna* (The evaluation of the Structural Funds: a regional perspective). Krakow: MSAP UEK, 59–74.

Brown, R., and Mason, C. (2017). Looking inside the spiky bits: a critical review and conceptualisation of entrepreneurial ecosystems. *Small Business Economics*, *49*(1), 11–30.

CEM Instytut Badań Rynku i Opinii Publicznej, (2009). *Ocena transferu wiedzy i powiązan sfery B+R oraz instytucji otoczenia biznesu z przedsiębiorstwami w wojewodztwie malopolskim w 2009 roku* (Assessment of knowledge transfer and links between the R&D sector and business environment institutions with enterprises in Malopolska in 2009). Warsaw: CEM. At https://www.obserwatorium.malopolska. pl/wp-content/uploads/2016/05/Ocena-transferu-wiedzy-i-powi%C4%85za%C5% 84_2009.pdf (accessed on 16 July 2019).

Edquist, C. (2011). Design of innovation policy through diagnostic analysis: identification of systemic problems (or failures). *Industrial and Corporate Change*, *20*(6), 1725–53.

European Commission (2009, 2012, 2016, 2017). *Regional Innovation Scoreboard*. Brussels: European Commission.

Eurostat (2018). Regional Statistics. At https://ec.europa.eu/eurostat/web/regions/ data/database (accessed on 4 February 2019).

Foray, D. (2014). *Smart Specialisation: Opportunities and Challenges for Regional Innovation Policy*. Abingdon and New York, NY: Routledge.

Foray, D. (2017). The economic fundamentals of smart specialization strategies. In Radosevic, S., Curaj, A., Gheorghiu, R., Andreescu, L., and Wade, I. (eds), *Advances in the Theory and Practice of Smart Specialization*. London: Academic Press, 38–50.

Foray, D., Morgan, K., and Radosevic, S. (2018). *The role of smart specialisation in the EU research & innovation policy landscape*. Brussels: European Commission. At: http://ec.europa.eu/regional_policy/sources/docgener/brochure/smart/role_sm artspecialisation_ri. pdf (accessed on 5 March 2018).

Fundacja GAP (2014). *Analiza weryfikacyjna obszarów inteligentnej specjalizacji regionalnej województwa malopolskiego* (Verification analysis of areas of regional smart specialisation of the Malopolska region). At https://www.malopolska.pl/pu blikacje/gospodarka/analiza-weryfikacyjna-obszarow-inteligentnej-specjalizacji-regionalnej-wojewodztwa-malopolskiego (accessed on 16 July 2019).

FundEko (2012a). *Badanie stopnia wdrażania Regionalnej Strategii Innowacji Województwa Malopolskiego w ramach dedykowanego systemu monitoringu: III etap prac* (Examination of the degree of implementation of the RIS Malopolska within the framework of a dedicated monitoring system: stage III of works). At http://pliki.wrotamalopolski.pl/Raport_koncowy.pdf (accessed on 16 July 2019).

FundEko (2012b). *Ocena transferu wiedzy i powiązań sfery B+R oraz instytucji otoczenia biznesu z przedsiębiorstwami w województwie malopolskim w 2012 roku* (Assessment of knowledge transfer and links between the R&D sector and business environment institutions with enterprises in the Malopolska region in 2012). At

https://www.obserwatorium.malopolska.pl/wp-content/uploads/2016/05/Ocena-tr
ansferu-wiedzy-i-powi%C4%85sza%C5%84.pdf (accessed on 16 July 2019).

FundEko (2015). *Ewaluacja systemu monitoringu wdrażania Regionalnej Strategii Innowacji Wojewodztwa Malopolskiego 2008–2013* (Evaluation of the monitoring system of the RIS Malopolska 2008–2013). At http://pliki.wrotamalopolski.pl/RaportEwaluacjaMonitoringu.pdf (accessed on 16 July 2019).

Georghiou L. (2007). What lies beneath: avoiding the risk of under-evaluation. *Science and Public Policy*, *34*(10), 743–52.

González-López, M. (2019). Understanding policy learning in regional innovation policies: lessons from the Galician case. *Innovation: The European Journal of Social Science Research*, *32*(1), 104–18.

Grillitsch, M. (2018). Following or breaking regional development paths: on the role and capability of the innovative entrepreneur. *Regional Studies*, *53*(5), 1–11.

Haber, A. (2007). *Proces ewaluacji ex-post: konceptualizacja, operacjonalizacja, realizacja badania ewaluacyjnego* (The ex-post evaluation process: conceptualisation, operationalisation, implementation of the evaluation study). In: Haber, A. (ed.), *Ewaluacja ex-post: teoria i praktyka badawcza* (Ex-post evaluation: research theory and practice), Warsaw: PARP, 43–58.

Hassink, R. (2005). How to unlock regional economies from path dependency? From learning region to learning cluster. *European Planning Studies*, *14*(3), 521–35.

Hassink, R., Isaksen, A., and Trippl, M. (2019). Towards a comprehensive understanding of new regional industrial path development. *Regional Studies*, *53*(11), 1–10.

Hausner, J. (ed.) (2008). *Foresight technologiczny na rzecz zrownowazonego rozwoju Malopolski* (Technology foresight for the sustainable development of Malopolska). Krakow: MSAP UEK. At http://www.msap.uek.krakow.pl/doki/publ/foresight.pdf (accessed on 16 July 2019).

Isaksen, A., and Karlsen, J. (2011). Organisational learning, supportive innovation systems and implications for policy formulation. *Journal of the Knowledge Economy*, *2*(4), 453–62.

Isaksen, A.O., Jakobsen, S.E., Njøs, R., and Normann, R. (2019). Regional industrial restructuring resulting from individual and system agency. *Innovation: The European Journal of Social Science Research*, *32*(1), 48–65.

KPT (2010). *Foresight: perspektywa technologiczna Krakow-Malopolska 2020* (Foresight: technology perspective for Krakow-Malopolska 2020). Krakow: KPT. At http://foresight.kpt.krakow.pl (accessed on 16 July 2019).

Lundvall, B.Å., and Borrás, S. (1998). *The Globalising Learning Economy: Implications for Innovation Policy*. Brussels: EU Commission.

Malerba, F., and Nelson, R. (2011). Learning and catching up in different sectoral systems: evidence from six industries. *Industrial and Corporate Change*, *20*(6), 1645–75.

Malopolska Regional Government Office (2005). *Program strategiczny „Regionalna Strategia Innowacji Wojewodztwa Malopolskiego 2005–2013"* (Strategic programme, "Regional Innovation Strategy of the Malopolska Region 2005–2013"). Krakow: Malopolska Regional Government Office.

Malopolska Regional Government Office (2008). *Program strategiczny „Regionalna Strategia Innowacji Wojewodztwa Malopolskiego 2008–2013"* (Strategic programme, "Regional Innovation Strategy of the Malopolska Region 2008–2013"). Krakow: Malopolska Regional Government Office.

Malopolska Regional Government Office (2012). *Program strategiczny „Regionalna Strategia Innowacji Wojewodztwa Malopolskiego 2013–2020"* (Strategic programme, "Regional Innovation Strategy of the Malopolska Region 2013–2020"); updates approved by the Management Board of the Malopolska region in 2012, 2013, 2014, 2015, 2016. Krakow: Malopolska Regional Government Office.

Malopolska Regional Government Office (2018). *Aktualizacja poglebionej analizy innowacyjnosci gospodarki Malopolski* (The updated in-depth analysis of the innovativeness of the Malopolska economy). Krakow: Malopolska Regional Government Office.

Martin, R. (2010). Roepke Lecture in Economic Geography – Rethinking regional path dependence: beyond lock-in to evolution. *Economic Geography*, *86*(1), 1–27.

Martin, R., and Sunley, P. (2006). Path dependence and regional economic evolution. *Journal of Economic Geography*, *6*(4), 395–437.

Mason, C., and Brown, R. (2014). Entrepreneurial ecosystems and growth oriented entrepreneurship. *Final Report to OECD, Paris*, *30*(1), 77–102.

McCann, P., and Ortega-Argilés, R. (2015). Smart specialization, regional growth and applications to European Union cohesion policy. *Regional Studies*, *49*(8), 1291–1302.

Miedziński, M. (2008). *Wybrane zagadnienia ewaluacji polityki innowacyjnej* (Selected areas of evaluating the innovation policy). In Olejniczak, K., Kozak, M.W., and Ledzion, B. (eds), *Teoria i praktyka ewaluacji interwencji publicznych: podręcznik akademicki* (Theory and practice of evaluating the public intervention: an academic textbook). Warsaw: Wydawnictwa Akademickie i Profesjonalne, 480–98.

MSAP UEK (2016). *Oddziaływanie inteligentnych specjalizacji regionalnych na rozwój gospodarczy Malopolski* (The impact of regional smart specialisations on Malopolska's economic development). Krakow: MSAP UEK. At https://www.malopolska.pl/publikacje/gospodarka/oddzialywanie-inteligentnych-specjalizacji-regionalnych-na-rozwoj-gospodarczy-malopolski (accessed on 16 July 2019).

Ndofor, H.A., Sirmon, D.G., and He, X. (2015). Utilizing the firm's resources: how TMT heterogeneity and resulting faultlines affect TMT tasks. *Strategic Management Journal*, *36*(11), 1656–74.

North, D.C. (1990). *Institutions, Institutional Change and Economic Performance*. Cambridge: Cambridge University Press.

North, D.C. (2005). *Understanding the Process of Economic Change*. Princeton, NJ, and Oxford: Princeton University Press.

OECD (2019). *Local entrepreneurship ecosystems and emerging industries: case study of Malopolskie, Poland*. OECD Local Economic and Employment Development (LEED) Working Papers, No. 2019/03, Paris: OECD Publishing. At https://doi.org/10.1787/d99ba985-en (accessed on 16 July 2019).

Olejniczak, K. (2010). *Rola ewaluacji w krajowych politykach publicznych: analiza systemowa lat 1999–2010* (The role of evaluation in national public policies: system analysis of 1999–2010). In Haber, A., and Szałaj, M. (eds), *Ewaluacja w strategicznym zarządzaniu publicznym*, Warsaw: PARP, 39–62.

Ostrom, E. (2005). Governing the commons: The evolution of institutions for collective action. In Menard, C., and Shirley, M.M. (eds), *Handbook of New Institutional Economics*. Dordrecht: Springer, 819–48.

PARP (2013). *Regionalne systemy innowacji w Polsce: raport z badań* (Regional innovation systems in Poland: a research report). Warsaw: PARP.

Rodrik, D. (2014). Green industrial policy. *Oxford Review of Economic Policy*, *30*(3), 469–91.

Skulimowski A.M.J. (ed.) (2013). *Scenariusze i trendy rozwojowe wybranych technologii społeczeństwa informacyjnego do roku 2025, Raport Końcowy* (Scenarios and development trends of selected information society technologies by 2025, final report). Projekt WND-POIG.01.01.01-00-021/09. Wydawnictwo Naukowe Fundacji Progress & Business, Krakow. At www.ict.foresight.pl (accessed on 16 July 2019).

Stam, E. (2015). Entrepreneurial ecosystems and regional policy: a sympathetic critique. *European Planning Studies*, *23*(9), 1759–69.

Statistics Poland (2017). *Wybrane wskazniki przedsiebiorczosci 2011–2015* (Selected entrepreneurship indicators 2011–2015). Warsaw: Statistics Poland.

Statistics Poland (2018a). *Local data bank*. At https://bdl.stat.gov.pl/BDL/start (accessed on 16 July 2019).

Statistics Poland (2018b). *Wybrane wskazniki przedsiebiorczosci 2012–2016* (Selected entrepreneurship indicators 2012–2016). Warsaw: Statistics Poland.

Statistics Poland (2019a). *Local data bank*. At https://bdl.stat.gov.pl/BDL/start (accessed on 16 July 2019).

Statistics Poland (2019b). *Regional Statistics*. At https://bdl.stat.gov.pl/BDL/start (accessed on 16 July 2019).

STOS (2017). *Ocena transferu wiedzy i powiązań sfery B+R oraz instytucji otoczenia biznesu z przedsiębiorstwami w województwie małopolskim: ewaluacja ex-post wdrażania Regionalnej Strategii Innowacji Województwa Małopolskiego 2008–2013 w perspektywie jej oddziaływania na regionalną innowacyjność w horyzoncie 2016 roku* (Assessment of knowledge transfer and links between the R&D sphere and business environment institutions with enterprises in the Malopolskie voivodeship: ex-post evaluation of the implementation of the RIS Malopolska 2008–2013 in the perspective of its impact on regional innovation in the horizon of 2016). Krakow: Malopolska Regional Government Office. At https://www.malopolska.pl/publikacje/gospodarka/ewaluacja-expost-rsi-wm-w-perspektywie-jej-dlugoterminowego-oddzialywania-na-regionalna-innowacyjnosc (accessed on 16 July 2019).

Szlachta, J. (2014). *Nowe uwarunkowania trzeciej generacji strategii rozwoju regionalnego w Polsce* (The new conditions for the third-generation regional innovation strategies). Warsaw: SGH, *94*, 243–68.

Uyarra, E. (2010). What is evolutionary about "regional systems of innovation"? Implications for regional policy. *Journal of Evolutionary Economics*, *20*(1), 115–37.

Vatn, A. (2007). *Institutions and the Environment*. Cheltenham, UK and Northampton, MA, USA: Edward Elgar Publishing.

Williamson, O.E. (1998). Transaction cost economics: how it works; where it is headed. *De Economist*, *146*(1), 23–58.

12. The Agder region: an innovation policy case study

Roger Normann, Sissel Strickert and Jon P. Knudsen

1. INTRODUCTION

In this chapter we seek to identify and examine some of the key features of innovation policy in the Agder region. In the European Union (EU), regional innovation policies have become almost synonymous with Research and Innovation Strategies for Smart Specialisation (RIS3). Responsible and efficient use of structural funds is one of the drivers of RIS3 as a policy in the EU. As Norway is not a full member of the EU, Norwegian regions have not had access to EU structural funds, which has meant that this incentive is missing. However, over the last decades, regional innovation systems and related policies have had a significant impact in Norway, on policy instrument design, such as cluster policies, as well as on the design of several applied research programmes. This has become manifest in several regional policy documents, and in some higher education institution strategies.

The Norwegian system is historically characterised by a strong planning tradition and the leadership role in this regard is designated to the regional level. Therefore, Norway and Norwegian regions had a solid institutional foundation for implementing RIS3. Norway, for instance, was an early adopter of cluster programmes, and it would not have been a surprise if the country had become one of the frontrunners in implementing RIS3 as well. However, this did not happen. But Norway did not completely ignore the introduction of RIS3 and related policies. That said, the Norwegian responses were uncoordinated at the national level and fragmented at the regional level. In this chapter we ask why this was the case through an examination of the Agder region in the southernmost part of Norway. Specifically, we ask the following question: How can the Agder region response to RIS3 be explained?

We could foresee different types of rationales for choosing whether to implement a new policy, such as any smart specialisation policies, at the regional level or not. One way to implement these policies could be through hierarchical instruction, which means that the rationale for doing something is necessity. In a regional policy setting, this would resemble being hierarchically instructed through law, regulation or economic incentive by the national government or by the EU. However, even if one isn't instructed to do something, one might decide on free terms to make a choice to act. This would look like a situation where a regional political entity makes an informed and rational choice-based decision on careful assessment of the relevant pro and con arguments. Such would be the case if a new RIS3 policy is assessed as likely to be instrumental for realising existing strategic aims for industrial development, renewal and entrepreneurship, and/or if it is complementary to existing plans and actions, and/or if it represents a cost- and time-efficient way to realise policy goals. Another rationale for choosing to implement a new policy, discussed here, could be labelled adaptation to institutional norms. This is a mechanism that could be labelled as a variety of "organisational window dressing" and it is discussed in much detail by new-institutional theorists (Brunsson, 1989; DiMaggio and Powell, 1983; March and Olsen, 1989; Meyer and Rowan, 1977; Røvik, 1998). The mechanism works in situations where organisational entities make decisions about policy, strategy, organisation and ways of working based on the extent to which they contribute to achieving organisational legitimacy. Brunsson (1989) discusses this as an effective way of achieving organisational legitimacy in a world where organisations are exposed to an increasing number of inconsistent and conflicting norms and demands. In this perspective, it is not necessarily the end-effects of the new policy that are the most important, e.g. number of new jobs, but rather that surrounding agencies and institutions recognise the implementation of "fashionable", forward-leaning and cutting-edge policies. This then serves the purpose of generating legitimacy and attractiveness for the region. A final rationale could be ideological, based on social and cultural structures. An expression of this could be that regions with liberalist politicians in government would be less incentivised to support policy instruments that prescribe political intervention in the marked domain.

In the following sections, we briefly introduce the key theoretical concepts and constructs that we will use to discuss the research question, before identifying some of the defining components of the innovation system in the Agder region. Next, we discuss some characteristics of innovation policy in the region; and we conclude the chapter with a discussion of findings related to our research question.

2. THEORETICAL FRAMEWORK

2.1 Regional Innovation Policy

The regional innovation systems (RISs) approach was developed in the early 1990s by scholars such as Phil Cooke, Bjørn Asheim, Arne Isaksen and Franz Tödtling (Asheim and Isaksen, 1997; Cooke, 1992; Tödtling and Kaufmann, 1999). An RIS is conceptually outlined to consist of three core elements – actors, institutions and networks – where there is emphasis placed on the interdependencies between them. A key argument in RIS theory is that innovation does not happen in a vacuum but should be understood as the result of interactive learning in innovation networks that are embedded in specific socio-cultural and socio-economic settings (Asheim et al., 2019; González-López et al., 2019). Over the last decades, RIS theory has been presented in many different configurations and variations, but always containing the above-described core elements. Recently, more emphasis has for instance been put on the role played by agency in developing RIS, often conceptualised through concepts such as system entrepreneurs or place-based leadership (Isaksen et al., 2019; Normann et al., 2017).

RIS theory, together with the regional cluster paradigm (Porter, 2003) and triple-helix model (Etzkowitz and Leydesdorff, 1997), has increasingly come to inform a systems approach to regional economic policy and policy development worldwide (Normann, 2007). It has possibly been most influential in coordinated market economies and in countries with strong planning traditions. RIS3 conceptually shares significant features with RIS and therefore its emergence cannot be viewed in isolation from the family three. RIS3 is conceptually distinguished from RIS by its emphasis of the significance of concepts such as strategy, leadership and entrepreneurship. RIS theory has recently placed more emphasis on the role of agency in the development of RISs (Isaksen et al., 2019). Beginning in the early 2010s, RIS3 spread rapidly throughout Europe (Foray, 2015; Foray et al., 2011). However, before this, many European regions, in particular in the Nordic countries, developed their own set of RIS-informed policies (Henning et al., 2010; Jakobsen et al., 2012). The Agder region is one of several examples of a region that developed regional plans and industrial development policies that were influenced by RIS theory and thinking.

Innovation studies is a broad field with links to many disciplines. However, policy recommendations from researchers working with RIS theory tend to share some characteristics. Foremost is that regional innovation policies must always begin by assessing the regional context and subsequently develop place-based policies that consider and prey on regional preconditions. This particular point was notably articulated by Tödtling and Trippl (2005). Following from this, regional innovation policies informed by RIS theory will assess factors such as type of region, dominant modes of innovation, type of actors, industrial structure, collaborative structures, institutional configurations, opportunities for learning and differentiation, natural resources, mobility, endowment, etc. An important implication of this is that RIS policies in peripheral and specialised regions will be fundamentally different from RIS policies in thick and diversified regions with high innovation capacity.

This more nuanced approach to scale and type of policy intervention has led RIS researchers occasionally to find themselves in discussion with neo-classically oriented economists and policy makers about what the role of innovation policies should be. For instance, should innovation policy only be an instrument for correcting market failures or should it be utilised in full also in regions where innovation processes organically occur? These debates have often resulted in discussions of what constitutes a market failure. Asheim et al. (2019) suggest the reason this debate is often unproductive is that RIS theory addresses systemic and institutional failures, while neo-classical economists often emphasise the resources held by individual actors and agency in the local setting.

2.2   Policy Change, Policy Learning and Place-based Leadership

In recent years, management scholars, political scientists and action researchers have explored how agency in practice operates and can operate in order to facilitate desired changes to the RIS (Karlsen et al., 2012). One important consequence of this insight is that the role of agency has become more prominent in RIS theory (Isaksen et al., 2019), supplementing established systems/institutional theory (Asheim and Isaksen, 1997; Cooke, 1992). This interest has specifically targeted understanding the role played by actors in facilitating regional path development and creation (Boschma and Martin, 2010; Martin, 2010) and the role of place-based leadership therein (Sotarauta, 2014b; Sotarauta et al., 2012a). Researchers have therefore put emphasis on understanding how place-based leadership emerges and what kind of forms it takes in various institutional settings. It has subsequently been accepted that place-based leadership adds to our understanding of regional innovation systems, especially when it comes to recommending how insights from RIS theory can be of use to political change. Much discussed in the academic community, place-based leadership is still an emerging academic field (Audretsch, 2015; Beer, 2014; Beer and Clower, 2014; Collinge et al., 2010; Gibney, 2014; Gibney et al., 2009; Hidle and Normann, 2013; Normann, 2013; Normann et al.,

2017; Sotarauta, 2014a, 2014b; Sotarauta et al., 2012b). More specifically, leadership is often emphasised as a significant factor for regional growth and path development (Beer, 2014; OECD, 2009, 2010, 2012). Place-based leadership has also been suggested as a missing link in our current understanding of regional growth processes (Rodríguez-Pose, 2013). Others have pointed to place-based leadership as the key element for places and regions to systematically harness the underlying determinants of economic performance (Audretsch, 2015). Nevertheless, the difficulty of grasping the nature of place-based leadership has led some researchers to label it a "black box" for practitioners and academics alike (Sotarauta et al., 2012a). Place-based leadership can, following this, take the form of system-level agency (Isaksen et al., 2019), meaning actors that exert influence outside their institutional or organisational border. It can be defined as "the leadership of interdependent actors and institutions that are operationally autonomous and not necessarily connected in a formal system of steering and authority" (Normann et al., 2017, p. 275). Isaksen et al. (2019) give the following examples of system agency that transcends institutional spheres: A regional cluster manager and a dean who align an industry strategy with a regional university strategy, for instance in developing a joint educational programme or a user-oriented research centre. Another example could be an agency in the public support system that develops and implements new policy measures to which actors and institutions can respond and adapt. One important facet of the role performed by place-based leadership in regions is often that they facilitate policy learning processes. This could come about through importing and introducing regional actors to new concepts, working methods, development trends, etc. and translating and communicating these to facilitate policy change.

3. THE REGIONAL INNOVATION SYSTEM

3.1 Structure of the Regional Innovation System

The Agder region is by most standards a peripheral region with approximately 300,000 inhabitants. Most of the citizenry is located in smaller cities along the coastline. Agder is the southernmost region in Norway and its industry is dominated by processes industries and medium high-tech manufacturing and shipping. It is one of the most export-intensive regions in Norway based on processed goods. Key challenges for regional authorities regarding innovation policy are renewal of the existing industry, such as finding ways to incorporate global trends such as digitalisation and greening of the economy into the regional industry. This has been understood as a challenge in a region characterised as "thin" regarding research and development (R&D), concentration of employment opportunities and access to R&D resources. In the period stretching from about 2005 to 2015, the region alongside several other Norwegian regions incorporated policies and plans for facilitating innovation and renewal based on support for cluster projects, university development, R&D projects and infrastructure developments. Given the initial resources and funding structure, the Agder region can be described as having been moderately successful in generating new collaborative R&D activities aimed at industrial renewal. Collaboration in R&D and innovation projects between the regional and national R&D institutions is also increasing in importance. Notable examples include university status given to the University of Agder (2007), a 100MNOK award for a Centre for Research-based Innovation (SFI) and 200MNOK national funding for a mechatronics testing facility. Further on, the GCE NODE was one of the two first Norwegian business clusters promoted to Global Center of Expertise (GCE) status. Many of the institutional developments in the Agder region have in this sense been "by the book" in terms of RIS theory.

However, the positive developments within the Agder RIS are not all encompassing but limited to a few industries. Outside these industries, there are also examples of some very competitive firms that are connected to the region through supply chains or other resources. If we follow Asheim et al. (2019, p. 92) and their classification scheme, the RIS type in the Agder region can be described as thick and specialised, where at the core of the collaboration are R&D projects, labour mobility and leadership expressed as strategic collaboration. This is a description that fits well as a description of the collaborative patterns that have emerged in the two university campus towns Grimstad and Kristiansand between firms and the university. However, if we were to include the whole geographical region and all its 300,000 inhabitants, it would probably be more precise to describe the region as having a thin RIS.

3.2 Regional Policy

Regional policy has been of paramount importance in post-Second World War Norwegian politics, and more so than in the other Nordic countries (Gløersen, 2013; Knudsen, 2018b). From the late 1960s and onwards regional university colleges and regional research institutes were established in most of the then existing counties in what can be labelled a wave of regionalisation. Furthermore, several programmes and instruments have been established to foster innovation in a regional context throughout the 1990s and beyond. On the regional level, Agder has participated in most of these system-driven initiatives. Among them, the "Programme for Regional R&D and Innovation (VRI)" was the Norwegian Research Council's main support mechanism for research and innovation in Norwegian regions. The VRI project is probably one of the R&D programmes that contributed the most in shaping Norwegian regional innovation policy as an RIS-informed practice through the direct influence of internationally recognised Norwegian innovation scholars such as Arne Isaksen, Jan Fagerberg and Bjørn Terje Asheim.

3.3   Firms and Industrial Specialisation

During the VRI project period (2007–2016), all regions in Norway experienced centralisation and concentration regarding R&D efforts (Herstad and Sandven, 2017), as industry reduced its commitment to regional development work indirectly by strengthening the linkages between regional industry and national/international research institutions. In particular, SINTEF, one of the largest research institutes in Northern Europe, gained a position as the dominating collaborative partner for Norwegian firms. Herstad and Sandven (2017, p. 10) write that the exception among Norwegian regions is the Agder region, where relations between regional industrial networks and local research institutions were strengthened in the same period.

Figure 12.1 compiles and presents data covering the period 2006–2016 and thus includes market fluctuations and consequences of the financial

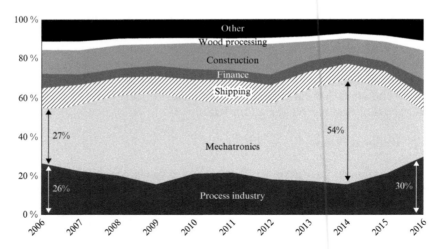

Source: Adapted from Rypestøl (2018).

Figure 12.1   Per industry percentage of total regional turnover, 2006–2016

crisis in 2008, in addition to the international fall in oil and gas prices in 2014. It illustrates the development of the relative importance measured in turnover of the largest industries in the Agder region.

However, specialised regions face the challenge of lock-in, described as a situation where development has followed the same track for so long that change is difficult. In Agder, a high and stable share of export and international ownership in the private sector serve as opposing forces to lock-in. Further, entrepreneurship and new establishments contribute with new ideas and ways of co-working as they challenge traditional ways of doing business and push to renew existing industries. Another challenge in Agder is the relatively low share of R&D activity compared with the national average. Many of the specialised industries combine experience-based knowledge with research knowledge, known as the Combined and Complex mode of Innovation (CCI), in their innovation process (Isaksen and Karlsen, 2011). Due to the relatively low share of R&D activity, continued efforts to strengthen R&D in the Agder region become important.

4.   REGIONAL INNOVATION POLICIES

4.1   Legal Framework

The Nordic countries are generally described as close in institutional arrangements regarding the integration of the economy and politics. All have mixed economies and a capitalistic system with a tradition for a strong state (Christensen, 2003). In Norway, there are currently 11 county councils following a recent merger of the former 19 counties into fewer and larger regions decided by the national Parliament (Norwegian Government, 2016).

The counties all have a formal role as *regional development actors* in a national division of labour on political tasks and responsibilities. In the mid-2000s, the counties were given the task of leading regional partnerships, although their role and authority are constantly being contested, discussed and changed. The counties are also responsible for developing regional plans on innovation, industrial development, education, climate, infrastructure, etc. They were also given autonomy in terms of deciding how to respond to RIS3 by the government. This eventually resulted in a relatively diverse Norwegian response to smart specialisation (Knudsen et al., 2019).

A problem arising for the counties is that their ability to finance new initiatives and processes in the fields of regional and innovation policies has been severely lowered in recent years. Between 2013 and 2018, the yearly lump sum allocated to them by the state to freely pursue their own policy initiatives was cut by almost one-third in nominal prices and close to half in fixed prices from the start to the end of the period (Knudsen, 2018b). This budgetary turn followed in the wake of a shift from a red–green to a liberal–conservative government. The paradoxical situation is, then, that the rhetoric of a more competent county council level, politically speaking, goes along with a weakened county council level, financially speaking.

The Norwegian county councils reacted differently to the challenge offered by the advent of RIS3. RIS3 came about when the whole county structure was under pressure from a government that ideally wanted the counties to dissolve. Parliament counteracted this development, and the government responded with indifference and budget cuts (Knudsen et al., 2019). This move was reinforced by the government's market-friendly liberal position on industrial development. Hence, different regional strategies towards RIS3 emerged. Some counties responded by ramping up their efforts to match policy initiatives from the EU and implementing fully fledged RIS3. Some counties responded to RIS3 through a more symbolic exercise, often because they were encouraged to do so by regional R&D institutions. Lastly, some counties ignored RIS3 or refused to partake. In the Agder region, and as a part of work performed in the VRI, the region completed its registration on the RIS3 platform.[1] This is an association with RIS3 in name only, because, as of 2019, the region has not completed any RIS3 activities such as monitoring, benchmarking or entrepreneurial discovery.

4.2   Institutional Framework

As mentioned earlier in this chapter, socio-cultural configurations are important for understanding, describing and prescribing policy changes in RISs. Socio-cultural configurations can be understood as a broad framework for understanding the relationship between the workings of the economy and the cultural and political sphere in which it is embedded (Knudsen, 2018a). If we use the Nordic countries as an example, the literature describes an east–west polarisation, where Denmark and Norway are characterised as exhibiting more liberalistic traits than Finland and Sweden, which offer more organic qualities – and in the case of Finland, even communitarian traits (Todd, 1990). The Norwegian political scientist Stein Rokkan (1987) explained this as an heritage that is passed on through generations with decisive consequences for contemporary institutions within all sectors of society (Knudsen, 2018a). Knudsen et al. (2019) use this type of scheme to explain divisions of capitalist practices between a coordinated market economy (CME)-based organic type and a liberal market economy (LME)-based liberalistic type, as outlined by Hall and Soskice (2001) and anticipated by authors such as Albert (1993) and Todd (1998). They further discuss how such differences appear to be especially apparent in the way regional innovation is dealt with when creating national and regional policies. Some of the Nordic countries, especially Norway and Finland, show distinct internal regional disparities with regard to ideological disposition that are as strong as those found between countries (Knudsen, 2011; Rokkan, 1987; Todd, 1990; Wicken, 2004). The CME sphere in Norway should in this regard be divided into two distinct subtypes (Knudsen et al., 2019). The first reflects the traditional hierarchic CME configuration as described by Hall and Soskice (2001) and is typically hierarchical as represented in countries like Germany and Sweden (CME type 1), whereas the second represents a more egalitarian organic structure, found in the western part of Norway, labelled *hierarchic egalitarianism* (CME type 2), known for its propensity to spur network-based innovations of the Doing, Using, Interacting (DUI) mode (Asheim and Grillitsch, 2015).

Following Emmanuel Todd (1990, pp. 37–8), a strain of literature has emerged linking economic macro-patterns to demographic micro-patterns as a means of explaining linkages and processes between socio-cultural and socio-economic structures in European regions (Duranton et al., 2009; Knudsen, 2018a; Luiten van Zanden et al., 2017; Schultenover, 1999). The main idea in this tradition is to highlight that socio-cultural and socio-economic forms (re-)produce each other so as to create fairly stable informal institutional fields that are only slowly and reluctantly responding to (external) pressures for formal institutional change. As such, a deeper understanding is presented concerning why the one-size-does-not-fit-all argument prevails. Linking the Toddian family typology with Hall and Soskice's (2001) Varieties of Capitalism (VoC) scheme, we obtain the following sequence (Table 12.1) as regards forms that are empirically found in Norway.

Table 12.1 Operationalisation of Todd family types based on VoC scheme

Family type	VoC category
Absolute Nuclear Family (ANC)	LME (Liberal Market Economy)
Stem Family (SF) type 1 (following Todd)	CME type 1
Stem Family (SF) type 2 (Hierarchic Egalitarian)	CME type 2

Source: Based on Knudsen et al. (2019).

Knudsen (2018a) argues that there are different ways of dealing with innovation within these different configurations. The ANC/LME combination seems to result in practices of innovation that come close to Anglo-American models for such behaviour, while the SF/CME 1 model offers a rather static and eventually reluctant position and the SF/CME 2 model seems to foster a strong drive for DUI- or CCI-like innovation. Knudsen et al. (2019) apply this framework to propose a tentative and mapped Norwegian typology of regional VoCs that contributes to a socio-cultural explanation for how counties responded to RIS3. They write:

> In our case, the significant point is to underline that the historical hegemony of the absolute nuclear family seems to align with the rising of the North Sea geographic core area of the Liberal Market Economy (LME), while the hegemonic regions of the stem family seem to have formed the North European stronghold of the Coordinated Market Economy (CME). (Knudsen et al., 2019)

The LME counties are located in the southwest of Norway and typically mirror policies and values in the business community and at the political level with a liberalist heritage. For instance, RIS3 was rejected in Vestfold county based on a negative ideological attitude to state intervention in the market. Counties classified with a classical CME (type 1), responded to RIS3 with a top-down response, embracing RIS3 in Nordland and rejecting it in Hedmark. In our case county, oscillating between the LME type and the CME type 2 classification (hierarchic egalitarian), the response was generally positive to RIS3. The county offering the most typical bottom-up response was the CME type 2 county Møre og Romsdal. Here, the county served as a facilitator to engaging partners. In this county, it is even a cluster manager who de facto leads the regional partnership and decides whether the region should "go for it" with respect to RIS3 (Knudsen et al., 2019).

4.3 Policy Changes and Leadership

In the Agder region, the main R&D actor, which is also one of the largest employers in the region, is the University of Agder. Universities and R&D institutions have a pivotal role in RIS, in how they operate, and in how their strategies and capabilities are alike. These are all among the key identifying characteristics of an RIS. The evolution of the RIS and the RIS policy in Agder can therefore be illustrated with the development of the third role of the University of Agder, which is a relatively young university. Normann and Pinheiro (2018) argue that the development of third-role strategies at the new universities follows a relatively predictable pattern given the national policies in the field and the existing practices of the more established universities. The public policy associated with performing the third role may be somewhat simplified and divided into three time periods: before 1970, between 1970 and 1995, and after 1995. Prior to 1970, the then university colleges, which now form the new universities, were understood as educational institutions. External commitments and research were neither expected nor desired to any extent. After 1970 and up to 1995, there was a softening of national policies where research was accepted but mainly limited to some less resource-intensive disciplines that were defined by the authorities. Following 1995, it is required by law that all activities performed by the universities must be research based. These changes have important implications for how the third role has been interpreted and operationalised. Based on this, Normann and Pinheiro (2018) divide the development of the third role into four phases at the University of Agder, which conclude with the strategic decision to pursue the third role through collaboration with regional industries in general and through "excellence" in an extended research collaboration with the regional mechatronics industry.

The development of regional innovation policy rationales and political decision-making processes in the Agder region is probably best illustrated with the development of the mechatronics industry in the region. In the 1970s and 1980s, no regional collaboration in and around the oil and gas industry took place in Agder, simply because there was nobody to collaborate with either on the public policy side or on the academic side. This can be contrasted with the neighbouring region of Rogaland, where Stavanger in the end became the de facto oil capital of Norway. In the late 1960s, the Mayor of Stavanger fought hard with the cities of Bergen and Trondheim and succeeded to establish Stavanger in this position. The situation in Kristiansand was different. Even though the city was located nearer to the oil fields and had great harbour facilities, the then city council declared that the city was not interested in hosting the oil industry (Hidle and Normann, 2013). There was also very little contact and interaction between the regional university college and the industry at the time (Normann et al., 2016).

However, after the NODE cluster was established in 2005, and the regional policy makers observed an exponential growth in the oil and gas supply industry within the Agder region, increased political and economic support both for firm projects and for cluster development initiatives followed suit. The NODE cluster was also instrumental in developing an academic mechatronics field. It arguably played a similar role in developing a political argument for facilitating a mechatronics field in the region. An industry chief executive officer informant describes the role of the cluster manager as follows:

[The cluster manager] was brilliant when he formed NODE. This created a platform for collaboration between companies and for speaking to the politicians – this also led the way for the SFI [Centre for Research-based Innovation]. NODE is an important entity that has created a regional force and shown the politicians that we are world leading – and also shown the international actors that this region is world leading and that they cannot move out of this region.

5.   CONCLUSIONS

In this chapter, we raised the question of how the Agder region's response to RIS3 can be explained. The Agder region had, following the discussion above, a symbolic response to RIS3. The region registered on the European Commission's smart specialisation platform and made use of references to RIS3 in regional plans, but it never executed any peer-review processes or implemented any entrepreneurial discovery processes. Given the region's previous experience and partial success with utilising policy instruments, partly designed and based on RIS theory combined with proven strategic and leadership capabilities demonstrated in facilitating the collaboration between the mechatronics industry and the university of Agder, the expectation should be that the region would be first in line to implement RIS3 policies and utilise opportunities for financing and collaboration therein. Our findings discussing this are briefly illustrated in Table 12.2 below.

With the findings presented and summarised like this, perhaps for a reader unfamiliar with the internal processes in the Agder region it is unsurprising and understandable why the Agder region had only a symbolic response to RIS3. For the authors of this chapter, who for decades have been working with innovation and regional development policies in the region, it was both puzzling and surprising that the region did not respond more forcefully at the time.

NOTE

1.   See http://s3platform.jrc.ec.europa.eu/

Table 12.2   Summary of findings

Type of explanation	Agder region
Hierarchical instruction	
Economic incentive	There were no specific economic incentives outside what could have been generated through international R&D collaboration. An RIS3 strategy would not give Norwegian regions access to EU structural funds.
National law or regulation	RIS3 development was neither required nor encouraged by the national government. The counties were free to perform their role as regional development agents. Simultaneously, a regional reform was launched to bring the number of counties down.
National budgets	The budgetary turn that followed in the wake of a shift from a red–green to a liberal–conservative government meant that between 2013 and 2018 the yearly lump sum allocated to regions by the state to freely pursue their own policy initiatives was cut close to half in fixed prices from the start to the end of the period.
Rational choice	
Leadership	The Agder region had proven that it had a place-based leadership capable of executing and realising complex innovation policy goals. However, responsibility for managing RIS3 was held by the counties, thereby they had the formal roles of leading regional partnership and coordinating regional planning.
Timing	RIS3 became the dominating innovation policy paradigm in Europe at a time when Norwegian counties were focused on structural reform. The number of counties was reduced from 19 to 11. Regions with merging counties, such as the Agder region, became increasingly preoccupied with internal processes and managing the planning and execution of the reform.
Resources	Given the cuts in national budgets, free resources that could be used for R&D became scarcer. Regions with more economic resources, such as Nordland and Møre og Romsdal, are among the eager adopters of RIS3.

Table 12.2 (*continued*)

Adaptation to institutional norms

Compatibility with internal existing rationales, processes and plans	RIS3 is by most observers said to complement, strengthen and build on previous work and policy rationales such as RIS theory and cluster policy. Thus, RIS3 in the Agder region would have the potential to be a useful amendment to existing ways of working, planning, developing and executing a new set of effective regional innovation policies in the Agder region. This is something that was discussed in a report commissioned by the counties written by Johnsen et al. (2016).
Compatibility with external norms	The Agder region registered on the EU RIS3 platform quite early; only one other region had previously registered. Given that Norwegian regions in sum were quite passive with respect to RIS3, the regional "peer" pressures seem to have been of little relevance for the decision-making process.

Ideological

Socio-cultural structure	The Agder region, oscillating within the VoC scheme discussed above, tends mostly to follow the self-reliance response pattern of an LME-scheme classification response.

Source: Own elaboration.

266

REFERENCES

Albert, M. (1993). *Capitalism Against Capitalism*. London: Whurr Publishers.

Asheim, B.T., and Grillitsch, M. (2015). *Smart specialisation: Sources for new path development in a peripheral manufacturing region*. Papers in Innovation Studies (No. 2015/11). Lund: CIRCLE – Center for Innovation, Research and Competences in the Learning Economy.

Asheim, B.T., and Isaksen, A. (1997). Location, agglomeration and innovation: Towards regional innovation systems in Norway? *European Planning Studies, 5*(3), 299–330.

Asheim, B.T., Isaksen, A., and Trippl, M. (2019). *Advanced Introduction to Regional Innovation Systems*. Cheltenham, UK and Northampton, MA, USA: Edward Elgar Publishing.

Audretsch, D.B. (2015). *Everything In Its Place: Entrepreneurship and the Strategic Management of Cities, Regions, and States*. New York, NY: Oxford University Press.

Beer, A. (2014). Leadership and the governance of rural communities. *Journal of Rural Studies, 34*, 254–62.

Beer, A., and Clower, T. (2014). Mobilizing leadership in cities and regions. *Regional Studies, Regional Science, 1*(1), 5–20.

Boschma, R., and Martin, R. (eds). (2010). *The Handbook of Evolutionary Economic Geography*. Cheltenham, UK and Northampton, MA, USA: Edward Elgar Publishing.

Brunsson, N. (1989). *The Organization of Hypocrisy: Talk, Decisions and Actions in Organizations*. Chichester: John Wiley.

Christensen, T. (2003). Narratives of Norwegian governance: Elaborating the strong state tradition. *Public Administration, 81*(1), 163–90.

Collinge, C., Gibney, J., and Mabey, C. (2010). Leadership and place. *Policy Studies, 31*(4), 367–78.

Cooke, P. (1992). Regional innovation systems: Competitive regulations in the new Europe. *Geoforum, 23*, 365–82.

DiMaggio, P.J., and Powell, W.W. (1983). The iron cage revisited: Institutional isomorphism and collective rationality in organizational fields. *American Sociological Review, 48*(2), 147–60.

Duranton, G., Rodríguez-Pose, A., and Sandall, R. (2009). Family types and the persistence of regional disparities in Europe. *Economic Geography, 85*(1), 23–47.

Etzkowitz, H., and Leydesdorff, L. (eds). (1997). *Universities and the Global Knowledge Economy: A Triple Helix of University–Industry–Government Relations*. London: Continuum.

Foray, D. (2015). *Smart Specialisation: Opportunities and Challenges for Regional Innovation Policy*. Abingdon: Routledge.

Foray, D., David, P.A., and Hall, B.H. (2011). *Smart specialisation: From academic idea to political instrument, the surprising career of a concept and the difficulties involved in its implementation*. Working Paper, No. 2011-001, Lausanne MTEI École Polytechnique Fédérale de Lausanne.

Gibney, J. (2014). Don't lose sight of context: A commentary on mobilizing cities and regions. *Regional Studies, Regional Science, 1*(1), 25–7.

Gibney, J., Copeland, S., and Murie, A. (2009). Toward a "new" strategic leadership of place for the knowledge-based economy. *Leadership, 5*(1), 5–23.

Gløersen, E. (2013). *La Finlande, la Norvège, la Suède face au projet d'une Europe polycentrique. La centralité à la marge de l'Europe. Espace et Territoires.* Rennes: Presses Universitaires de Rennes.

González-López, M., Asheim, B.T., and Sánchez-Carreira, M.d.C. (2019). New insights on regional innovation policies. *Innovation: The European Journal of Social Science Research, 32*(1), 1–7.

Hall, P., and Soskice, D. (2001). *Varieties of Capitalism: The Institutional Foundations of Competitive Advantage.* Oxford: Oxford University Press.

Henning, M., Moodysson, J., and Nilsson, M. (2010). *Innovation och regional omvandling: Från skånska kluster till nya kombinationer.* Malmö: Region Skåne.

Herstad, S.J., and Sandven, T. (2017). *Towards regional innovation systems in Norway? An explorative empirical analysis, Report 2017:8.* Oslo: Nordic Institute for Studies in Innovation, Research and Education (NIFU).

Hidle, K., and Normann, R. (2013). Who can govern? Comparing network governance leadership in two Norwegian city-regions. *European Planning Studies, 21*(2), 115–30.

Isaksen, A., and Karlsen, J. (2011). Combined and complex mode of innovation in regional cluster development: Analysis of the light-weight material cluster in Raufoss, Norway. In B. Asheim and M.D. Parilli (eds), *Interactive Learning for Innovation: A Key Driver within Clusters and Innovation Systems* (pp. 115–36). Basingstoke: Palgrave Macmillan.

Isaksen, A., Jakobsen, S.-E., Njøs, R., and Normann, R. (2019). Regional industrial restructuring resulting from individual and system agency. *Innovation: The European Journal of Social Science Research, 32*(1), 48–65.

Jakobsen, S.E., Byrkjeland, M., Båtevik, F.O., Pettersen, I.B., Skogseid, I., and Yttredal, E.R. (2012). Continuity and change in path-dependent regional policy development: The regional implementation of the Norwegian VRI programme. *Norwegian Journal of Geography, 66*, 133–43.

Johnsen, H.C.G., Knudsen, J.P., Karlsen, J., Isaksen, A., Normann, R.H., et al. (2016). *Smart spesialiseringsanalyse for Agder, del I & II.* FoU-rapport nr. 2/2016, Kristiansand: Agderforskning.

Karlsen, J., Larrea, M., Wilson, J., and Aranguren, M.J. (2012). Bridging the gap between academic research and regional development: A case study of knowledge cogeneration processes in the Basque Country. *European Journal of Education, 47*(1), 122–38.

Knudsen, J.P. (2011). Innovation, culture and politics: An outline for investigating criss-crossing Nordic cleavages. In H.C.G. Johnsen and Ø. Pålshaugen (eds), *Hva er Innovasjon? Perspektiver i Norsk Innovasjonsforskning. Vol. 1: System og Institusjon* (pp. 314–42). Kristiansand: Høyskoleforlaget.

Knudsen, J.P. (2018a). The socio-cultural basis for innovation. In A. Isaksen, R. Martin and M. Trippl (eds), *New Avenues for Regional Innovation Systems: Theoretical Advances, Empirical Cases and Policy Lessons* (pp. 61–83). New York: Springer.

Knudsen, J. (2018b). Towards a new spatial perspective: Norwegian politics at the crossroads. *Norsk Geografisk Tidsskrift, Norwegian Journal of Geography, 72*(2), 67–81.

Knudsen, J.P., Schulze-Krogh, A.C., and Normann, R. (2019). Smart specialisation – Norwegian adoptions. *Journal of the Knowledge Economy.* https://doi.org/10.1007/s13132-019-00610-7

Luiten van Zanden, J., Rijpma, A., and Kok, J. (eds). (2017). *Agency, Gender and Economic Development in the World Economy 1850–2000: Testing the Sen Hypothesis*. London: Routledge.

March, J.G., and Olsen, J.P. (1989). *Rediscovering Institutions: The Organizational Basis of Politics*. New York: Free Press.

Martin, R. (2010). Roepke lecture in economic geography – rethinking regional path dependence: Beyond lock-in to evolution. *Economic Geography, 86*(1), 1–27.

Meyer, J., and Rowan, B. (1977). Institutional organizations: Formal structure as myth and ceremony. *American Journal of Sociology, 83*(2), 340–63.

Normann, R. (2007). *Democracy in Development: A Critical View on Regional Governance, Theses at NTNU nr. 88*. Trondheim: Norwegian University of Science and Technology.

Normann, R. (2013). Regional leadership: A systemic view. *Systemic Practice and Action Research, 26*(1), 23–38.

Normann, R., and Pinheiro, R. (2018). University collaboration at a cross-road: Evolution and tensions in third-mission engagement. In R. Pinheiro, M. Young and K. Šima (eds), *Higher Education and Regional Development: Tales from Northern and Central Europe* (pp. 167–89). Cham, Switzerland: Palgrave Macmillan.

Normann, R., Johnsen, H.C.G., Knudsen, J.P., Vasström, M., and Johnsen, I.G. (2017). Emergence of regional leadership: A field approach. *Regional Studies, 51*(2), 273–84.

Normann, R., Vasström, M., and Johnsen, H.C.G. (2016). *The role of agency in regional path development*. Paper presented at the Regional Studies Association Annual Conference, 3–6 April, Graz, Austria.

Norwegian Government (2016). *Meld. St. 22 (2015–2016): Nye folkevalgte regioner – rolle, strukturer og oppgaver*. Oslo: Regjeringen.

OECD (2009). *Entrepreneurship and the Innovation System of the Agder Region, Norway: A review by the Local Economic and Employment Development (LEED) Programme of the Organisation for Economic Co-operation and Development (OECD)*. Paris: OECD.

OECD (2010). *Regions Matter: Economic Recovery, Innovation and Sustainable Growth*. Paris: OECD Publishing.

OECD (2012). *Growth in all Regions*. Paris: OECD Publishing.

Porter, M.E. (2003). The economic performance of regions. *Regional Studies, 37*(6/7), 549–78.

Rodríguez-Pose, A. (2013). Do institutions matter for regional development? *Regional Studies, 47*(7), 1034–47.

Rokkan, S. (1987). *Stat, nasjon klasse: Essays i politisk sosiologi*. Oslo: Universitetsforlaget.

Rypestøl, J.O. (2018). *Det regionale innovasjonssystemet i Agder*. Prosjektrapport nr. 2/2018. Kristiansand: Agderforskning.

Røvik, K.A. (1998). *Moderne organisasjoner: Trender i organisasjonstenkningen ved årtusenskiftet*. Oslo: Fagbokforlaget.

Schultenover, D.G. (1999). An anthropological view of the modernist crisis. *Journal of Religion and Society, 1*(1), 1–19.

Sotarauta, M. (2014a). Reflections on "Mobilizing leadership in cities and regions". *Regional Studies, Regional Science, 1*(1), 28–31.

Sotarauta, M. (2014b). Territorial knowledge leadership in policy networks: A peripheral region of South Ostrobothnia, Finland as a case in point. In

R. Rutten, P. Benneworth, D. Irawati and F. Boekema (eds), *The Social Dynamics of Innovation Networks* (pp. 42–59). Abingdon: Routledge.

Sotarauta, M., Horlings, L., and Liddle, J. (2012a). Leadership and sustainable regional development. In M. Sotarauta, L. Horlings and J. Liddle (eds), *Leadership and Change in Sustainable Regional Development* (pp. 1–29). Abingdon: Routledge.

Sotarauta, M., Horlings, L., and Liddle, J. (eds). (2012b). *Leadership and Change in Sustainable Regional Development*. Abingdon: Routledge.

Todd, E. (1990). *L'invention de l'Europe*. Paris: Seuil.

Todd, E. (1998). *L'illusion économique: Essai sur la stagnation des sociétés développées*. Paris: Gallimard.

Tödtling, F., and Kaufmann, A. (1999). Innovation systems in regions of Europe: A comparative paper. *European Planning Studies, 7*(6), 699–717.

Tödtling, F., and Trippl, M. (2005). One size fits all? Towards a differentiated regional innovation policy approach. *Research Policy, 34*(8), 1203–19.

Wicken, O. (2004). Politikk som konkurranse mellom industrialiseringsformer. In P. Arbo and H. Gammelsæter (eds), *Innovasjonspolitikkens scenografi* (pp. 50–65). Trondheim: Tapir.

Index

absorptive capacity 15, 26, 35, 60–61
adaptation to institutional norms 253, 265
administrative capacity 104, 105
Agder innovation policy 252–3, 264
  firms and industrial specialisation 258–9
  institutional framework 260–62
  legal framework 259–60
  place-based leadership 254–6, 265
  policy change 256, 260, 262–3
  R&D 257, 258, 259, 260, 262, 265
  regional policy 257–8
  smart specialisation policies 252–3, 259–60, 262, 264, 265–6
  structure of RIS 256–7
  theoretical framework 254–6
Albert, M. 261
ANC (Absolute Nuclear Family) type 261–2
APQ (Framework Programme Agreement) 214
Apulia region innovation policy 207–8, 219–21
  GDP measures 211, 212, 213
  innovation indicators 211, 212–13
  legal and institutional frameworks 214–18
  methodology of study 211–19
  R&D 212, 213, 214, 215, 216–19
  R&I 214, 216–18, 220
  regional production system 211–12
  science and technology system 212–14
  Smart Specialisation Strategies 208, 218–19, 220–21
  SmartPuglia 2020 strategy 218–19, 220–21

SMEs 212, 216–18, 219
  theoretical framework 208–11
AR (action research) 47–8, 50, 51, 53, 59, 60, 61, 62
Armstrong, H. 140
Arnold, E. 73
ARTD (action research for territorial development) 47–8, 53–8, 59, 60, 61
ARTI (Regional Agency for Technology and Innovation) 213–14, 215, 220
Asheim, Bjørn 2, 33, 254, 255, 257, 258

Baier, E. 75
Barca, F. 30, 36–8, 39, 40, 72
Barcelona Summit (2002) 117
Bardone, E. 50–51
benchmarking 34, 49, 84, 115, 227, 246, 260
Bennett, C. J. 48–9
Benneworth, P. 209
Benz, A. 53
BFOR (Budget Focused on Results) initiative 96
Borrás, S. 126, 190
Boschma, R. 3, 209
Bovaird, T. 105
Brexit 139
broad-based innovation policies 16, 17, 19–20, 21
Brunsson, N. 253
BSS (Business Service Sector) 229–30, 245
Bush, Vannevar 13

CAP (Common Agricultural Policy) 93–4
CCI (Combined and Complex mode of Innovation) 259, 262

Charron, N. 105
Citroën 193
cluster programmes 23, 124–5, 193
    Agder innovation policy 252, 257,
        262, 263, 266
    Apulia region innovation policy 219,
        220
    Malopolska innovation system 233,
        242, 243
    place-based policies 32, 33, 40
Cluster Theory 1, 2, 14, 15, 16, 17
CME (Coordinated Market Economy)
    practices 261, 262
Coenen, L. 34–5, 39
co-generative research methodologies
    47–8, 53, 54, 56, 58–61, 62
Cohesion Fund 67, 71, 94, 100, 101,
    131, 132, 133
Cohesion Policy 3, 72, 117, 190, 243
    EU innovation policy 125, 130, 131,
        132, 133
    European Regional Development
        Policy 92, 93, 94–6, 99–101,
        102–4, 108–9
    role of RIS approach in
        contemporary regional policy
        17, 19
collective knowing 53–4
community initiatives 96, 99, 126
compassionate compensations 37
competitive advantage 15, 16, 17–18,
    19–20, 31, 66, 75, 210
Cooke, Phil 209, 254
Copus, A. 210
CORDIS (Community Research
    and Development Information
    Service) dataset 162–3, 168
COST (Cooperation in Science and
    Technology) 116
CRA (Constructing Regional
    Advantage) 16, 17
Crescenzi, R. 144

Dahl, R. 69
decentralisation
    Apulia region innovation policy 212
    European Regional Development
        Policy 103, 109
    place-based policies 33–4, 35, 36
    regional autonomy 68, 71–2

decision-making
    Agder innovation policy 253, 263,
        266
    European Regional Development
        Policy 102–3, 105
    place-based policies 37–8, 40
    policy learning 53, 56, 61
    regional autonomy 66, 67, 69, 85,
        86
devolution 70–71
diffusion-oriented policies 32
distributed agency 24
DRs (developed regions) 168, 169, 171,
    174, 177, 179–80, 183, 184, 185
DUI (Doing, Using, Interacting)
    innovation 261, 262

EAFRD (European Agricultural Fund
    for Rural Development) 100
Economic Geography schools 1–2
EEs (entrepreneurial ecosystems) 227
EFSI (European Fund for Strategic
    Investment) 124
EIT (European Institute of Innovation
    & Technology) 117
Elazar, D. 69
EMFF (European Maritime and
    Fisheries Fund) 100
EMU (Economic and Monetary
    Union) area 139, 141, 142–6,
    149–57
entrepreneurial discovery process 3,
    31, 202
    Agder innovation policy 260, 264
    EU innovation policy 125, 129
    Malopolska innovation system 225,
        247
    role of RIS approach in
        contemporary regional policy
        17–18, 19, 20, 21
EPO (European Patent Office) 195, 213
EQI (European Quality of
    Government Index) 105–7
ERA (European Research Area) 117,
    124, 130, 162, 163, 183, 185
ERA-NETs (European Research Area
    networks) 124
ERDF (European Regional
    Development Fund)
    Apulia region innovation policy 215

EU innovation policy 124, 126, 128, 133
European Regional Development Policy 93, 97–100
regional autonomy 67, 71, 76, 77–9, 80–81, 84–5
role of RIS approach in contemporary regional policy 17
ERDP (European Regional Development Policy) 92–3, 108–9
appearance of 93
Cohesion Policy 92, 93, 94–6, 99–101, 102–4, 108–9
consolidation of 93–5
ERDF 93, 99–100
ESIF 94, 99–102
multilevel governance 102–3
policy principles 102–4
quality of government index 105–7
regional capacity 104–8
shifting rationale of 95–6
structural objectives 96–9
ESF (European Social Fund) 100
ESIF (European Structural and Investment Fund)
EU innovation policy 130–31, 133
European Regional Development Policy 94, 99–102
Framework Programmes 162, 184, 185–6
regional autonomy 72, 79, 82, 85
EU innovation policy 113–14, 132–3
alternative funds for research and innovation 124–6
context of 114–15
evolution and recent trends 126–7
foundation and evolution of 114–18
Framework Programmes 113, 118–24, 126–7, 129–31, 132–3
Horizon 2020 programme 102, 118–19, 121–3, 125, 126, 127, 130–31
key moments and rationales 116–18
linear model of innovation 113, 114, 116, 126, 128, 132
linking EU innovation and regional development policies 127–31
Lisbon Strategy 117, 130, 131, 132
main tools of 119–27

R&D 115, 117, 118, 126, 130
smart specialisation 113–14, 125, 126, 128, 129, 130, 131–2
SMEs 116, 119, 123, 126, 128, 130–31
Structural Funds 113, 118, 124–5, 126, 128, 129, 130, 132
Eureka programme 116
EURIPER (EU Regional and Innovation Policies and Peripheral Regions) 4
Europe 2020 strategy 3, 17
EU innovation policy 117, 118, 132
European Regional Development Policy 94, 95, 96, 102, 109
European Innovation Council 127
European Innovation Scoreboard 148–9
Eurostat database 168
Apulia region innovation policy 211, 212, 213
Malopolska innovation system 230–34
regional disparities 139, 142–5, 150–52, 154–5
Evolutionary School 1, 2, 189, 190, 208
experimental governance 37–8

Fagerberg, Jan 114, 208, 258
Farole, T. 105
FDI (foreign direct investment) 144, 230, 242, 245
Fernández, I. 126
FIR (Future in Research) 219
firm-level agency 23–6
First Action Plan for Innovation in Europe (1996) 117
fiscal authority 69
Fitjar, R. D. 52
Flexible Production Systems approach 1
Fordism 15
foundational economy 36, 41
FPs (Framework Programmes)
effects on regional innovation and scientific performance 162–3
analytical framework and data 166–9, 170–74
developed regions 168, 169, 171, 174, 177, 179–80, 183, 184, 185

discussion and policy implications
183–5
GDP measures 163, 165, 166, 168,
177, 185
less developed regions 168, 169,
171–2, 177–8, 183, 184, 185–6
main features and recent dynamics
163–5
main results 169, 175–83
methodology of study 165–9
middle income regions 169, 171,
173, 177, 181–3, 184, 185–6
OLS regression 163, 169, 175–9,
181
SMEs 163, 166–8, 170–81, 183
Tobit regression 163, 169, 175–8,
180, 182, 183
EU innovation policy 113, 118–24,
126–7, 129–31, 132–3
Freeman, R. 50
Fürst, D. 53

Galician Innovation Agency 197,
199
Galician innovation system and
policies 188, 204–5
changes in industrial specialization
191–4
exports 192–4, 195
institutional set-up 195, 197–204
legal framework and institutional
organization 197–9
policy learning 199–205
R&D 194–5, 196, 197–9, 200–201,
202, 203–4
relative specialization 191–2
Smart Specialisation 199, 201, 202,
203, 204–5
Galician Plans of Research and
Innovation 197
garden argument 34
Garud, R. 24
GCE NODE (Global Center of
Expertise) 257
GDP (gross domestic product) data
Apulia region innovation policy 211,
212, 213
EU innovation policy 117
European Regional Development
Policy 96–8, 100–101

Framework Programmes 163, 165,
166, 168, 177, 185
Galician innovation system and
policies 194, 196
Malopolska innovation system 229,
232–3
regional disparities 140, 141–5, 148,
150–55
'General regional autonomy' (regional
autonomy indicator) 76–7, 80–81,
84, 85
globalization 12, 30
González-López, M. 191, 193, 197,
198, 204
grand challenges 50
Great Recession 96, 156
Green Paper on Innovation (1995) 117
Grillitsch, M. 24
Grjebine, T. 144
Growth Centres/Poles 13–14

Hall, P. 261
Harmaakorpi, V. 209
Heclo, H. 48
Herstad, S. 258
hierarchic egalitarianism 261, 262
hierarchical instruction 253, 265
Hirschman, A. 14
Horizon 2020 programme 19, 163, 184
EU innovation policy 102, 118–19,
121–3, 125, 126, 127, 130–31
Howlett, M. 48–9
human resources 38, 123, 146, 203,
219–20, 227, 231, 233, 245

Iammarino, S. 38–9, 184
IAs (Innovative Actions) 124
ILO (Industrial Liaison Office) 215,
217
improvement of programme efficiency
(ARTD framework) 57, 58
INDITEX (Industria de Diseño Textil)
193, 204
InnovaPuglia 215
Innovation Union 117–18, 130, 132
input characteristics 225, 227, 233, 245
instrumental learning 49–50, 52
interactive learning approach 1, 15, 18,
23, 49, 147, 190, 254
Interreg Europe 126

Isaksen, Arne 207, 254, 256, 258
Italian National Institute of Statistics 211

Jacobsen, S. E. 207
Jiao, H. 209
Juncker Plan 124
'just-in-time' practices 193

Karnøe, P. 24
Keeble, D. 210
KETs (key enabling technologies) 19, 219
KICs (knowledge and innovation communities) 117
KIS (knowledge-intensive services) 152, 154, 204, 229, 231
Knudsen, J. 260–61, 262
Kuhlmann, S. 73

Lagging regions report (2017) 108
Lambooy, J. 3
Lapuente, V. 105
LDRs (less developed regions) 168, 169, 171–2, 177–8, 183, 184, 185–6
learning agents 49
learning-by-doing 199, 200–201, 202
Learning Region approach 1
Lind, M. 50–51
linear model of innovation 2, 203
    EU innovation policy 113, 114, 116, 126, 128, 132
    regional disparities 147, 149
    role of RIS approach in contemporary regional policy 13, 14, 15
Lisbon Strategy 94, 95, 102, 117, 130, 131, 132
Living Labs 221
LME (liberal market economy) practices 261, 262
lock-ins 22, 41, 208, 209, 210, 226, 245, 259
Löffler, E. 105
Lundvall, Bengt-Åke 126, 190, 209

Malopolska innovation system 225–6, 245–7
    firms and industrial specialisation 229–31

GDP measures 229, 232–3
    innovation indicators 232–5, 236
    input characteristics 225, 227, 233, 245
    institutional and governance framework 235–8
    methodology of study 228
    monitoring and evaluation 243–5
    output characteristics 225, 233–4, 245
    policy documents 228, 240–41
    policy instruments and budgets 236, 240–43, 245–6
    policy learning 225, 226, 227, 246–7
    R&D 227, 228, 230, 231, 232–4, 240, 243, 244–5
    regional specialisation development 238–40
    RIS Malopolska 2005–2013 strategy 235–7, 241, 242
    RIS Malopolska 2020 strategy 237–8, 240, 241–3, 244
    science and technology system 231
    smart specialisation 225, 226–7, 228, 237, 238–40, 246–7
    structure of RIS 229–32
    theoretical framework 226–8
Managing Authorities 71, 78, 84–5
market failures 2, 19, 70, 114, 208, 209, 255
Marks, G. 69
Marshall Plan 13
Marx, Karl 146
McCann, P. 3
Mellizo-Soto, M. 197
Metcalfe, J. 208
MFF (multiannual financial framework) 94, 96, 100
Milio, S. 104–5
MIRs (middle income regions) 169, 171, 173, 177, 181–3, 184, 185–6
mission-oriented innovation policies 21, 36
Moedas, Carlos 126
Monnet, Jean 4
Morgan, K. 34–5, 39
multi-level governance 37, 41, 70, 75, 102–3, 104, 125, 191, 200–201, 204, 214
Musiolik, J. 24–5

Myrdal, G. 14
Mytelka, L. 190, 203

National Systems of Innovation 12,
    14–19, 73, 189, 209
Neffke, F. 3
neoclassical perspectives 2, 114, 141,
    208, 209
neoliberalism 30, 31, 141
New Industrial Districts school 1
new-institutionalism 253
NODE cluster 257, 263–4
Normann, R. 262–3
NUTS-1 regions 166
NUTS-2 regions 139, 140, 141, 144,
    145, 150–52, 163, 166
NUTS-3 regions 98

Oates, W. 67
OECD (Organisation for Economic
    Co-operation and Development)
    14–15, 20–21, 35
oil crisis (1970s) 14
OLS (ordinary least squares) regression
    153, 155, 163, 169, 175–9, 181
'one-size-fits-all' innovation policies 16,
    32, 39, 108–9, 148, 211, 261
Openlabs Initiative 219
Operational Programmes 76, 78, 84–5,
    214, 237, 238
organisational legitimacy 253
Oughton, C. 32, 210
output characteristics 225, 233–4,
    245

Padoa-Schioppa, Tommaso 93
participation (RRI pillar) 50
patents 33, 148, 151, 152, 166, 186,
    195, 213, 233–4
path dependency 1, 70, 212, 226
path development 3, 16–17, 22, 36, 226,
    255–6
path transformation 3, 4, 22–3, 190
Patient Innovation Lab 20
Pearson correlation coefficients 150,
    152
Pekkarinen, S. 209
Percoco, M. 35
Perroux, F. 13–14
Pinheiro, R. 262–3

place-based policies 2, 3, 4, 30–31, 41,
    49, 72, 184, 207
    advancement of 39–41
    Agder innovation policy 254–6,
        265
    conceptualization of place 40–41
    contemporary discussion 36–9
    EU innovation policy 132, 133
    general trends in regional innovation
        policy 32–6
    new understanding of innovations
        35–6
    place-neutral policies 30–31
    place-sensitive distribution
        development policies 38–9
    populism 30, 31, 38, 40, 41
    role of RIS approach in
        contemporary regional policy
        16, 19, 21
    spatially blind policies 30–31, 34–5,
        38, 41
    standardization of regional
        innovation policies 34–5
    surge in regional innovation policies
        33–4
policy change 85, 190, 211
    Agder innovation policy 256, 260,
        262–3
    Galician innovation system and
        policies 199, 202–3
    policy learning 46, 48, 49
policy evaluation 190, 200–201, 202,
    227, 243, 246
policy learning 46–8, 62, 190–91, 215
    absorptive capacity 60–61
    Agder innovation policy 255–6
    analytical ARTD framework 57–8
    AR/ARTD strategies 47–8, 50, 51,
        53–8, 59, 60, 61, 62
    co-generative research
        methodologies 47–8, 53, 54, 56,
        58–61, 62
    Galician innovation system and
        policies 199–205
    Malopolska innovation system 225,
        226, 227, 246–7
    perspectives on 48–50
    policy change 46, 48, 49
    praxis 54, 55, 56, 57, 58, 59
    regional autonomy 84, 87

responsible innovation 46, 47, 48,
50–53, 57, 58–60, 61, 62
role of research and researchers 47
policy scope 69
political discourse (ARTD framework)
57, 58
POP (Progetto Operativo Plurifondo)
214, 216
populism 30, 31, 38, 40, 41
POR (Regional Operational
Programme) 214, 216–17, 218, 221
Porter, M. 2, 14, 15, 17
Post-Fordism 15
PPI (public procurement of
innovation) policy 20
PPS (Purchasing Power Standards)
167, 168, 229, 232
praxis 54, 55, 56, 57, 58, 59
process-focus (RRI pillar) 50–51
PSA Group (previously Citroën) 193
Puglia Sviluppo 215

quadruple-helix model 21, 23, 219

R&D (research and development)
Agder innovation policy 257, 258,
259, 260, 262, 265
Apulia region innovation policy 212,
213, 214, 215, 216–19
EU innovation policy 115, 117, 118,
126, 130
Evolutionary School 208
Framework Programmes 162–3,
185–6
discussion and policy implications
183–5
GDP measures 163, 165, 166, 168,
177, 185
main features and recent dynamics
163–5
main results 169, 175–83
methodology of study 165–9,
170–74
SMEs 163, 166–8, 170–81, 183
Galician innovation system and
policies 194–5, 196, 197–9,
200–201, 202, 203–4
Malopolska innovation system 227,
228, 230, 231, 232–4, 240, 243,
244–5

peripheral areas 209
place-based policies 32–3
regional disparities 146, 148, 151,
152–4, 157
role of RIS approach in
contemporary regional policy
12, 13–14, 15
R&I (research and innovation) 17, 162,
184, 185–6, 214, 216–18, 220
rational choice 253, 265
RD&I (research, development and
innovation) funding 118, 124, 126,
130
recipe book for policy (ARTD
framework) 57–8
recognition inequalities 30, 37
reflexive learning 49, 50, 52
reflexivity (RRI pillar) 51
regional autonomy 66–8, 86–7
analysing innovation policy 68–75
conceptualising 69–70
decentralisation 68, 71–2
decision-making 66, 67, 69, 85, 86
devolution 70–71
empirical results 79–85
ERDF 67, 71, 76, 77–9, 80–81, 84–5
ESIF 72, 79, 82, 85
framework for policymakers 73–5
indicators of 75–81, 83–5, 86, 87
innovation systems 67, 68, 73, 74, 75,
79, 86
map of 83–4
operationalisation of 75–9
processes of transformation 71
self-rule and shared rule 69, 72, 75,
79, 86
regional capacity 104–8
'Regional competences with regard
to innovation policy' (regional
autonomy indicator) 77, 80–81,
84, 85
Regional Competitiveness Index 148–9
'Regional influence on Structural
Fund allocations' (regional
autonomy indicator) 77–9, 80–81,
84, 85
Regional Information Society Initiative
16
Regional Innovation Index 149,
150–51, 157

regional innovation paradox 35
Regional Innovation Scoreboard 140,
	148–9, 150, 151, 152, 154, 155,
	156, 166, 211, 233
regional structural change 3, 22–6, 190
regionalisation 33–4, 66–7, 70, 76, 79,
	103–4, 163, 188, 257
Regions of Knowledge Programme
	124–5
Reillon, V. 164, 184
rent-seeking 37, 39
Report on economic, social and
	territorial cohesion (2017) 109
representative committees 190
Research Potential Programme 124,
	125
responsible innovation 46, 47, 48,
	50–53, 57, 58–60, 61, 62
RIS (Regional Innovation Strategies)
	124, 128–9, 132, 133
RIS (Regional Innovation System)
	approach 1
	Agder region *see* Agder innovation
		policy
	Apulia region *see* Apulia region
		innovation policy
	Economic Geography schools 1–2
	Galician region *see* Galician
		innovation system and policies
	Malopolska region *see* Malopolska
		innovation system
	peripheral areas 208, 209–11
	regional disparities 139–41, 156–7
		convergence 139, 140–42, 144–5,
			156
		data 148–9
		divergence 139, 140–42, 144, 149
		empirical assessment 149–56
		GDP measures 140, 141–5, 148,
			150–55
		R&D 146, 148, 151, 152–4, 157
		SMEs 148, 152–6, 157
		systemic perspective 146–9,
			150–51, 156, 157
		trends of 140–46
	role in contemporary regional policy
		12–13, 26
	National Systems of Innovation
		12, 14–19
	R&D 12, 13–14, 15

regional structural change 22–6
	relevance of 12, 18–19, 22, 26
	S3 strategy 16–20, 21
	transformation of RIS 22–6
	transformative change 12, 13,
		19–22
RIS Malopolska 2005–2013 strategy
	235–7, 241, 242
RIS Malopolska 2020 strategy 237–8,
	240, 241–3, 244
RITTS (Regional Innovation and
	Technology Transfer Strategies)
	16, 124, 128, 132
Rodríguez-Pose, A. 30, 184
Rokkan, Stein 260
Rosenfeld, S. 210
RRI (responsible research and
	innovation) 50–52, 62
RTDI (Research, Technological
	Development and Innovation)
	policies 77
RTPs (Regional Technological Plans)
	16, 124, 128

S&T (Science & Technology) policies
	2, 188, 190
S3 (Smart Specialisation Strategies) 3,
	190
	Agder innovation policy 252, 253,
		259–60, 262, 264, 265–6
	Apulia region innovation policy 208,
		218–19, 220–21
	EU innovation policy 113–14, 126,
		128, 130, 131–2
	European Regional Development
		Policy 92, 108, 109
	Galician innovation system and
		policies 199, 202, 203
	Malopolska innovation system
		226–7, 237, 238–40
	regional autonomy 72, 82
	role of RIS approach in
		contemporary regional policy
		16–20, 21
Sandven, T. 258
Sanz-Menéndez, L. 190
Schot, J. 12
Schumpeter, Joseph 146, 208
Science: The Endless Frontier 13
self-rule 69, 75, 79, 86

SF (Stem Family) types 261–2
SFI (Centre for Research-based
    Innovation) 257, 264
SFs (Structural Funds) 113, 118,
    124–5, 126, 128, 129, 130, 132
shared rule 69, 72, 79, 86
Silicon Valley 35
Single European Act (1986) 94, 116
SINTEF 258
SmartPuglia 2020 strategy 218–19,
    220–21
SMECO (SMEs collaborating with
    others) 153, 154–6
SMEIH (SMEs innovating in house)
    153, 154–5
SMEs (small and medium-sized
    enterprises)
    Apulia region innovation policy 212,
        216–18, 219
    EU innovation policy 116, 119, 123,
        126, 128, 130–31
    Evolutionary School 208
    Framework Programmes 163, 166–8,
        170–81, 183
    Malopolska innovation system
        233
    peripheral areas 210
    place-based policies 32–3
    regional disparities 148, 152–6, 157
    role of RIS approach in
        contemporary regional policy
        15
Smith, K. 190, 203
social and political participation 190,
    200–201, 202, 205, 227
social learning (ARTD framework)
    57, 58
socio-cultural configurations 260
Soskice, D. 261
Sotarauta, M. 24
spatially blind policies 30–31, 34–5,
    38, 41
SS (Smart Specialisation) approach
    2–3, 189–90, 253
    EU innovation policy 113–14, 125,
        129, 130, 131–2
    European Regional Development
        Policy 92, 108, 109
    Galician innovation system and
        policies 201, 202, 203, 204–5

Malopolska innovation system 225,
    226, 228, 238–40, 246–7
place-based policies 33
role of RIS approach in
    contemporary regional policy
    16–17
standardization of regional innovation
    policies 34–5
Steinmueller, E. 12
Stone, D. 59
STRIDE initiative 116, 128, 133
Suksi, M. 69
sustainability
    EU innovation policy 117, 120–21,
        128
    European Regional Development
        Policy 105, 109
    Framework Programmes 184
    Malopolska innovation system 226,
        234, 238, 239
    place-based policies 37, 40
    policy learning 46, 50, 62
    role of RIS approach in
        contemporary regional policy
        17, 19–20, 21
system building 24–5
system innovation policy 20–21
system-level agency 24–6, 256

technology assessment and forecasting
    190, 200–201, 202, 227, 246
technology transfer 16, 32–3, 66
    Apulia region innovation policy 217,
        221
    EU innovation policy 123, 124, 128
    Malopolska innovation system 236,
        237
territorial inequality 30
theoretical rationales 200–201, 203–4
Tobit regression models 163, 169,
    175–8, 180, 182, 183
Todd, Emmanuel 261
Tödtling, F. 32, 39, 207, 209, 210, 254,
    255
transformative change 12, 13, 19–22,
    23
Treaty of Lisbon (2009) 94, 95, 101,
    116
Treaty of Maastricht (1992) 94, 116,
    118, 212

Treaty of Rome (1957) 93, 115
triple-helix model 21, 26, 219,
    254
Trippl, M. 32, 39, 207, 209, 210,
    255

Uyarra, E. 3, 189

Vanguard Initiative 124, 125, 129
Varela-Vázquez, P. 168, 185

VINNOVA (Swedish government
    agency) 18, 19
VoC (Varieties of Capitalism) scheme
    261–2
VRI (Programme for Regional R&D
    and Innovation) project 258, 260

wearing apparel industry 192–3, 194,
    195
Witt, U. 208